Networks of Power in Digital Copyright Law and Policy

In this book, Benjamin Farrand employs an interdisciplinary approach that combines legal analysis with political theory to explore the development of copyright law in the EU. Farrand utilises Foucault's concept of 'Networks of Power' and Culpepper's 'Quiet Politics' to assess the adoption and enforcement of copyright law in the EU, including the role of industry representatives, cross-border licensing, and judicial approaches to territorial restrictions. Focusing in particular on legislative initiatives concerning copyright, digital music and the internet, *Networks of Power in Digital Copyright Law and Policy: Political Salience, Expertise and the Legislative Process* demonstrates the connection between copyright law and complex network relationships.

This book presents an original socio-political theoretical framework for assessing developments in copyright law that will interest researchers and post-graduate students of law and politics, as well as those more particularly concerned with political theory, EU and copyright law.

Benjamin Farrand is Lecturer in Intellectual Property Law and Policy at the University of Strathclyde, UK. His research predominantly focuses on the interaction between political processes and intellectual property law, with particular interest in principles of networked governance, technology regulation and human enhancement technologies.

Networks of Power in Digital Copyright Law and Policy

Political salience, expertise and
the legislative process

Benjamin Farrand

Routledge
Taylor & Francis Group

LONDON AND NEW YORK
a GlassHouse Book

First published 2014
by Routledge

Published 2014 by Routledge

2 Park Square, Milton Park, Abingdon, Oxfordshire OX14 4RN

and by Routledge
711 Third Avenue, New York, NY 10017

a GlassHouse Book

Routledge is an imprint of the Taylor and Francis Group, an informa business

First issued in paperback 2015

British Library Cataloguing in Publication Data
A catalogue record for this book is available from the British Library

Library of Congress Cataloging-in-Publication Data
Farrand, Benjamin, author.
Networks of power in copyright law: the role of policy makers,
policy takers and industry in the development of digital music law
and policy/Benjamin Farrand.
    pages cm
    'Loosely based' on dissertation (doctoral) – European University
    Institute, 2011, under title: The Pan-European Licensing of Digital
    Music – The Effect of the Harmonisation of Copyright and the
    Role of Collecting Societies. 1. Copyright – Music – European
    Union countries. 2. Digital media – Law and legislation –
    European Union countries. 3. Copyright licenses – European
    Union countries. 4. Copyright – Political aspects – European Union
    countries. I. Title.
    KJE2665.F37 2014
    346.2404'8 – dc23   2013037758

ISBN 978-0-415-85442-9 (hbk)
ISBN 978-1-138-94484-8 (pbk)
ISBN 978-0-203-79792-1 (ebk)

Typeset in Galliard by
Florence Production Ltd, Stoodleigh, Devon, UK

For Lena, my wife, my friend and my academic companion. None of this would have been possible without you.

Contents

Introduction

Copyright law, or more precisely the changes to copyright law beginning in the 1990s as a response to the widespread use of the internet, are the subject of frequent criticism and debate among academics, economists, civil society organizations, and on occasion, European citizens. International treaties on intellectual property protection have existed now for more than a hundred years, and the EU has legislated in the field of intellectual property law since the 1970s. However, it appears that these developments are perceived as making copyright an increasingly restrictive form of regulation, expanding substantially the scope of protection, while limiting the exceptions and limitations to that protection. The term of duration of copyright has also increased, as have the number and severity of enforcement mechanisms used to prevent or punish copyright infringement. Furthermore, despite the borderless nature of the internet, the ability of European institutions to facilitate cross-border trade in digital media appears to be somewhat limited, resulting in the territorial partitioning of the digital market in the EU. Academics have criticized EU copyright policies both with regard to the substance of proposed changes to copyright law and with regard to the processes by which those proposals are transformed into legal instruments. Many of these critiques of process, or criticisms of certain substantive provisions, make reference to the role of copyright-holding organizations and entertainment industry representatives in influencing policymakers through lobbying (see, for example, Hugenholtz 2000; Kohli 2001; Kierkegaard 2005; Hilty *et al.* 2009; Mazziotti 2010 – this list should not be viewed as criticism of these statements, but evidence of arguments concerning lobbying). Within critiques of legislative process in copyright law it is often argued that such changes would not have come about if not for the lobbying by groups with vested interests in strong copyright protections. These arguments suggest that this influence subverts copyright law, and that lobbying prevents the passing of copyright legislation that is based on objective evidence. To take one example, the Foreword to the Hargreaves Review in the UK states that 'We urge Government to ensure that in future, policy on Intellectual Property issues is constructed on the basis of evidence, rather than weight of lobbying' (Hargreaves 2011, p. 1). Furthermore, 'lobbying on behalf of rights owners has been more persuasive to Ministers than economic impact assessments' (2011, p. 6). This discourse suggests that lobbying and evidence are two separate and distinct phenomena. The first, lobbying, is perceived as a negative phenomenon that achieves the 'wrong' result, and the other, 'evidence', is perceived as the basis for good policy, helping to ensure the 'right' result. Such a perception could lead to the question 'why do EU institutions bow to lobbying pressures in the field of copyright law?' being asked. However, it must be stated that all acts that are intended to influence the decisions of policymakers are forms of lobbying, whether performed by industry representatives, academics, civil society organizations, or individual voters (see Kollman 1998, chap. 1; Mahoney 2007, p. 35; Mack 2005, pp. 339–40). Whether evidence is submitted by an industry representative, by a civil society organization, or by an academic commissioned to perform a study, the use of that evidence to recommend a policy constitutes a form of lobbying. For this reason, referring solely to 'lobbying' without deeper analysis does not appear to be a significant explanation for the drivers for European copyright law and policy. If all attempts to influence the form, substance, or indeed, the passing or not of legislation constitute forms of lobbying, then the question 'why do EU institutions bow to lobbying pressures in the field of copyright law?' does not help to explain how policy develops at the EU level.

The purpose of this book is to reformulate this question. Instead of asking 'why do EU institutions bow to industry lobbying in the field of copyright law and policy?', this book asks 'why are some lobbyists more successful than others in having their preferred policy outcomes taken into account?'. Why are attempts to influence policy by the entertainment industry more successful than those attempts by academics, civil society or industries such as the telecoms sector? To address this question requires the use of a cross-disciplinary approach, incorporating both political and legal analysis. In particular, this book will seek to explain these developments in terms of power, demonstrating how the relationships between different actors impact upon legislative development. The framework for assessing these relationships is that of Foucault's 'networks of power' (Foucault 2004, p. 29). In networks of power analysis, the power relations between different actors are demonstrated, as are the ways in which knowledge is transferred between them resulting in a particular discourse, or way of thinking about and discussing a certain issue, becoming dominant. Power is not something that is possessed, but something that is exercised through social relations, creating dominant discourses and establishing certain ideas as 'true'. The networks of power approach is useful in determining how the relationships between actors may lead to the adoption of certain policies or legislative acts in the field of copyright law. This book will demonstrate that lobbying is not simply a case of 'big business getting what big business wants', but is the result of more complex relationships based strongly on perceptions of industry expertise and the ability of industry representatives to effectively frame the discourses in which these developments take place. It is because of the fact that industry representatives are perceived as best understanding their sectors that they are influential in policy development – often these areas of work are technically complex and difficult to understand, meaning that external expertise is required by policymakers to determine whether or not to legislate, and if so, how to legislate in a particular area.

In this respect, treating 'lobbying' and 'evidence' as separate categories of information production creates something of a false dichotomy, as the form that lobbying generally takes is that of 'expert' knowledge, be it in the form of economic evidence, statistics, or considerations of 'problems' existing within a particular area, as will be expanded upon in Chapter 1. Through the production of knowledge that is useful to policymakers, industry representatives contribute to the perception of possessed expertise. The provision of this evidence/expertise also helps to frame issues, determining what exactly constitutes a problem, and what the potential solutions for that problem are. There may of course be competing views on how best to solve that particular problem, or indeed, whether the issue identified is a problem at all. Which view becomes dominant can largely be explained by networks of power, and by the political salience of an issue. If an issue is politically salient, it is important to voters, who are likely to vote on the basis of political responses to that issue. Where an issue is highly salient, then policymakers are more likely to take the views of voters into account. If, however, an issue is considered highly complex and of low political salience, meaning that the average voter is unlikely to consider an issue particularly important, they are more likely to not invest time in seeking to understand that subject, and will defer to perceived experts. Culpepper refers to this environment of high complexity and low salience as 'quiet politics' (2011). In an environment of 'quiet politics', business or corporate actors are more likely to be able to influence policy outcomes. This book will demonstrate that copyright policy, while highly topical in academic scholarship, is generally an issue characterized by high complexity and low salience, with the result that well-placed industry representatives that possess 'expert' knowledge of both their business areas and legislative processes are more able to influence policy than other actors, such as those academics and civil society organizations that prefer different outcomes. Should an issue become salient, however, then it is more likely that these groups will be able to resist legislative changes preferred by industry representatives and their supporters (academic or otherwise), being more effectively able to lobby policymakers to avoid or change a particular approach. It is intended that through application of the approaches of networks of power and quiet politics analysis to the issue of copyright law in the EU, a greater understanding will develop of how lobbying practices in this sector function. It is also intended that this explanation may assist in demonstrating where resistance to copyright policy development may be successful, by highlighting how the issue may become more politically salient.

In order to apply these theories, this book will focus on copyright developments applicable to the internet and digital music distribution. This is because legislative initiatives concerning copyright law and the internet in the EU are considered highly contentious by many academics in this field, in part due to the perception that this legislation is the result of strong lobbying by the entertainment industry. Furthermore, the application of copyright law to digital music and its distribution is the predominant focus of the analysis in this book as many of the legislative developments covered relate to musical works specifically, and much of the academic discussion of copyright and the internet has concerned music. However, the findings in this book are likely to apply equally to other forms of digital media such as film and 'ebooks', and have the potential to be applicable to copyright law development more generally. This shall now be expanded upon by providing an overview of the key issues and themes discussed in this book.

Overview

The first three chapters of this book provide the framework for analysis, both in terms of the theoretical approach and in the substance of the law being assessed. The first chapter of this book shall explore the theoretical framework of the research, expanding upon the central notions of 'networks of power'. The chapter will detail how the theory of networks of power, which considers the relationships between actors based on dominant discourses, the production of knowledge and the perception of expertise, may help to explain the reason why legislative or executive bodies pass legislation in the field of copyright law that favours certain actors. Theories on political salience and quiet politics, it will be argued, help to support this analysis by demonstrating why complex issues may often be left to certain industry representatives due to the low political salience of an issue, which results in policymakers deferring to perceived expertise. This chapter will demonstrate how the networks of power approach fits into existing discussions about governance more generally, demonstrating the fact that policymaking institutions such as the European Commission do not draft legislation in splendid isolation, but constitute a node in a network of interrelated policy actors that influence the creation of legislation. It is important to note, however, that this book is not intended as being a general study of Foucault's philosophy. The intention of this theoretical chapter is to provide a framework for assessing copyright policy, insofar as it is useful to the study of EU lobbying processes in this area.

Whereas Chapter 1 provides the theoretical framework for assessment of power relations in copyright law, Chapter 2 provides the substance of analysis; this chapter will introduce the legislative acts that form the basis for the analysis of power relations, namely the Information Society Directive (2001/29/EC), Term Extension for Sound Recordings Directive (2011/77/EU), Enforcement Directive (2004/48/EC) and the Collective Rights Management Recommendation (2005/737/EC). This chapter will provide an overview of the key provisions and academic debates over these legislative acts, demonstrating why each act was perceived as contentious by those academics, as well as the arguments that the finalized legal instruments were the result of lobbying by the entertainment industry. One of the themes drawn from Chapter 2 is that the market for digital music distribution in the EU is fragmented along Member State boundaries. Chapter 3 will continue with this analysis, discussing in more detail the territorial nature of digital music services and demonstrating the relative inability of the Court of Justice of the European Union to successfully remove territorial restrictions on the provision of digital music services in the EU. As this chapter will show, removing territorial restrictions is one area in which legislative and judicial action has been unsuccessful. The analysis in Chapter 3 is particularly relevant for the discussion of collecting societies in Chapter 6.

Chapter 4 is the first chapter applying the networks of power analysis to copyright law-making processes in the EU. This chapter will expand upon the dominant discourses concerning the scope and duration of copyright and how the internet has fundamentally changed the way in which creative works can be disseminated, resulting in a need to change the way in which copyright is protected. Entertainment industry representatives have been particularly successful in establishing these discourses and, as this chapter will demonstrate, the low political salience of changes to copyright law in the EU results in these industry representatives being able to operate in an environment of quiet politics in which policymakers are willing to defer to their perceived expertise. Chapter 5 continues the networks of power analysis, explaining the development of discourses concerning the threat posed by copyright infringement, and the use of this discourse as a driver of copyright policy. This chapter will assess the way in which entertainment industry representatives have been involved in establishing a discourse in which copyright infringement is linked to more serious forms of crime, and in constructing a discourse in which internet intermediary service providers are perceived as responsible for the actions of their service users. Through being able to rely on an environment of quiet politics, these entertainment industry representatives are both able to frame the 'problem' of and 'solution' to copyright infringement on the internet, through the close proximity in the networks of power between those representatives and bodies such as the European Commission and Parliament. Chapter 6 concludes the focus on networks of power and the role of industry representatives in influencing copyright law and policy by considering the issue of territoriality in the provision of digital music services, expanding upon the analysis in Chapters 2 and 3. This chapter will demonstrate how entertainment industry representatives have framed the difficulties in providing multi-territory licenses for music content in the EU as the result of the ineffective application of competition law to collective rights management organizations, 'problematizing' the existence of these bodies as national monopolies, and influencing the European Commission's approach to collecting society reform. This chapter will also demonstrate how the music industry has been able to deter the Commission from considering increased harmonization, or the creation of a Copyright Code, as a means of ending the territorial partitioning of the digital market. Due to the low political salience of copyright generally and collecting society practices specifically, entertainment industry representatives have been able to ensure certain clauses are contained or approaches adopted in legislation, and to ensure that non-preferred approaches are not pursued by the European Commission.

The final two chapters of this book focus on the possibility of transforming the networks of power in copyright law and policy. Chapter 7 will begin the consideration of 'resistance' within networks of power, discussing how resistance is interrelated to and dependent upon power. If power is the exercise of influence over actors in the networks of power, then resistance is the act of exercising influence as a means of combating that exercise of power. This chapter will discuss how resistance can operate at a personal or 'micro' level, or at a general 'macro' level, and how resistance can act within a dominant discourse or as a means of transforming that discourse. This theoretical discussion will be linked to acts of resistance in the face of proposed changes in copyright law, through the use of the court system and academics writing critiques of changes to copyright. This chapter will discuss how low political salience and the limited nature of the resistance posed means that this resistance is either successful only at the micro level, or unsuccessful. Chapter 8 will demonstrate, however, that resistance is possible, even if it is difficult, using the negotiation and rejection of the Anti-Counterfeiting Trade Agreement as an example. This chapter will discuss the contentious provisions of the Agreement, and the way in which increased media and public attention coupled with protests by European citizens and lobbying of the European Parliament by citizens and civil society organizations transformed the discourse surrounding the Agreement from one concerning the need for intellectual property protection to one concerning the undemocratic nature of the Agreement and the resultant threat to civil liberties and internet freedoms. Through this reframing of the Agreement, the issue was transformed from a high technical complexity and low political salience issue concerning copyright protection into a high salience issue of democratic accountability and transparency. This chapter will conclude by discussing that if fundamental change to copyright is desired, resistance to the current framing and direction of copyright law is possible, so long as copyright is transformed into an issue of high political salience, in which policymakers are more likely to take into account the views of ordinary voters than those of industry representatives.

Bibliography

Culpepper, P.D., 2011. *Quiet politics and business power: Corporate control in Europe and Japan*. Cambridge: Cambridge University Press.

Foucault, M., 2004. *Society must be defended: Lectures at the Collège de France, 1975–1976*. London: Penguin.

Hargreaves, I., 2011. *Digital opportunity: A review of intellectual property and growth*. London: UK Intellectual Property Office.

Hilty, R.M., Kur, A., Klass, N., Geiger, C., Peukert, A., Drexl, J., and Katzenberger, P., 2009. 'Comment by the Max-Planck Institute on the Commission's proposal for a

Directive to amend Directive 2006/116 concerning the term of protection for copyright and related rights'. *European Intellectual Property Review*, 31(2), pp. 59–72.

Hugenholtz, P.B., 2000. 'Why the copyright directive is unimportant, and possibly invalid'. *European Intellectual Property Review*, 11, pp. 501–2.

Kierkegaard, S., 2005. 'Taking a sledge-hammer to crack the nut: The EU Enforcement Directive'. *Computer Law and Security Report*, 21(5), p. 488.

Kohli, V., 2001. 'Mutilating music: A critical look at the copyright and business issues in online music distribution'. *Entertainment Law Review*, 121(1), pp. 15–24.

Kollman, K., 1998. *Outside lobbying: Public opinion and interest group strategies*. Princeton, NJ: Princeton University Press.

Mack, R., 2005. 'Lobbying effectively in Brussels and Washington: Getting the right result'. *Journal of Communication Management*, 9(4), pp. 339–47.

Mahoney, C., 2007. 'Lobbying success in the United States and the European Union'. *Journal of Public Policy*, 27(1), pp. 33–56.

Mazziotti, G., 2010. 'New licensing models for online music services in the European Union: From collective to customized management'. *Columbia Journal of Law and the Arts*, 34, p. 757.

Chapter 1

Networks of power, quiet politics and political salience

Establishing a framework for analysing European digital copyright initiatives

> The relationship proper to power would therefore be sought not on the side of violence or of struggle, nor on that of voluntary contracts (all of which can, at best, only be instruments of power), but rather, in the area of that singular mode of action, neither warlike nor juridical, which is government
>
> (Foucault 2002b, p. 341)

The purpose of this chapter is to introduce readers to the theoretical concepts and framework for analysis that is used in this book. In so doing, this chapter seeks to provide readers unfamiliar with Foucault's work with a brief overview of some of the central concepts of his political thought, seeking to somewhat simplify a complex and dense body of literature. It must be stated clearly, however, that this is not a book about Foucault. Nor is it a book about political philosophy (or at least, not entirely). This is a book about copyright law and policy development that is significantly influenced by a Foucauldian perspective and the way that policy development can be reinterpreted or reconceptualized as a result of such a perspective. For this reason, the overview of Foucault's work will be largely confined to his thoughts on political processes, namely those of networks of power, governmentality and resistance. An approach that assesses networks of power is one that considers that power is not something that is possessed by people or institutions at the top of a pyramid-like social structure, with that power being exerted upon the lower levels of that pyramid structure. Instead, power is relational; it is not possessed but exercised through network relations, multilaterally rather than hierarchically. The way in which these networks of power can be analysed is through the study of governmentality, or rather, the study of government both in terms of the processes, techniques and vocabularies through which power is exercised and by the way in which it establishes rules concerning the conduct of conduct. Central to this analysis is 'discourse', the way in which particular thoughts or ideas in the form of 'knowledge' construct truths about society more generally, or with respect to the analysis in this book, about copyright in particular. Quiet politics as a theory is intended to be used as a way of 'grounding' these more abstract notions, demonstrating how these networks of power do not solely result in powerful businesses achieving their intended objectives through lobbying alone, but through the provision of expert knowledge, involvement in political processes, and the ability to frame issues in the media. However, the theory of quiet politics holds that this power is exercised in environments of low political saliency, where the average voter is not particularly concerned with the outcome of policy development in a particular sector. Where an issue becomes salient, and is considered important by voters, the power of corporate lobbyists to influence policies is reduced. Finally, this chapter will link the theory of networks of power to the concept of networked governance, indicating the similarities and differences between these conceptualizations of regulation, before discussing how this analytical framework will be applied to the rest of the book. For now, however, this chapter will begin by introducing the work of Michel Foucault.

Michel Foucault and networks of power

Michel Foucault (1926–84) was a highly influential French writer active during the second half of the twentieth century, although he himself would likely have denied such a claim. He was a social historian, political philosopher and activist, both influenced by and disillusioned with the rigidity and intolerance of Marxist politics in France in the 1950s (Downing 2008, pp. 3–5). While turning his back on the Marxist politics and political institutions of the time, Foucault nevertheless had a continuing interest in Marxist thought, particularly with regard to the conceptualization of power and power relations. As is stated by Downing, where Foucault differed from Marx is in methodological approach. 'Where Marx proposes a global philosophy, Foucault is concerned with specificity. Where Marx puts forward a system, Foucault seeks to demystify the working of systemisation' (Downing 2008, p. 5). Foucault was a prolific and diverse writer, writing on topics as diverse as mental health and institutions for the mentally ill in *The history of madness* (2006), crime, prisons and self-regulation in *Discipline and punish* (Foucault 1991a) and the history and construction of human sexuality in *The history of sexuality: The will to knowledge* (1978). In his work, Foucault sought to question commonly understood views of rationality, the existence of universal truths and the perception of history as a natural and inevitable progression (see generally Kelly 2012; Lemke 2011; Downing 2008; Bennett 2013, pp. 23–5). Through the concept of genealogy, Foucault instead sought to demonstrate how such views are constructed or invented, through dominant discourses and the exercise of knowledge (Foucault 2002a; Kelly 2012, pp. 18–20). For Foucault power determines what discourses become dominant, who has the ability to construct a dominant discourse, and through which methods.

According to Kelly, 'in a sense, all Foucault's work has to do with power' (2012, p. 31). In an interview conducted by Duccio Trombadori in 1978, Foucault stated that 'every time I think about the experiences lived in contemporary societies, or about the investigations I have made, I always come up against the question of "power"' (Foucault 1991b, pp. 148–9). Foucault, however, dismissed the idea of creating a general theory of power, which in his view would 'provide an answer to everything, which is just what I don't want to do' (Foucault 2004, p. 13). Instead, the purpose of his works on power were to 'determine what are, in their mechanisms, effects, their relations, the various power-apparatuses that operate at various levels of society.' (Foucault 2004, p. 13). In other words, Foucault's writings on power were not intended as creating a general theory of power, but a way of analysing power in practice (Kelly 2012, pp. 34–5; Foucault 1991b, p. 148). In particular, Foucault sought to challenge the pervading view of power in what he described as its 'juridical conception', in which power can be possessed, and is treated as a commodity that can be transferred or otherwise treated as a form of property through juridical acts (Foucault 2004, p. 13). Or, as Veyne has incisively put it, law and 'political philosophy is too often inclined to reduce power solely to the central authority, Leviathan' (2010, p. 94). Instead, Foucault considered power as being relational. In a lecture given at the Collège de France in January 1976, Foucault stated:

> Do not regard power as a phenomenon of mass and homogenous domination – the domination of one individual over others . . . power is not something divided between those who have it and hold it exclusively, and those who do not have it and are subject to it. Power must . . . be analysed as something that circulates . . . Power functions. Power is exercised through networks.
>
> (Foucault 2004, p. 29)

Through a process of 'extrapolation', Kelly identifies the following characteristics of Foucault's conception of power: power is impersonal (and not to be found as an attribute of a particular individual or group); relational; decentered (not being concentrated on a single individual or group); multidirectional, not only operating hierarchically from the more powerful unto the less powerful but multilaterally; and strategic (2012, pp. 37–8). By 'strategic', Foucault meant that the exercise of power has a certain intentionality; 'action and reaction, question and answer, domination and evasion, as well as struggle' (Foucault 2002b, p. 2). Power, in other words, is exercised as a means of achieving certain objectives, such as to enact legal change, or to resist legal change (the notion of resistance will be discussed in much more detail in Chapters 7 and 8 of this book). Strategy constitutes the means employed to attain a certain end, the way in which one actor seeks to gain advantage over another actor, and the means perceived as resulting in victory (Foucault 2002b, p. 346). According to Downing, these means may be employed surreptitiously or indirectly, as well as overtly or directly (Downing 2008, p. 78). Power is everywhere, insofar as these networks of power comprise the everyday interactions that take place in society (Downing 2008, p. 90) – power relations include the relations between family members, between teacher and student, or law-making institution and the individual. To reiterate, these relations are not hierarchical; the exercise of power need not be by parent over child, or by teacher over student, but could be by child over parent, or student over teacher. And, as shall be demonstrated throughout this book, the individual can also exercise power over the lawmaker or governing institution, or between different actors within the same institution. In this way, the effects of power are 'not exercised from a single vantage point, but are mobile [and] multivalent' (Downing 2008, p. 83).

So, if we take power to be something that is exercised, or a relational function rather than an attribute possessed, the question then becomes 'how is power exercised?' Foucault argues that power can only be exercised over 'free' subjects. By this, Foucault means that power is exercised over 'individual or collective subjects who are faced with a field of possibilities in which several kinds of conduct, several ways of reacting and modes of behavior are available' (Foucault 2002b, p. 342). Power is exercised through one actor influencing or inducing the actions of another actor (whether that actor is an individual, group or institution). This influence can extend from the power exercised by a sovereign, such as the medieval King who had the right of life and death over his subjects (Foucault 2004, p. 240). This was not a power held by the sovereign, but a right exercised by a sovereign when killing (or ordering the death of) a subject. This power was exercised through acts of violence. Power can also be disciplinary, 'the technology by which men's bodies are controlled and trained in prisons, factories, schools, et cetera' (Kelly 2012, p. 43). This power is not exercised through violence, but through regulation, self-regulation and surveillance, as explained in significant detail in *Discipline and punish* (Foucault 1991a). 'Discipline consists of a concern with control which is internalized by each individual' (Mills 2003, p. 43). These self-regulating impulses begin as an external exercise of power that then becomes internalized as a matter of 'second-nature', forms of regulation that we do not give any great thought to. They may include practices relating to hygiene, such as washing one's hands before eating. They may concern when we eat, what time we sleep, or how we respond to emotionally fraught circumstances. Drawing from analysis of schools, prisons, factories and the military, Foucault argued that discipline is the exercise of power through controlling the way in which people circulate and the activities they perform (Foucault 1991a, pp. 141–56). So, for example, children within a school are divided into year groups. They may again be sub-divided into groups relating to aptitude, and allocated different rooms for different forms of activity. They will have timetables that dictate how long each activity will be performed, and strict parameters set on how those activities will be performed. While initially a form of power exercised upon those students, that power ultimately results in self-regulation, the internalization of these rules regarding circulation and activity. Students will know where they are supposed to go at a particular time and what they are supposed to be doing at that time, without the need for external pressures to be exerted in directing that activity. 'Discipline is a set of strategies, procedures and ways of behaving which are associated with certain institutional contexts and which then permeate ways of thinking and behaving in general' (Mills 2003, p. 44). Related to this, and of the most relevance to the study undertaken by this book, was Foucault's focus on 'governmentality'. By governmentality, Foucault means:

> The ensemble formed by the institutions, procedures, analyses, and reflection, the calculations and tactics that allow the exercise of this very specific, albeit complex form of power, which has as its target population, as its principal form of knowledge political economy.
>
> (Foucault 2002b, pp. 219–20)

According to Gordon, Foucault understood governmentality in a 'narrow' sense and a 'wide' sense (Gordon 1991, p. 2). In the narrow sense, governmentality is about Western liberal governmental rationality; it can be used to 'describe the emergence of a government that saw that the object of governing power was to optimise, use and foster living individuals as members of a population' (Dean 1999, p. 19). In its wider sense, it refers to the 'conduct of conduct', or the way in which activities intended to shape, guide or affect the conduct of individuals, groups or institutions are undertaken (Gordon 1991, p. 2). Kiersey considers that this wide definition of governmentality 'suggests, simply, that the intentionality of power is immanent to diverse and reversible sites and scales of social interaction' (2011, p. 17), or as Downing puts it, 'Foucault's concept is designed to counter notions of state power as unidirectional . . . or as static' (2008, p. 18). Butler states that 'marked by a diffuse set of strategies and tactics, governmentality gains its meaning and purpose from no single source, no unified sovereign subject' (2004, p. 52). Instead, the relationship between state institutions such as government and groups or individuals is multi-directional, including the relations between government and social institutions, or relations concerning political sovereignty (Gordon 1991, p. 3). Governmentality asks 'by what means, mechanisms, procedures, instruments, tactics, techniques, technologies and vocabularies is authority constituted and rule accomplished?' (Dean 2010, p. 42). In this wide sense, governmentality is a grid of analysis for these power relations (Kelly 2012, p. 61). Governmentality will be used in both senses in this book; it will be used both as a means of discussing the way in which copyright is governed within the EU area and the ways in which governing institutions guide conduct concerning copyright, and as a means of analysing the 'conduct of conduct' of those governing institutions. To put it another way, in the wide sense, governmentality will be used as a means of analysing the way in which those means of governing copyright are developed by assessing the roles of, and relations between governing institutions and other actors in formulating copyright laws.

Finally, it is important to state clearly that for Foucault, power is not by its very nature repressive (or, at the very least, not *solely* repressive). Instead, power is also productive, insofar as it can be ' "positive" (in the non-normative sense of asserting something), not inherently "repressive" or "forbidding" ' (Hearn 2012, p. 88). If power can be productive as well as repressive, 'then it is difficult to see power relations as simply negative and restraining' (Mills 2003, p. 47). Lemke argues that for Foucault, power is often considered in terms of its ability to repress, to censor or in terms of violent or forceful conduct without considering this productive element – the power to produce knowledge, or construct individual or community identities (2011, p. 11). 'We must cease once and for all to describe the effects of power in negative terms . . . In fact, power produces . . .' (Foucault 1991a, p. 194). For this reason, in the discussions of networks of power in subsequent chapters the intention of the analysis is not to demonstrate the negativity of the power relations apparent, but to analyse how the exercise of power shapes legal and regulatory approaches. As shall be demonstrated in the final chapters of this book, that power can be productive as well as repressive becomes important for analysing resistance.

Power/knowledge and discourse

Central to the analysis in this book is the relationship between power and knowledge. In *Power/knowledge*, Foucault argued that 'knowledge and power are integrated with one another . . . It is not possible for power to be exercised without knowledge, it is impossible for knowledge not to engender power' (1980, p. 51). Kelly however argues that it is important to note that this does not mean that knowledge and power are one and the same (2012, p. 169), but that there is a certain mutuality between power and knowledge. Instead, the relationship is that knowledge requires an apparatus of knowledge production in which relations of power are invested, and cannot exist without that apparatus. In turn, Kelly states, 'there is no apparatus invested in power relations which does not itself produce knowledge' (2012, p. 44). According to Foucault, 'the delicate mechanisms of power cannot function unless knowledge, or rather, knowledge apparatuses, are formed, organized and put into circulation' (2004, pp. 33–4). In other words, knowledge production is the result of the exercise of power, but knowledge production also facilitates the exercise of power. By apparatus, Foucault meant the 'heterogeneous ensemble consisting of discourses, institutions . . . regulatory decisions, laws, administrative measures, scientific statements, philosophical, moral and philanthropic positions . . . the apparatus itself is the system of relations that can be established between these elements' (1980, p. 194).

It is the interplay between these apparatuses that result in knowledge production – for example, the bringing together of discourses concerning efficiency with institutions such as the European Central Bank and scientific statements regarding economic indicators can lead to the production of a certain type of knowledge. This knowledge may very well result from certain power relations and also result in the realignment of power relations in the wake of the knowledge produced. One recent example is that of the controversy surrounding what is known as the 'Rogoff-Reinhart Study', also known as 'Growth in a Time of Debt' (Reinhart and Rogoff 2010). The 2010 study determined that across a broad range of countries and historical periods, economic growth declines dramatically when a country's level of public debt exceeds 90 per cent of gross domestic product (Pollin and Ash 2013). According to Rogoff and Reinhart, 'seldom do countries "grow" their way out of debts ... As countries hit debt tolerance ceilings, market interest rates can begin to rise quite suddenly, forcing painful adjustment' (2010, p. 577). This study followed on from an earlier study using the same dataset, in which it was deduced that commonly shared indicators such as a high debt-to-GDP ratio often precipitated a financial crisis. Rogoff and Reinhart argued that:

> the main cause of debt explosions is not the widely cited costs of bailing out and recapitalizing the banking system ... In fact, the big drivers of debt increases are the inevitable collapse of tax revenues ... as well as often ambitious countercyclical fiscal policies.
>
> (Reinhart and Rogoff 2009, p. 3)

In other words, these studies argued that the use of counter-cyclical policies such as governmental spending as a means of boosting the economy during a financial downturn, also known as 'Keynesian economics', fails to result in growth and contributes to increasing debts. According to *The New Yorker*, in 2008 many states in Europe were engaged in Keynesian programs as a means of tackling the financial crisis, before changing tack and adopting austerity programs in 2010. In February 2010, MP George Osborne (who became Chancellor of the Exchequer in May 2010) stated in Parliament that 'As Ken Rogoff himself puts it, "there's no question that the most significant vulnerability as we emerge from recession is the soaring government debt."' (as reproduced in Cassidy 2013). According to the same report, European Commissioner for Economic and Monetary Affairs and the Euro Olli Rehn also directly quoted the Rogoff-Reinhart study as a means of justifying policy choices made (Cassidy 2013). In a letter addressed to the Euro Area Finance Ministers, Rehn stated that:

> it is widely acknowledged, based on serious academic research, that when public debt levels rise above 90 per cent they tend to have an impact on economic dynamism, which translates into low growth for many years. That is why consistent and carefully calibrated fiscal consolidation remains necessary in Europe.
>
> (2013, p. 3)

We see here, then, the way in which knowledge has been produced and prioritized. Actors within institutions make scientific statements (in this instance, Harvard-based economists), and then these statements are adopted and reiterated by other institutional actors, such as a European Commissioner or parliamentary representative. These statements are then used as one basis for policy decisions made by those institutional actors. Power is exercised multilaterally – institutional actors deemed experts influence the decision-making policies of other actors, who in turn exercise power to create economic policies as a result of that produced knowledge. As a result, the position of Rogoff and Reinhart is influenced by the discourse of actors such as Osborne and Rehn, who produce knowledge that states that Rogoff and Reinhart are experts in this particular field. In turn, through the adoption of the discourse of Rogoff and Reinhart and its dominance in debate, a certain 'truth' is produced. By this, Foucault did not mean the production of true utterances, 'but the establishment of domains in which the practice of true and false can be made at once ordered and pertinent' (Foucault 2002b, p. 230). In other words, it is not that the findings of Rogoff and Reinhart are objectively true, but that through the power/knowledge apparatuses, their claims are accepted as being true. That the claims cannot be judged as being objectively true can be found in the previously mentioned controversy that developed upon subsequent findings by other academics that there were errors in the dataset used by Rogoff and Reinhart, resulting in questions over the validity of their research (Pollin and Ash 2013; Cassidy 2013). Nevertheless, the claims made were accepted as being true. According to Shiner, 'in Western societies, for example, "truth" is centred on scientific discourse and institutions; it is central to economic production and political power ... produced and disseminated by great economic and political apparatuses like the university, or media.' (1982, p. 384). Academics such as Rogoff and Reinhart, and particularly academics at highly respected institutions such as Harvard University, constitute actors with significant ability to exercise power through discourse. Shiner goes on to argue that Foucault believed that those in 'lower' positions within societies' institutions, such as prisoners in the jail as in *Discipline and punish*, or patients in an asylum in *Madness and Civilization*, have their knowledge discounted or suppressed.

> They are part of a system of power that invalidates their discourse ... continuously by a set of implicit rules concerning what sorts of concepts and vocabulary are acceptable and what credentials and status are requisite for one's discourse to count as knowledge.
>
> (1982, p. 384)

Others, such as academics, economists, and politicians, who are considered as being more senior in societies' institutions, are more likely to have their discourses considered as valid. For while power may be exercised multilaterally, and from below up, Foucault specifically viewed the ability to exercise power as inegalitarian, with privileged nodes within the networks of power more effectively able to exercise power than others (Kelly 2012, p. 41; Lemke 2011, pp. 19–20). In this context, a Harvard-based Professor in Economics has the status to be empowered to say what is true with regard to the impact of Keynesian economics on fiscal policy, in the way that (for example) a struggling worker in Greece, the governable subject of such a policy, cannot (see Shiner 1982, p. 384; Dean 2010, pp. 26–7).

Another way of putting it is that the regimes of practice give rise to and are informed and reshaped by various forms of knowledge and expertise (Dean 2010, p. 32). Knowledge defines the 'objects of such practices, codifies appropriate ways of dealing with them, set the aims and objectives of practice, and define the professional and institutional locus of authoritative agents of expertise' (Dean 2010, p. 32). Networks of power analysis, therefore, can be used to show how through discourse, 'conceptions themselves have their genesis and come to achieve regulatory dominance' (Prado 2000, p. 20). It also helps to demonstrate how certain discourses come to be viewed as true, by looking at imbalances between different actors in the ability to exercise knowledge power (see also Dean 2010, p. 27 on truth production). By achieving regulatory dominance in this manner, claims become regarded as true, or as Rehn puts it in his letter, 'widely acknowledged', to the extent that they become hegemonic, 'incorporated into the common-sense way we interpret, live in, and understand the world' (Harvey 2007, p. 23).

Lemke argues that the emergence and stability of state agencies is 'intimately tied to the incessant generation, circulation, storage, and repression of knowledge' (2011, p. 28). State agencies then use the knowledge produced, be it in the form of economic studies, legal reports, bureaucratic rules or censuses to then produce further knowledge that enable those actors to act upon the governed reality – in this sense, knowledge power both constitutes actors and the policy decisions of those same actors (Lemke 2011, pp. 28–9). The purpose of this study of the development of digital copyright laws is in essence to apply the perspective of an analytics of government to legal developments. As Dean states, 'an analytics of government attempts to show that our taken-for-granted ways of doing things and how we think about and question them are not entirely self-evident and necessary' (2010, p. 31). With regard to this book's study, the intention of this study is to identify how discourses and practices that have constituted digital copyright law emerge, through the analysis of how the regime of copyright both gives rise to and depends upon particular forms of knowledge (Dean 2010, p. 31). Furthermore, it shall seek to demonstrate the influence of particular forms of knowledge and discourse that help to achieve the goals of certain actors within the networks of power, and the techniques used to achieve such goals.

Quiet politics, business power and political salience

It is not only Foucault's theories on networks of power that inform the approach taken in this book. The general approach, and in particular the approach taken in the final chapters of this book on resistance to copyright policy development, is significantly influenced by the work of Pepper Culpepper on 'Quiet Politics' (2011). Describing his work on quiet politics as being 'about what happens in democracies when the people are not watching' (2011, p. xv), Culpepper analyses the approach taken to corporate control in the very different political regimes in

Germany, France, the Netherlands and Japan. The intention of Culpepper's work is to offer 'a framework for understanding the sources of managerial power in the politics of corporate control' (2011, p. 4). In his study, Culpepper determined that even where managerial preferences may vary among the selected countries, each influenced by the socio-political, cultural and economic contexts in which those businesses operate, the power exercised by those managerial actors did not. 'In each case, managers got the regime of corporate control they wanted' (Culpepper 2011, p. 4). The method through which these objectives were achieved, according to Culpepper, were having 'access to superior weapons for battles that take place away from the public spotlight ... [and] are decided through what I call "quiet politics"' (Culpepper 2011, p. 4). These 'weapons' include the use of direct lobbying tactics, involvement in working groups and framing issues favourably in the press (Culpepper 2011, pp. 8–9). In describing these apparatuses, Culpepper draws upon the work of academics such as Baumgartner (2009), Bernhagen and Braüninger (2005), and Eberle and Lauter (2008) on the topic of lobbying, and Iyengar (1991), Baum and Potter (2008), and Guber and Bosso (2007) on the topic of media framing.

Lobbying, as this book will demonstrate, is about more than just money, as is discussed by Baumgartner (2009, pp. 190–214). While money may have an impact on the development of laws and policies as subsequent chapters of this book will discuss, and has been argued as being particularly influential on US politics in particular (Lessig 2012), lobbying is a much more complicated issue than large corporations throwing money at sensitive issues. Successful lobbying is largely based on perceptions of expertise (Esterling 2004) and information asymmetry (Bernhagen and Braüninger 2005). 'Special interest groups enjoy informational advantages *vis-à-vis* policymakers due to the latter's capacity constraints, and because of interest groups' own strong incentives to pool resources and routinely conduct research on issues of concern to their members' (Bernhagen and Braüninger 2005, p. 47). Similarly, in a more recent study by Lutz *et al.* on corporate self-governance, it was determined that 'corporate governance codes are not instruments of "civil regulation" in a broader sense, given that code development is shaped by an "inner circle" of law experts, corporate and financial leaders and investor representatives' (Lütz *et al.* 2011, p. 331). Amable describes the creation of self-regulatory codes as being shaped by key coalitions, 'socio-political groups which have the power to shape the rules, institutions and governance mechanisms of a national political economy and to negotiate changes in them' (2003, pp. 10–12). This power stems from the perception of the objects of regulation as being best placed to regulate based on superior knowledge and expertise. As Culpepper puts it, 'company managers know more about the effect of legal changes on their companies than do politicians, and politicians know this' (2011, p. 9). For this reason, policymakers may defer to the requests of industries with regard to the wording of legislation, or indeed whether legislation is to be introduced at all. Members or representatives of business organizations may be invited to sit on 'expert committees' with politicians (forming one of these types of 'key coalition' described by Lütz *et al.*), influencing the findings of these committees in a way that may not necessarily be possible if regulation were to be discussed by a legislative committee without industry representation (Culpepper 2011, p. 9). By way of example, Lütz *et al.* describe the way in which a post-Enron review of the UK's Combined Code on corporate regulation known as the Higgs Review was highly influenced by corporate actors. The Review, which adopted a voluntary approach to strengthening companies' internal control and account-ability mechanisms, was strongly supported by stakeholders such as investors, companies and auditors (in addition to the general public), and the sections on the independence of non-executive directors as defined by Higgs 'largely followed the classification used by investors' (Lütz *et al.* 2011, p. 322). Where changes were contentious, and subject to significant criticism by corporate bodies, a working group was set up that included 'Higgs, members of the CBI [Confederation of British Industry], the ICAEW [Institute of Chartered Accountants in England and Wales] and the investment community' (Lütz *et al.* 2011, p. 323). According to Lütz *et al.*, the finalized Code that resulted from this working group had a distinctly 'investor-friendly character' (2011, p. 323). Through the active involvement of corporate or industry representatives in the law-making process, combined with the perception of expertise on the part of those representatives, business is able to favourably modify the content of legislation or regulatory codes, or even prevent them from being passed entirely.

Another means by which business may be able to influence legislative initiatives is through the use of the media. According to Iyengar, press or media framing refers to 'subtle alterations in the statement or presentation of judgment and choice problems' (1991, p. 11). Examples Iyengar gives include the framing of financial outcomes so as to 'manipulate' preferences regarding tax policies, the framing of cancer survival rates so as to 'manipulate' preferences regarding invasive surgery, or so as to 'manipulate' political preferences more generally, relying upon political discourse being ambiguous and levels of public knowledge about and interest in politics being low (1991, pp. 12–13). For a managerial actor, this framing could entail promotion of a discourse that links the continued health or success of a particular organization with the effective functioning of the economy (Culpepper 2011, p. 10). For a copyright holding business, as will be demonstrated throughout this book, it may be the promotion of a discourse in which increased protection is beneficial to the economy generally, or to creators specifically. While sceptical of the view that the media is merely a passive conduit for the opinions of elite actors such as corporate organizations or politicians, Baum and Potter nevertheless hold the view that 'the public is typically ill-informed . . . Thus, the information equilibrium tends to favour leaders, and, hence, the media are more responsive to leaders' preferences than to those of the public' (2008, p. 50). According to Guber and Bosso, this responsiveness means that public opinion on a particular issue can be molded by those leaders, with the result that 'without a clear understanding of the issue to anchor their responses, most were willing to be persuaded by the arguments they were offered' (2007, p. 43).

This is not to say, however, that 'big business' always gets the legislation (or lack of) that it desires. The successful use of techniques within the framework of quiet politics is ultimately dependent on the political salience of a particular issue. According to Culpepper, political salience is the importance of that issue 'to the average voter, relative to other political issues' (2011, p. 4). Put another way, the more politically salient an issue is, the more likely it is to be a 'vote winner', or perhaps of more concern to policymakers, a 'vote loser'. Kollman describes political salience as being about how important an issue is to a constituent, rather than their support of the proposed approach to that issue (1998, p. 25). For example, a constituent may consider crime to be a highly important issue, and wants to vote for a representative that promises to 'do something' about crime. However, two politicians may run for office on an anti-crime platform, albeit suggesting radically different approaches to the perceived problem. One may advocate for 'tough on crime' or 'zero tolerance' approaches with strict sentencing guidelines and longer sentences, whereas the other may advocate for tackling social issues, investing in rehabilitation or outreach programs. The preferred approach by the constituent is phrased in terms of popularity. The importance of the issue for the constituent is phrased in terms of salience. So, one constituent may consider the issue to be highly salient, and will vote accordingly (and specifically) for the representative advocating for their preferred method of tackling crime, such as zero tolerance. In comparison, a second voter may not consider the issue of crime to be of particular importance to them – while they may prefer the rehabilitation approach to crime they are unlikely to vote for a candidate on the basis of their crime-related platform. They have a preference, but for them, the issue is not politically salient.

While policy preferences appear to change infrequently on key policy issues such as crime, salience changes frequently as issues come to be perceived as either less or more important (See Page and Shapiro 1992). This salience, Kollman argues, 'rises and falls with news coverage, presidential speeches, world events … and the activities of interest groups' (1998, p. 25). Again using crime as an example, Gardner discusses the perceptions of the general public on crime-related risk, stating that 'crime makes up a large and growing portion of the stories told by the news media. The numbers vary depending on the country, but most surveys show crime makes up about 10 to 30 per cent of newspaper content' (2008, p. 195). The result is that the issue of crime becomes highly visible and frequently discussed by both politicians and the public. On an issue such as crime, constituents are more likely to vote for politicians who propose approaches to crime they support, or alternatively to 'punish' politicians who do not take their preferred approach. If an issue is not politically salient, however, this is unlikely to be the case. '"Read my lips; No new poison pills" is an unlikely campaign slogan in any country' (Culpepper 2011, p. 5). Where an issue is low visibility, or appears relatively unimportant to voters, then the apparatuses of 'quiet politics', such as the use of industry expertise or positive media framing can be relied upon by businesses. Issues that are perceived by the public and media to be technically complex and to have uncertain effects on issues that are of concern to voters (such as tax policy or crime levels) are likely to be issues of low salience. For this reason, voters are likely to pay little attention to the issue, and the media is unlikely to report on those issues, save perhaps for in specialized publications or newspapers such as the *Financial Times* and its international equivalents. 'When an issue is of little interest to voters, the press has little incentive to cover it and ambitious politicians gain little by acquiring expertise in it' (Culpepper 2011, p. 5). Where an issue becomes politically salient, however, this ability to substantially impact the content or form of policymaking is reduced. According to Culpepper, this is because when the general public becomes aware of a particular issue, politicians then pay attention to the preferences of that visible group and pay less attention to the interests of interest groups (2011, p. 6). Interest groups will then rely on what Kollman (1998) refers to as 'outside lobbying', in which those interest groups will attempt to convince voters that the interest group's preferred option is the most favourable one, or alternatively mobilize support for that option should they believe that the public is on their side (Culpepper 2011, p. 6). This shall be discussed in greater detail, particularly with regard to processes through which issues become politically salient, in Chapter 8.

The interaction between networks of power and quiet politics

As may be apparent from the preceding sections of this chapter, the analytical approaches taken by Foucault and Culpepper are strikingly different. Whereas Foucault's work is somewhat abstract and highly theoretical, Culpepper's is theoretically grounded in data analysis. Whereas Foucault takes a genealogical approach to case studies, tracing the apparent origins and development of ideas in particular fields such as psychiatry or criminality, Culpepper takes an empirical approach to the issue of corporate regulation, analysing managerial power in four delimited case studies in Germany, France, the Netherlands and Japan. Foucault and Culpepper would seem to speak in very different languages, and appear to have little in common. Nevertheless, there are similarities between the works of Foucault and Culpepper, and ways in which the different approaches of the two may be complementary. In particular, although their conceptualizations may be different, both authors ultimately deal with power. Whereas Foucault's discussion of power focuses on its multilateral nature, and that it is something exercised by actors rather than possessed by them, and Culpepper discusses 'managerial' or 'business' power in a way that may be inferred as suggesting that it is something possessed rather than exercised, this does not necessarily render the two approaches incompatible.

The first similarity identified is in the way in which both authors conceptualize the way power operates. The Foucauldian perspective explicitly refers to the networked nature of power. Power is something that is exercised through social relations. Power is not something wielded exclusively by a sovereign or state power in a vertical manner, but is something that is exercised multilaterally, between institutional actors, family members, and business and social structures of all kinds. While there may be asymmetries in the ability to effectively exercise power, individuals or institutions perceived as holding low positions in localized power structures (such as prisoners in the criminal justice system) are nevertheless able to exercise power upon other actors deemed more senior in those networks (such as prison wardens). Culpepper does not specifically refer to power in a networked sense, but the way in which the concept of quiet politics is described is indicative of the importance of relations between actors for the effective exercise of power. Quiet politics describes a process by which state actors defer to managerial actors in the field of corporate control. Business leaders, industry representatives and other non-state officials are influential in regulatory processes, exercising power over state actors and the media. In turn, when an issue becomes politically salient, individual voters are able to exercise some power over state actors. The media in both low and high salience issues is also able to exercise power, through the framing of the issues being discussed. In Culpepper's approach, then, there is also an understanding that power is not exercised in a purely hierarchical manner – it is multilateral, and while there may be asymmetries that impact the ability to effectively exercise power, that exercise of power functions within a network.

Another similarity is that both authors highlight the importance of the role of expertise in policymaking. Foucault, as has been discussed, focused on the role of the expert as a key node within the relationships of power that are involved in knowledge production, and thereby able to dominate discourses (Dean 2010, p. 32). The expert is thereby in a position to influence policies, by presenting evidence that is instrumental in establishing 'truth' (Foucault 2002b). Culpepper also highlights the importance of expertise in policymaking, referring to the 'deference of legislators and reporters towards managerial expertise' (2011, p. 4). As was mentioned in the preceding section, politicians perceive company managers as knowing more about their businesses than politicians do. The perception is one of expertise held by a particular actor within the network of power. Bernhagen and Braüninger quote an anonymous industry representative who states that 'I am actually surprised how often [ministerial civil servants] ring me up looking for information I would have assumed they would have at their fingertips.' (as quoted in 2005, p. 47), noting that businesses often accumulate knowledge that is important for policymaking (2005, p. 47). From a Foucauldian perspective, this knowledge accumulation also constitutes knowledge production. Knowledge is produced regarding the running of the business, but knowledge is also produced that states that businesses are best placed to provide this information, influencing policymaking both in terms of the data supplied, but also in the creation of the perception of the business as expert. In this respect, industry or business representatives can be considered as an epistemic community, 'a network of professionals with recognised expertise and competence in a particular domain and an authoritative claim to policy relevant knowledge within that domain or issue-area.' (Haas 1992, p. 3). This perception of expertise and authority also disadvantages those seeking to challenge the policies made as a result of business expertise, as is indicated by Esterling. 'The theory and analysis that inform expert policy draw on specialized knowledge that is often communicated in the technical language of social science learned only through rigorous professional training . . . citizens lack the capacity to comprehend [this] analytical information' (2004, p. 24). Similarly, Culpepper argues that effective lobbying is down to the expertise of managers and their lawyers, who possess knowledge that politicians (and arguably the general public) find difficult to challenge (2011, p. 9). The role and power of the expert would therefore appear to be important in analysing how policies develop from both the perspective of Foucault, and that of quiet politics.

Closely related to the role of experts is that of the role of discourse in policy-making. Foucault's approach was one of genealogy – uncovering or revealing the way in which discourses are constructed, and how certain truths are produced as a result. As discussed in the section on power/knowledge, apparatuses exist that facilitate the construction of particular discourses (such as that mentioned of high debt-to-GDP ratios exacerbating the economic crisis), determining what sort of statements will be considered 'true' and which 'false', and which discourses will achieve regulatory dominance and which will be discarded (Foucault 2002b; Shiner 1982; Dean 2010 as previously cited). Those that achieve regulatory dominance come to be accepted as 'common sense', both forming the basis of policy action and being difficult to challenge or resist. Culpepper in comparison refers to the 'agenda-setting' powers of businesses, and their ability to set the terms of the debate (2011, p. 9). While this language is substantially different, they nevertheless refer to the same phenomenon – the ability of an actor within a network of power to influence or shape how an issue is perceived, discussed and acted upon. Both also recognize the role of the media as an actor in framing discourse, Foucault considering the media more generally as one of a number of nodes with the ability to produce knowledge and construct truths (Foucault 1980; Shiner 1982), and Culpepper referring to the importance of the role of the media in issue framing (Culpepper 2011; Iyengar 1991; Guber and Bosso 2007). In particular, Guber and Bosso refer specifically to the importance of the media in framing an issue so as to construct particular images and reinforce favourable discourses (Guber and Bosso 2007, p. 45). One particularly interesting similarity between the two approaches is that despite the differences in language, both emphasize the explanatory potential of the analysis of power relations as a means of revealing how policy develops 'behind the scenes'. In other words, both approaches to analyses of power attempt to render visible political struggles, whether legislative or otherwise. Foucault attempted to reveal the hidden discourses of power that underpin many issues that we take for granted, seeking to demonstrate that they do not represent absolute truths, but may instead be indicative of the dominant discourses at a particular point in history (for example, who today would use phrenology, the study of the size and proportions of the human skull, as a means of assessing criminality?). Culpepper's focus on quiet politics, although using somewhat different terms, is a focus on what happens when the public is not paying attention, or where policymaking occurs in arenas hidden from public view (2011, p. xv). Quiet politics focuses on the role of businesses in issues considered as having low political salience in which policy-making is largely undertaken behind the scenes, involving lobbying, framing issues indirectly through the media, and participating in working groups or providing expert knowledge. By uncovering these processes by which policies are developed in low salience issues, Culpepper aims to provide an explanation for how businesses are able to secure favourable regulatory conditions. In this way, both networks of power analysis and quiet politics analysis seek to explain otherwise hidden processes.

It is for these reasons that adopting an approach that incorporates both the Foucauldian approach to power and the quiet politics approach to power is neither inconsistent nor incoherent. Both approaches appear to recognize the importance of perceiving the functioning of power in policy development as being through networks, and that power is not exercised in a solely hierarchical manner. In networks of power and quiet politics, the role of experts in policy development is of particular importance, and the role of discourse in these power relations is emphasized, albeit in different terms. Finally, both approaches seek to uncover hidden discourses of power. These approaches can both provide an explanation for processes that are taken for granted, providing an opportunity to reassess the role of actors in policy development, and a means of analysing the way in which policies develop in particular issue areas.

Networks of power and networked governance

A theme that will quickly become apparent throughout this book is that of 'networked governance', a topic that will be covered in some depth in Chapter 5. Governance and governmentality are somewhat different concepts, but share some similarities. Where governmentality is a frame for analysis, in which one seeks to understand the apparatuses that are used for governing subjects, governance is more of a descriptive-normative assessment of the institutional structures by which something is governed. Governance, according to Marcussen and Torfling, is based in a recognition that political decision making is not restricted to formal governmental institutions (2003, p. 2), and is highly focused on the creation, construction and establishment of policy networks (see for example Koimann 2000). For Marcussen and Torfling, networked governance can be defined as:

1) a horizontal articulation of interdependent, but operationally autonomous actors; 2) who interact through negotiations; 3) transpiring within a regulative, normative, cognitive and imaginary framework; 4) that to a certain extent is self-regulating; and 5) which contribute to the production of public purpose within a particular area.

(2003, p. 7)

This understanding of networked governance shares distinct similarities with Foucault's networks of power, with its focus on multilateral exercises of power. For Castells, each interdependent actor constitutes a node in this network, the importance of which varies depending on the particular activity being undertaken, and the level of competence and information possessed by that particular node (2011, pp. 18–19). Nodes can cooperate or compete, depending on the situation (as shall be seen when considering entertainment industry representatives and telecoms representatives in Chapter 5), operating through communication (2011, p. 20). This is similar to Foucault's perception of relationships within governmentality. In both analyses, information/knowledge plays an important role in determining whose ideas are more effectively communicated/which discourses become dominant. Where Castells and Foucault differ, however, is in their consideration of power in itself, with Foucault (as discussed) considering it something that is exercised, whereas Castells refers to power as something 'held' (2011, p. 28). Nevertheless, despite this difference in conceptualization, both Castells and Foucault perceive power as being something that operates through multilateral networks, rather than hierarchical ones.

With regard to frameworks, networked governance fits effectively into the conceptualization of Western liberal government (or, depending on the author, neoliberal government (Harvey 2007)), in which the power of the state is limited, and reliant on the technical expertise and reach of large transnational organizations such as multinational companies in many activities. For Braithwaite, this can be summarized as 'regulatory capitalism' (2008, p. 1), a concept developed by Levi-Faur (2005) in which regulation is performed by networks of connected actors, both public and private, and through systems of self-regulation and regulated self-regulation (Parker 2002). Regulatory capitalism holds that rather than seeing a significant decrease in regulatory structures as a result of globalization and the neoliberal ideology, regulatory structures, both formal and informal have flourished, with interdependent, yet autonomous and self-regulatory nodes, able to exert control/guidance over particular state and non-state functions. In general, within this form of networked governance, these institutions or actors are able to act without the need for direct oversight (Christou and Simpson 2006). Because of this level of interdependence, the importance of deliberation and the ability for competing discourses to be communicated within these networks, it is difficult to refer to certain actors acting purely as policymakers, and others as policy-takers. Instead, the relationship is more complex, with a particular policy filtering back and forth through various levels of a network system, in such a way that a policy initiative that begins in one form may be affected by certain dominant discourses, leading to a change in that policy. For this reason, a conceptualization of power as operating multilaterally through networks rather than hierarchically between policymaker and policy-taker may better explain the development of copyright policies in the EU.

In a Foucauldian analysis, networked governance would constitute a mentality of rule (Foucault 2010, pp. 3–12), or as Lemke puts it, a rationalization of how power is exercised (2001, p. 191). The rationalization of a theory of governance, such as networked governance, is not neutral knowledge and 'objective description', but an 'intellectual processing of the reality which political technologies can then tackle' (Lemke 2001, p. 191). This is the reason why the description 'descriptive-normative' was used earlier in the discussion of networked governance. Networked governance is the term used to explain the observed relations between actors, but one that is subject to certain stated or unstated normative positions. How one perceives networked governance will result in a different understanding or conceptualization of problems in governance, or which issues are issues to be tackled. For example, for a proponent of neoliberalism (and one which shares its ideological convictions), markets regulated are markets distorted. Therefore, government intervention becomes a problem that must be combated through the 'shrinking' of the state, the deregulation of financial markets and the privatization of state assets. For a proponent of networked governance, the increased involvement of non-state actors, whether civil society organizations or private business entities with particular expertise, may represent a beneficial 'opening up' of government, allowing for knowledge production and a more democratic form of decision making. For those who are more sceptical of networked governance, it may entail regulatory capture and the running of state functions (or functions perceived as being best run by the state) by undemocratic and unaccountable business interests. Nevertheless, as Marcussen and Torfling make clear, networked governance is a popular metaphor for contemporary understandings of how governance currently functions (2003, p. 3). It also appears to be a discourse that has significant influence at the European level, as shall be explored in Chapter 5. It is important to note, however, that the use of networked governance in this book is within the frame of governmentality, seeking to explore a possible explanation for political decisions taken by institutional actors. Or to put it another way, networked governance may be the rationality of government that influences institutional actors to make the policy decisions they make. If the European Commission perceives networked governance through the cooperation of public and private entities in regulation as a beneficial or effective way of tackling perceived issues, then this belief may have an impact on the Commission's policy decisions. With this in mind, the final section of this chapter will provide an explanation of how the networks of power and quiet politics framework will be used throughout this book.

Concluding remarks: the application of networks of power and quiet politics to the development of digital copyright law and policy in the EU

As was stated explicitly at the beginning of this chapter, this book is neither dedicated to Foucault's political philosophy specifically, nor to corporate governance more generally. For this reason, the works and theories of Foucault more generally will not be referred to throughout the book, but will be limited to ways of exploring relations of power between institutional and non-institutional actors. The purpose of this book is to demonstrate how the networks of power present in this field of study have come to shape the digital copyright policies and law making of the EU, and the role of discourse in giving effect to these networks of power. The Foucauldian conceptualization of networks of power, coupled with the study of quiet politics in the field of digital copyright law constitutes a frame for analysis. These approaches are useful for their explanatory potential, allowing for the development of copyright law in the EU to be reassessed, or perhaps reinterpreted. Through an approach to copyright legislation and legislative initiatives that is informed by the networks of power analysis, it becomes possible to identify and to an extent deconstruct the dominant discourses that either influence or inhibit the development of copyright law, and the tensions inherent between competing discourses in copyright policy. It allows for hidden discourses of power to be revealed, showing how perceptions of expertise on the part of industry representatives and hegemonic discourses of economic efficiency, or in some instances threat, influence the timbre of legislative responses to issues identified in copyright law. It also helps us to understand why particular 'issues' are viewed as 'problems' that require legislative responses at all. Through the influence of the quiet politics approach, it is possible to link the more abstract approach of the networks of power to a means of analysing practical case studies of legislative development – how lobbying in a particular instance was undertaken, the specific role of experts in that process, and whether that issue was perceived as being one of high or low political salience. The two approaches interact, with quiet politics helping to explain how certain discourses may become dominant, while the networks of power analysis will help to explain why lobbyists are able to exert influence over policy development.

It is intended through the analysis being undertaken in this book, particularly in Chapters 4 through to 8, to provide those with a legal background with a deeper explanation of the processes by which copyright law and policy develop in the EU through reference to non-legal sources, providing an interdisciplinary approach to a field that has predominantly been studied doctrinally. It is hoped that through performing this analysis, the usefulness and relevance of adopting a critical perspective to legislative development that looks beyond legal texts and analyses processes will be demonstrated. In particular, an approach that sees law-making as part of a complex network of relationships that can be understood in terms of political saliency may help to provide legally trained readers with additional instruments for assessing legislative change. For non-legal readers, this book may give insight into a particular area of the European Union's internal market policies, focusing on copyright law, a subject not often covered in significant detail in political analysis, in part due to its relatively low political salience in comparison to issues such as taxation, social welfare or external action policies. The next two chapters will provide an overview prior to the assessment of networks of power. Chapter 2 will briefly introduce the legislative initiatives that will form the basis for the assessment in Chapters 4 to 6, providing basic information about key provisions in those texts and some of the academic response to the successfully enacted Directives, and information on legislative initiatives relating to harmonization that failed. Chapter 3 will provide an overview of decisions of the Court of Justice of the European Union, demonstrating that despite judicial efforts to create a single market in the area of digital media distribution, those efforts have been somewhat unsuccessful. Upon concluding these summaries of the current state of the law and market, the analysis of networks of power will begin in Chapter 4, concerning initiatives regarding the scope and duration of protection, continue in Chapter 5, concerning copyright enforcement measures, and conclude with Chapter 6, in which the problematization of the digital single market and the role of collecting societies will be considered in more detail. Finally, Chapters 7 and 8 will continue with analysis of resistance within networks of power.

Bibliography

Amable, B., 2003. *The diversity of modern capitalism.* Oxford. Oxford University Press.

Baum, M.A. and Potter, P.B.K., 2008. 'The relationships between mass media, public opinion, and foreign policy: Toward a theoretical synthesis'. *Annual Review of Political Science, 11*(1), pp. 39–65.

Baumgartner, F.R., 2009. *Lobbying and policy change: Who wins, who loses, and why.* Chicago, IL: University of Chicago Press.

Bennett, T., 2013. *Making culture, changing society.* London: Routledge.

Bernhagen, P. and Bräuninger, T., 2005. 'Structural power and public policy: A signaling model of business lobbying in democratic capitalism'. *Political Studies, 53*(1), pp. 43–64.

Braithwaite, J., 2008. *Regulatory capitalism: How it works, ideas for making it work better.* Cheltenham: Edward Elgar.

Butler, J.P., 2004. *Precarious life: The power of mourning and violence.* London: Verso Books.

Cassidy, J., 2013. 'The Reinhart and Rogoff controversy: A summing up'. *The New Yorker Blogs.* Available at: www.newyorker.com/online/blogs/johncassidy/2013/04/the-rogoff-and-reinhart-controversy-a-summing-up. html [Accessed 19 June 2013].

Castells, M., 2011. *Communication power.* Oxford: Oxford University Press.

Christou, G. and Simpson, S., 2006. 'The internet and public-private governance in the European Union'. *Journal of Public Policy, 26*(1), pp. 43–61.

Culpepper, P.D., 2011. *Quiet politics and business power: Corporate control in Europe and Japan.* Cambridge: Cambridge University Press.

Dean, M., 1999. *Governmentality: Power and rule in modern society.* London: Sage.

Dean, M., 2010. *Governmentality: Power and rule in modern society*, 2nd edn. London: Sage.

Downing, L., 2008. *The Cambridge introduction to Michel Foucault*. Cambridge: Cambridge University Press.

Eberle, D. and Lauter, D., 2008. 'Corporate governance codes and the "Varieties of Capitalism", a comparison between Germany and Great Britain'. In Sixteenth International Conference of Europeanists. Chicago, IL.

Esterling, K.M., 2004. *The political economy of expertise information and efficiency in American national politics*. Ann Arbor, MI: University of Michigan Press.

Foucault, M., 1978. *The history of sexuality: The will to knowledge*. London: Penguin.

Foucault, M., 1980. *Power/knowledge: Selected interviews and other writings. 1972–1977*, C. Gordon, ed. New York: Random House.

Foucault, M., 1991a. *Discipline and punish: The birth of the prison*. London: Penguin.

Foucault, M., 1991b. *Remarks on Marx: Conversations with Duccio Trombadori*. New York: Semiotext(e) Foreign Agents.

Foucault, M., 2002a. *Archaeology of knowledge*, 2nd edn. London: Routledge.

Foucault, M., 2002b. *Power: The essential works of Michel Foucault 1954–1984*, J. Faubion, ed. London: Penguin.

Foucault, M., 2004. *Society must be defended: Lectures at the Collège de France, 1975–1976*, London: Penguin.

Foucault, M., 2006. *The history of madness*. New York: Routledge.

Foucault, M., 2010. *The birth of biopolitics: Lectures at the Collège de France, 1978–1979*, F. Ewald, A. Fontana and Collège de France, eds. Basingstoke, UK: Palgrave Macmillan.

Gardner, D., 2008. *Risk: The science and politics of fear*. London: Virgin Books.

Gordon, C., 1991. 'Governmental rationality: An introduction'. In G. Burchell, C. Gordon, and P. Miller, eds, *The Foucault effect: Studies in governmentality*. Chicago, IL: University of Chicago Press.

Guber, D.L. and Bosso, C., 2007. 'Framing ANWR: Citizens, consumers, and the privileged position of business'. In M.E. Kraft and S. Kamieniecki, eds, *Business and environmental policy corporate interests in the American political system*. Cambridge, MA: MIT Press.

Haas, P.M., 1992. 'Introduction: Epistemic communities and international policy coordination'. *International Organization*, 46(1), pp. 1–35.

Harvey, D., 2007. 'Neoliberalism as creative destruction'. *The ANNALS of the American Academy of Political and Social Science*, 610(1), pp. 21–44.

Hearn, J., 2012. *Theorizing power*. Basingstoke, UK: Palgrave Macmillan.

Iyengar, S., 1991. *Is anyone responsible?: How television frames political issues*. Chicago, IL: University of Chicago Press.

Kelly, M.G.E., 2012. *The political philosophy of Michel Foucault*. London: Routledge.

Kiersey, N.J., 2011. 'Neoliberal political economy and the subjectivity of crisis: Why governmentality is not hollow'. In N.J. Kiersey and D. Stokes, eds, *Foucault and international relations: New critical engagements*. New York: Routledge.

Koimann, J., 2000. 'Societal governance: Levels, modes, and orders of social-political interaction'. In J. Pierre, ed., *Debating governance: Authority, steering, and democracy*. Oxford: Clarendon.

Kollman, K., 1998. *Outside lobbying: Public opinion and interest group strategies*. Princeton, NJ: Princeton University Press.

Lemke, T., 2001. '"The birth of bio-politics": Michel Foucault's lecture at the Collège de France on neo-liberal governmentality'. *Economy and Society, 30*(2), pp. 190–207.

Lemke, T., 2011. *Foucault, governmentality, and critique.* Colorado, CO: Paradigm.

Lessig, L., 2012. *Republic, lost: How money corrupts congress – and a plan to stop it.* New York: Twelve.

Levi-Faur, D., 2005. 'The rise of regulatory capitalism: The global diffusion of a new order'. *The ANNALS of the American Academy of Political and Social Science, 598*(1), pp. 12–32.

Lütz, S., Eberle, D. and Lauter, D., 2011. 'Varieties of private self-regulation in European capitalism: Corporate governance codes in the UK and Germany'. *Socio-Economic Review, 9*(2), pp. 315–38.

Marcussen, M. and Torfing, J., 2003. 'Grasping governance networks'. *Centre for Democratic Network Governance Working Paper Series,* 2003: 5, pp. 1–31.

Mills, S., 2003. *Michel Foucault.* New York: Routledge.

Page, B.I. and Shapiro, R.Y., 1992. *The rational public: Fifty years of trends in Americans' policy preferences.* Chicago, IL: The University of Chicago Press.

Parker, C., 2002. *The open corporation: Effective self-regulation and democracy.* New York: Cambridge University Press.

Pollin, R. and Ash, M., 2013. 'Austerity after Reinhart and Rogoff'. *Financial Times.* Available at: www.ft.com/cms/s/0/9e5107f8-a75c-11e2-9fbe-00144feabdc0.html#axzz2WaWLHhrf [Accessed 18 June 2013].

Prado, C.G., 2000. *Starting with Foucault: An introduction to genealogy.* Boulder, CO: Westview Press.

Rehn, O., 2013. 'Letter to Euro area finance ministers'. Available at: http://ec.europa.eu/commission_2010–2014/rehn/documents/cab20130213_en.pdf [Accessed 19 June 2013].

Reinhart, C.M. and Rogoff, K.S., 2009. *The aftermath of financial crises,* National Bureau of Economic Research. Available at: www.nber.org/papers/w14656 [Accessed 18 June 2013].

Reinhart, C.M. and Rogoff, K.S., 2010. 'Growth in a time of debt'. *American Economic Review, 100*(2), pp. 573–8.

Shiner, L., 1982. 'Reading Foucault: Anti-method and the genealogy of power-knowledge'. *History and Theory, 21*(3), pp. 382–98.

Veyne, P., 2010. *Foucault: His thought, his character.* Cambridge: Polity.

Chapter 2

European digital copyright law

As was stated in the introduction, the purpose of this chapter is to provide the reader with a basis for the arguments made in the subsequent chapters of this book. As the intent of the book is to demonstrate the networks of power that have framed the development of European laws pertaining to copyright on the internet, and in order to limit the scope to an area of research that can feasibly undertaken, analysis has been restricted to four principle topics. These are the passing of the Information Society Directive (2001/29/EC) and the framing of the scope of copyright; the Term Extension Directive (2011/77/EU) and the framing of the extension of protection for sound recordings; the framing of the Enforcement Directive (2004/48/EC) and proposals for strengthened enforcement mechanisms; and the framing of the Collective Rights Management Recommendation (2005/737/EC) and subsequent proposals for a Directive on Collective Rights Management.

This chapter will begin by defining what is meant by 'European' or 'EU' copyright law, making clear that the legislation adopted by the EU thus far in the field of copyright law does not represent the creation of a unified or supranational system of copyright protection, but instead represents the harmonization of nationally existing rights. The legal basis for legislative developments will be expanded upon, demonstrating that harmonization has not only been the aim of the Community in the field of intellectual property law, but also the legal justification for forays into law-making in the field of copyright. The creation of an explicit competence in the field of intellectual property law post-Lisbon Treaty will also be discussed, and the possibility of Article 118 forming the legal basis for the creation of a unified copyright code, as opposed to continued approximation through harmonization, which has been considered as forming a major impediment to the provision of cross-border services in copyrighted works. This chapter will then provide an overview of the traditional justifications for granting copyright protection as a means of familiarizing the reader with concepts that will be expanded upon in the networks of power chapters, discussing the differences between the 'economic incentive' and 'natural rights' approaches to copyright, and a brief consideration of the discourse concerning the UK's copyright system and continental Europe's *droit d'auteur* system being based on these two different conceptualizations.

Discussion of the four main legislative acts forming the basis of this book's analysis will be preceded by a brief overview of the international agreements impacting upon the development of 'European' copyright law such as the World Intellectual Property Organization Treaties (hereafter WIPO Treaties) and the TRIPS Agreement, discussing the perception of these international agreements as being the result of concerted lobbying practices, noting the involvement of the Community in framing these agreements. The subsequent sections will consider the Information Society, Term Extension and Enforcement Directives, and the Collective Management Recommendation respectively, providing an overview of the sections of these acts most relevant to the analysis, and demonstrating that where harmonization has been successful, it has generally been of a contentious and contested 'upwards' form. The fact that 'lobbying' is usually referred to as a key element of these developments will also be discussed, providing a frame of reference for Chapters 4 to 6.

'European' copyright law?

Certain harmonizing measures in copyright law have existed for much longer than the European Union. Arguably the most important international agreement on copyright is the Berne Convention of 1886, an agreement to which 163 states are now party. The aim of this Convention was to ensure 'national treatment' for creative works, as guaranteed under Article 5. In other words, the purpose of this Convention was to ensure that authors and publishers from other nations were granted the same rights and remedies that were available to domestic authors. The reason for this was the belief of policymakers that large-scale piracy of books was taking place during that time, and the exploitation of loopholes in national laws that provided no national protection for foreign nationals whose works were copied outside of their own jurisdiction (Drahos and Braithwaite 2002, pp. 31–4; Johns 2011, pp. 1–16). Prior to the Convention, protection was subject to bilateral agreements, leading to undue complexity and uneven protection based on the bargaining positions of the parties involved (Tritton and Davis 2008, p. 469). The purpose of this Convention, however, was to ensure some mitigation of the difficulties in ensuring effective copyright protection through equal treatment, not, as Torremans equivocally states, 'to create a supranational copyright system' (Torremans 2010, p. 31).

The European Union does not have a supranational copyright system, and it is technically incorrect to refer to the copyright law of the EU. At the time of writing, at least, there is no European Copyright Code. Instead, when EU copyright law or European copyright law is referred to, it is in fact a reference to the harmonizing legislation and jurisprudence of the Court of Justice of the European Union (CJEU). The reason for this has been explicitly referred to by the CJEU in the 2005 *Lagardère* case. In this case, Lagardère had a transmitter in France, and a second transmitter in Germany. The transmitter in Germany was used to broadcast into France on a long-wave signal, as the FM signal of the French transmitter was not powerful enough to cover the entirety of the country. The company was involved in no commercial activity in Germany, yet some satellite owners on the German side of the border could view the broadcast content. Lagardère agreed with SPRE, the French broadcasting collecting society, that from the royalties paid, an amount would be deducted that would be paid to the German collecting society. However, the CJEU ruled that the royalty payment must be made in full in both Member States. In its decision, the CJEU stated that with regard to copyright:

> The principle of the territoriality of those rights . . . is recognised in international law and also in the EC Treaty. Those rights are therefore of a territorial nature and, moreover, domestic law can only penalise conduct engaged in within national territory.
>
> (*Lagardère* (2005), para. 46)

In other words, European copyright law refers to the harmonization of aspects of copyright law among the Member States, but those harmonized aspects are implemented and enforced within the national territory of a Member State. As Hugenholtz notes, 'despite extensive harmonisation, copyright law in the EU is still largely linked to the geographic boundaries of sovereign Member States' (2012, p. 4; see also Eechoud *et al.* 2009, chap. 9; Hugenholtz 2009). Harmonization is aimed primarily at removing disparities between national copyright laws, in areas such as the duration of copyright. The impetus for law-making, and indeed the legal justification for endeavors in the field of copyright, has predominantly concerned barriers to trade within the internal market. Prior to the Treaty on the Functioning of the European Union (TFEU), the European Union did not possess an explicit competence for law-making in the field of intellectual property. Therefore, an alternative legal basis within the EC Treaties was required. As Georgopoulos states, 'harmonization of copyright law is by far the most common method of regulation chosen by EU institutions . . . justified by the impact of copyright on the internal market' (Georgopoulos 2012, sec. 1.1). This legal basis could be found in Article 95 EC (now 114 TFEU). Article 95(1) EC stated that in order to remove barriers to the functioning of the internal market allowing for the free movement of goods, services, workers and capital, the Council could 'adopt the measures for the approximation of the provisions laid down by law, regulation or administrative action in Member States which have as their object the establishment and functioning of the internal market'. This legal basis can be identified in the recitals to Directives such as the Information Society Directive, in which it is stated in recital 1 that:

> The Treaty provides for the establishment of an internal market and the institution of a system ensuring that competition in the internal market is

not distorted. Harmonisation of the laws of the Member States on copyright and related rights contributes to the achievement of these objectives.

This justification was the basis for the 'first phase' of copyright harmonization in the EU, which was initiated in the late 1980s with the Green Paper 'Copyright and the Challenge of Technology' (European Commission 1988). The Green Paper stated that 'to the maximum extent possible, creators and providers of copyright goods and services should be able be able to treat the Community as a single internal market' (1988, sec. 1.3.2), thereby necessitating the removal of barriers to trade posed by copyright. This need to harmonize in order to remove barriers to trade formed the legal basis for Directives such as the Rental Rights Directive 92/100/EEC (repealed and replaced by Directive 2006/115/EC) and the Copyright Duration Directive 93/98/EEC (repealed and replaced by Directive 2006/116/EC), which stipulated that copyright protection should last for the life of the author plus seventy years.

However, post-TFEU, the EU appears to have the ability to create law in the field of intellectual property as an explicit, individual competence under Article 118 TFEU, which states that the European Parliament and Council can 'establish measures for the creation of European intellectual property rights to provide uniform protection of intellectual property rights'. In an analysis of the TFEU (under the name of the Treaty of Lisbon), the House of Lords in the UK made an assessment of Article 118, where they considered that Article 118 TFEU is merely a restating of pre-existing powers, but noted that 'although the Treaty of Lisbon would not confer additional IP powers on the EU, it marks a statement of political intent' (House of Lords European Committee 2008, sec. 9.24). In comparison, Georgopoulos argues that while the Article may give the impression of being merely a restatement of existing power, it has the potential to constitute 'new wine in new bottles', allowing for the European institutions to create a system of European intellectual property law that goes beyond the principle of harmonizing the national laws of Member States, and also allows for the EU to negotiate international treaties in the field of intellectual property law as part of a proactive commercial policy (2012, sec. 1.3).

The territoriality of copyright has been referred to as the Achilles heel of the EU's initiatives to harmonize copyright law, with deference to national property systems constituting a potential reason why (as shall be demonstrated in the analysis of the four legal initiatives discussed later in this chapter) there has been an observable trend of 'upwards' harmonization to the highest offered national level of protection in the EU (Eechoud et al. 2009, p. 308). As will be demonstrated in Chapters 4, 5 and 6, there are other possible explanations for this upwards harmonization trend that may be found in both explicit and hidden discourses, but nevertheless, territoriality in copyright has been identified as a significant issue within the harmonization process. In the 2011 Commission Communication 'A Single Market for Intellectual Property Rights', it was stated that a 'far-reaching overhaul of Copyright at European level could be the creation

of a European Copyright Code' (European Commission 2011, p. 11). Cook and
Derclaye, among others, have stated that a unitary copyright law in the EU would
potentially have significant benefits, such as having instant Community-wide
effect, thereby creating a true single market for copyright and related rights (2011,
p. 261). This is an initiative supported by a number of notable academics in
the field of intellectual property, who under the name 'The Wittem Group' have
recently drafted such a unitary Copyright Code, with the aim of promoting
'transparency and consistency in European copyright law' (The Wittem Group
2011, p. 76). Ginsburg and Hilty, however, have expressed skepticism concerning
the ability for a unified code to address the issues of territoriality in EU law
(Ginsburg 2011, p. 265), and whether there genuinely exists the political will
to implement such a code (Hilty 2012, sec. 18.1.3). This shall be explored further
in Chapter 6 in the context of discussion of networks of power and the cross-
border licensing of music content.

Dominant discourses concerning the protection of copyright

There are two major arguments in favour of copyright protection that are
dominant in contemporary discourse. The first is that of economic efficiency –
it argues that copyrightable works such as music are of value to society, and
without copyright protection, the production of such works would fail to happen
at an optimal level. For example, this line of reasoning goes, recording an album
involves considerable costs, including the recording itself in a studio, production
and advertising. If that work was to then be copied at little cost to the copier,
and then redistributed on a mass scale for free, these costs could not be recouped.
This argument becomes particularly pertinent given the ease at which music can
be digitally copied and distributed through the internet. The legal protection
given by copyright is intended to rectify this 'market failure' by providing
incentives that encourage the production and dissemination of works:

> [providing] a legal means by which those who invest time and labour in
> producing . . . goods can be confident that they will not only be able to
> recoup that investment, but also reap a profit proportional to the popularity
> of their work.
>
> (Bently and Sherman 2004, p. 35)

This incentivization-based justification is sometimes referred to as being a
'utilitarian' justification for intellectual property protection of creative works. As
one author states, 'utilitarian theorists endorse the creation of intellectual property
rights in order to induce innovation and intellectual productivity' (Zemer 2007,
p. 9). This is based on the belief that by encouraging creators through the
provision of economic incentives, more cultural works will be produced, resulting
in a greater public surplus. Zemer argues that this view constitutes the prime

justification for copyright protection in the Anglo-American intellectual property regimes (2007, p. 12), a view that is supported by UK and United States-based legislation. The Statute of Anne 1709, which is considered as being one of the first 'modern' copyright statutes, had the long title of 'An Act for the Encouragement of Learning, by vesting Copies of printed Books in the Authors, or Purchasers of such copies, during the Times therein mentioned'. It would appear, from the title of the Act, that protection was granted to literary works on the grounds that by providing an economic incentive for the creation and distribution of works, this would lead to a general improvement in the education standards of the population (See also Deazley 2004). Similarly, Article 1 s.8(8) of the US Constitution empowers Congress 'to promote the Progress of Science and useful Arts, by securing for a limited Time to Authors and Investors the exclusive Right to their respective Writings and Discoveries'. As Chapters 4 and 5 of this book shall demonstrate, many of the justifications given for expanding the scope and protection of copyright law at the EU level are made on these economic-incentive based justifications.

The second of these arguments focuses on the rights of the author as an individual. This argument for an authors right is that it is fair and equitable that the author be rewarded for the time and effort that went into the production of the work. While this appears to mirror the economic efficiency justification for copyright protection, it relates instead to what the author may 'deserve', rather than what is economically optimal. This is closely linked to the natural rights theory on property argued by the philosopher John Locke in his 'Two Treatsies on Government' (Spitzlinger 2011). As summarized by Zemer, this theory argues that everyone has a natural property right in his own 'person' and in the labour of his body (2007, pp. 11–13). This argument, therefore, is that as an artist has laboured in the creation of a work, they therefore have a property right in that created work. As Spitzlinger states:

> Arguments in favor of extending property rights to non-material goods tend to be based on traditional property theories. In particular, John Locke's labor appropriation theory is frequently cited as an adequate philosophical basis in support of strong natural property rights in ideas.
>
> (2011, p. 274)

It is worth noting, however, that Locke never specifically talked about intellectual property in his Two Treatsies on Government, referring only to real property (see Locke, 2010, Book II, Chapter 5 'Of Property'), such as land. Some authors nevertheless argue that Locke's lack of specific discussion of intellectual property does not lessen the validity of the labour-appropriation justification for intellectual property protection (Spinello and Bottis 2009; Epstein 2009; DeLong 2002). This argument considers that 'it would surely seem that this theory is naturally applicable to intellectual property as well. Intellectual property is surely as much the fruit of one's labor as is physical property' (Spinello and Bottis 2009, p. 155).

This approach to copyright therefore appears not to rely on incentive or utilitarian justifications, but upon natural rights theories of property ownership. A work deserves protection because it is the expression of an individual's personality and created through that individual's labour. Therefore, that individual deserves to enjoy the fruits of that creation. It has been argued that the Anglo-US conception of 'copyright' is representative of the economic incentive justification for copyright protection, whereas the continental *droit d'auteur* system is more reflective of a labour/personality conceptualization of copyright protection (see for example Grosheide 2009, pp. 243–4), making unification difficult to achieve due to their differing theoretical justifications. However, others such as Strowel have argued that these differences may be somewhat exaggerated (Strowel 1994).

The impact of international agreements on the harmonization of copyright law in the EU

The twenty-first century has seen globalization that the nineteenth century parties to the Berne Convention could hardly have imagined. After the Second World War, in a desire to ensure the effectiveness of free trade, states determined that an international organization would best serve this purpose. Negotiations over the forming of an international trade organization with full legal status ultimately failed (Drahos and Braithwaite 2002, pp. 108–10), but in its place the General Agreement on Tariffs and Trade Treaty of 1948 was created (hereby GATT). However, unlike a formal international institution, states signatory to the Treaty were not members, but instead contracting parties in a much more flexible arena (Drahos and Braithwaite 2002, p. 108). It was out of the Uruguay Round of GATT talks concluded in 1993 that the Trade Related Aspects of Intellectual Property Agreement, or TRIPS, was born. Signed on 15 April 1994 by 124 nations with entry into force on 1 January 1995, TRIPS was:

> The first comprehensive intellectual property agreement ever executed by most of the world's trading nations which establishes minimum standards of protection [and enforcement] for practically all categories of IP rights ... the adopted standards mirror those in force in the industrialized countries.
>
> (Moncayo von Hase 2008, p. 83)

TRIPS is administered by the World Trade Organization (WTO), an international organization also born out of the Uruguay Round talks. Among the main provisions of the TRIPS agreement is Article 9, which states that Member States party to the WTO are required to implement Articles 1–21 of the Berne Convention into their domestic law, noticeably with the exception of moral rights. One criticism of the TRIPS agreement often made, particularly by Drahos and Braithwaite, is that TRIPS is a primarily economic Treaty governed by the interests of corporate rights holders (2002). This will be discussed in much greater detail throughout Chapters 4, 5 and 6. Furthermore, the Berne Convention's 'three-step' test, which permits the limitation and exceptions to rights conferred by the Treaty, has been codified in Article 13. Very briefly, these steps specify that exceptions to copyright are (a) limited to certain special cases; (b) do not conflict with the normal exploitation of the work; and (c) do not unreasonably prejudice the legitimate interests of the right-holder. However, unlike the Berne Convention where this test only applies to the reproduction right as stated in Article 9(2), in TRIPS this test applies to all exclusive rights. This has led several commentators to refer to the Article 13 provision as 'plus-Berne' (Koelman 2006; Jehoram 2005). This test has been the subject of much controversy, and will be considered in greater depth later in this chapter.

Particularly important to the development of modern-day IP protection and enforcement are the Treaties of the World Intellectual Property Organization (WIPO), a United Nations institution established with competences in intellectual property generally, in comparison to the WTOs specific focus on IP in relation to trade. Described by Stokes as dealing with the digitization of copyright (Stokes 2009, pp. 8–15), the WIPO Copyright Treaty (WCT) and WIPO Performances and Phonograms Treaty (WPPT) are also known as the WIPO Internet Treaties. By the mid-1990s, use of the internet was becoming much more widespread, and with the development of peer-to-peer file sharing software such as Napster and the MP3 file format (allowing for high quality digital encoding of music in just a few megabytes), corporate right-holders were becoming increasingly concerned by the possibility of mass-scale piracy existing in an area where the law was not clear. As a result, 'pressure grew for international regulation covering the exploitation of works in the online . . . environment' (Tritton and Davis 2008, p. 483). It was established in Articles 7, 8 and 10, and 11, 12 and 14 of the WPPT that the acts of reproducing, distributing and/or making available music through the internet are solely rights held by performers and publishers respectively. In dealing with the risk of piracy, WCT Article 11 dictated that Contracting States prohibit in their national law methods of circumventing technological prevention measures (TPMs) used to prevent the copying of works, and in Article 13 that it is an offence to alter in any way digital rights management software. It was intended that these Treaties would update and improve the rights of performers on the internet, in order to ensure equal (or at least equivalent) protection in comparison to the offline environment (Keplinger 2003, p. 17). While it has been argued that the text of the treaties administered by WIPO emerged 'primarily as result of transnational corporations' consensus and the coincidence of the perceived interests of that group with key governments such as the US' (Lucchi 2006, p. 25), and that the TRIPS Agreement is the result of transnational lobbying practices (as has been covered in significant detail in Drahos and Braithwaite 2002 and therefore will not be reproduced here), the role of the European institutions in the formulation of these policies cannot be overlooked. After all, as the 1991 follow-up to the 'Challenges' Green Paper mentioned earlier stated, 'the Community proposals have succeeded in forming the main basis for discussion' (European Commission 1991, sec. 7). While the

Information Society Directive is ostensibly the result of the EU's obligation to incorporate the TRIPS Agreement and WIPO Treaties into European law, this by no means indicates that the EU played the role of a mere 'policy-taker' in these negotiations.

The Information Society Directive

The Information Society Directive (2001/29/EC) has been referred to in the past as the 'most lobbied Directive of all time' (see for example Hugenholtz 2000; Hart 2002), and the beginning of a 'second phase' of EU copyright harmonization. The general consensus appears to be that the main justifications for the passing of the Directive relates to the implementation of the TRIPS Agreement and WIPO Treaties and the necessity of ensuring that the internal market of the EU was 'ready' for the technological changes brought by the internet by harmonizing certain aspects of copyright and neighboring rights (Hart 2002, p. 58; Hugenholtz 2009, p. 16; Kretschmer 2003, p. 333 among others). Under Council Decision 94/800 of 1994, the Community became a party to the TRIPS Agreement, and by virtue of Community law is bound by international conventions, as stated in the *Poulsen* case (1992). As a result, all secondary Community legislation created or already existing must be interpreted as consistently as possible with the EC's international obligations, as stated at para. 52 of the *Germany v EC Commission* (1996) case, giving the Commission the necessary impetus for incorporating the international laws into the European legal system. The need to adapt to changes brought by new technologies was referred to in the Directive itself in terms of the multiplication and diversification of 'vectors' for the creation, production and exploitation of works as a result of technological changes (recital 5), and the need to ensure that responses to these technological changes were harmonized among the Member States, so that differences in protection would not cause barriers to the functioning of the internal market (recital 6). An important element of this harmonization, according to recitals 21, 23 and 24, concerned the definition of the scope of the reproduction right, communication right and the right to make available respectively. Furthermore, according to recital 32, exceptions and limitations to the reproduction and communication rights would be provided as an exhaustive list. Article 2 of the Directive states that right-holders should be granted the exclusive right to authorize or prohibit direct or indirect, temporary or permanent reproduction by any means. The Article was phrased in such a way in order to cover any type of copying that may be possible using new technologies – due to the speed at which technology adapts, it is reflective of the desire not to have the legislation hampered by, for example, a change in music format or distribution mechanism, and represents a broadening of the scope of the reproduction right, repealing Article 7 of the Rental Rights Directive (92/100/EEC) (Mazziotti 2008, p. 59). Whereas previous Directives such as the Software Directive (91/250/EEC) and Database Directive (96/9/EC) had already harmonized to an extent the reproduction right, Article 2 of the Information Society Directive expanded the protection, making no distinction between copyright and neighbouring rights (producers, for example, gaining exclusive rights over phonograms in the same way as an author had over their composition) (Ohly 2009, pp. 214–15). This Article was broader than the protection afforded under the WIPO Copyright Treaty, which did not include temporary reproduction within the exclusive right (Hart 2002, p. 58; Schloetter 2012, sec. 6.2.1–6.2.2). Mazziotti goes as far as to state that by defining reproduction in such a way, the right covers not only the reproduction of a digital work, but also its use, giving an intellectual property right something akin to a real property right (2008, p. 60; see also Hart 2002), an approach seemingly adopted in the creation of the definition of the reproduction right in the Information Society Directive (2008, pp. 61–4). The limitation of this expansive scope by means of Article 5(1) of the Directive, which allows for transient and incidental reproduction, has been criticized as lacking in any particular certainty (Mazziotti 2008, p. 62; Hart 2002, p. 58; Schloetter 2012, sec. 6.2.2).

Article 3 of the Directive provides for the exclusive right of 'communication' and/or 'making available to the public', described by Hart as protecting 'the transmission and distribution of copyright works other than in physical form to members of the public not present at the place where the communication originates' (2002, p. 58). This implements Article 8 of the WIPO Copyright Treaty, and appears to have been specifically implemented with the internet in mind. In particular, the principal of exhaustion does not apply to Article 3 under subsection 3, and Mazziotti argues that the wording of this right makes it clear that the Information Society Directive was intended as pursuing commercial policy objectives (2008, pp. 65–6). This right of 'making available' appears to have been created out of a concern that new technologies such as the internet made the old Berne 'right of communication' obsolete (Haque 2008, p. 376) and somewhat influenced by the highly mediatized rise and fall of Napster (see for example Haque 2008, pp. 375–6; Akester 2010, p. 374; Foged 2002, p. 525). It has been argued that Napster's users made available music in the form of MP3 files in a manner that breached this exclusive right, through the Napster's centralized database system, allowing users to browse other users' libraries, and if the a user was online, download songs from that library. Going public in June 1999, Napster was the first popular software for the distribution of digital media. By January 2000, 5 million internet users had downloaded the software and 60 per cent of the University of Indiana's bandwidth was reportedly being taken up by Napster-based file transfers (Topham 2000). Napster was inevitably closed in its initial copyright infringing form following the *A&M Records, Inc (and others) v Napster, Inc* (2001) case in the US after the company admitted it was unable to monitor the high volume of traffic on its service so as to prevent acts of copyright infringement (McIntosh 2001).

The right of distribution under Article 4 of the Directive was specifically divided between tangible goods, where the principle of first sale and exhaustion applies, and intangible works, in which the principle does not apply, as was categorically stated in recital 29 of the Directive. Exhaustion is a principle that the exclusive rights over a copyrighted work are 'exhausted' and can no longer be enforced by a copyright holder after the sale of that work in the form of a good to another, as a form of compromise between intellectual property and real property rights (see Schloetter 2012, sec. 6.3.2; Hart 2002, p. 59). The provision of copyrighted works on the internet, such as music in the form of digital music files, constitutes a service under recital 29, rather than a sale of goods (as shall be discussed in more detail in the next chapter). The wording of the Directive is that exhaustion does not apply to 'the original work or its copies', and the combination of this with the treatment of intangible copies of works as services in which the first sale rule does not apply prevents users from, for example, selling an MP3 file, or distributing copies of that file. Because this principle of exhaustion does not apply, it leads to a strict delimitation of the digital market along national boundaries, as there is no transfer of title but only a license to make available to users at the end of the commercial provider, and a license to use the intangible work at the end of the consumer (see Mazziotti 2008, pp. 68–9).

These exclusive rights are in turn protected not only by legal means, but technological, under Article 6 of the Directive, which applies to the use of TPMs (this book will not go deeply into the subject of TPMs, as it is not the main focus of the book, and has already been covered in significant detail by, for example, Mazziotti 2008; Lucchi 2006). Furthermore, the protection granted by the Commission to copyrighted works through TPMs is considered as being a 'TRIPS plus' provision, providing a higher level of protection than that afforded in the WIPO Treaties. Although transposing the WCT and WPPT Treaties word for word on the prohibition of circumvention or alteration, in order to give additional protection and help restrict the possibility of such circumvention or alteration being possible, the Commission inserted an extra section into the Information Society Directive. According to this section, not only are acts of circumvention are prevented, but also 'the manufacture, import, distribution, sale, rental, advertisement for sale or rental, the possession for commercial purposes of devices, products or components or the provision of services which are promoted . . . for the purpose of circumvention of . . . any effective technological measures'. Mazziotti is very critical of Article 6 of the Directive, arguing that the EU went further than the US, not allowing for circumvention for any reason, meaning that the technology restricts not only acts that could be considered as infringing, but also acts that would otherwise be exempt from copyright infringement under the exceptions and limitations provided for under Article 5 (2008, p. 72). Hart argues that the provisions on TPMs are highly unclear, unusual, and restrictive (2002, pp. 62–3), a view shared by others including Sun (2005), Favale (2008), Koelman (2000) and Dusollier (1999).

Article 5 of the Information Society Directive deals with exceptions and limitations to copyright. This section of the Directive provides for a list of twenty exceptions under which the reproduction or transmission rights are exempted, including exemptions for private copying for backup purposes that are not directly or indirectly commercial, and for teaching, review or research purposes. Under Article 5(1) temporary and incidental acts of reproduction which are 'essential and integral to a technological process' are specifically exempt, as to do otherwise could render service providers and search engines in breach of copyright through the act of providing a service and linking users to materials. Article 5 is the subject of contention particularly as the list of exemptions provided is an exhaustive list, as confirmed by recital 32 (see also Seville 2010, p. 900; Mazziotti 2008, p. 38; Hart 2002, p. 59). This, therefore, would appear to limit the ability of Member States to be able to introduce their own exceptions to copyright, and in the words of one author 'leaves no room for devising new exceptions and limitations that may be appropriate for present or future environments, including the Internet' (Heide 1999, p. 108). Furthermore, given the harmonizing intent of the legislation, the list of exceptions and limitations does not appear to be particularly effective. This is because the list of exemptions is voluntary, and Member States may pick and choose from that list which exceptions they will apply. The result of this has been that Member States have adopted very different solutions and exceptions (Favale 2008, p. 697; Westkamp 2007, pp. 11–48), where some Member States such as Italy, Germany, Greece and Sweden have only allowed private copying in analogue form, whereas States such as the UK and Ireland allow copying for the purposes of 'time-shifting', and post-Accession states generally allow for private-use copying without restriction (Favale 2008, pp. 703–4). The implementation of the three-step test in the Directive under Article 5(5) is also regarded as being 'TRIPS plus', going beyond what was prescribed in the TRIPS Agreement and WIPO Treaty. Article 5(5) states that the exceptions and limitations under Article 5 'shall only be applied in certain special cases which do not conflict with a normal exploitation of the work or other subject matter and do not unreasonably prejudice the legitimate interests of the right-holder'. TRIPS makes specific reference to the addressees of the test in Article 13, namely the Member States themselves. This is also true of Article 10 of the WCT. By addressing the provisions to the national executives and legislature, these provisions would guide lawmakers in making sure that any legislated exceptions or limitations of copyright would meet this test. Article 5(5) does not, however, leading Jehoram to speculate that 'it is not addressed to the national Governments, but to the populace at large and the courts in the Member States' (2005, p. 364). Koelman argues that 'the three-step test does not give judges sufficient latitude for considering other interests than the right-holders" (2006, p. 408).

Indeed, the Information Society Directive has been heavily criticized in academic literature for being overly-broad in scope, overly-restrictive of user rights/copyright limitations and apparently overly-sympathetic to business interests (see for example Hugenholtz 2000; Mazziotti 2008; Lucchi 2006). Ohly makes mention of the fact that rights are defined broadly, but exceptions to those rights narrowly, and the fact that while exceptions to copyright are exhaustive, the rights provided for in Articles 2, 3 and 4 are not (2009, p. 236). Boyle refers to the post-TRIPS laws such as the Digital Millennium Copyright Act in the US and the Information Society Directive as constituting the 'second enclosure movement' drawing an analogy with the enclosures by which land was taken from the 'commons' and placed in the hands of private landowners, arguably for the benefit of those new right-holders and to the detriment of the public at large (Boyle 2008, p. 45). This second enclosure seeks to restrictively control intangible works, following a logic of propertization and commodification (Boyle 2008, p. 67), leading to great boons to private businesses, but at the expense of user rights. Similarly, Peukert argues that the Information Society Directive is reflective of a mentality in which intellectual property is propertized, meaning that protection becomes an end in itself, and 'that these exclusive rights would be considered beneficial under all circumstances; therefore they are always good' (2011, p. 67). This property logic shall be returned to in Chapter 4, when consideration is given to the dominant discourses underlying the legislative process for the Directive.

The Term Extension for Sound Recordings Directive

Whereas the Information Society Directive significantly expanded the scope of copyright protection in the EU, the Term Extension for Sound Recordings Directive, or Terms Extension Directive 2011/77/EU, approved by the Council in September 2011, significantly extended the term of protection for sound recordings, whether tangible in the form of pressed CDs or intangible in the form of MP3 files. Article 1(2) of the Sound Recordings Directive states that Article 3(1) of the Copyright Duration Directive will be amended to state that the copyright over the fixation of a performance in a phonogram will expire after seventy years from first publishing or public communication, whichever is earlier (a reduction from the proposal of an extension to ninety-five years, equal with the protection granted in the US). All additional references to '50 years' with regard to sound recordings are also amended to read '70 years'. Article 1(1) also extends the protection for the 'the author of the lyrics and the composer of the musical composition, provided that both contributions were specifically created for the respective musical composition with words', irrespective of whether the individual in question is recognized as a co-author, giving them an equal 'life+70' term of protection afforded to an author under Directive 2006/116/EU. This additional level of protection was stated as seeking to afford equal protection to session musicians, who are considered as performers rather than authors under copyright law, and not entitled to the same protections (Farrand 2012, p. 298). The reason for the extension, it would appear, was in order to ensure 'fairness' and equal treatment between composers and performers. The then-Commissioner for Internal Market and Services, Charlie McCreevy, stated in February 2008 that:

> I have not seen a convincing reason why a composer of music should benefit from a term of copyright which extends to the composer's life and 70 years

beyond, while the performer should only enjoy 50 years, often not even covering his lifetime.

(McCreevy 2008)

The Directive nevertheless has proven very controversial among academics, many of whom argue that the extension for the term of protection over phonograms represents little more than a guarantee of income to record producers, with there being little suggestion that performers/session musicians will benefit from the additional twenty year term (Hilty *et al.* 2009; Helberger *et al.* 2008; Editorial 2008; Geiger 2009). An editorial published in the *European Intellectual Property Review*, written by a number of academics in the field of intellectual property law and economics and signed by a significant number of others, referred to the proposed Directive as constituting the result of 'years of fierce lobbying by the trade bodies of the record industry' (Editorial 2008, p. 341). With regard to the Commission's argument that the extension (to, as initially proposed, ninety-five years) was in the interest of performers, the editorial stated that 'if the Commission wants to support European artists, there are many possible measures that would not result in monopolising the back catalogue of recorded music for another 45 years' (2008, p. 345). Other arguments raised by critics of the Directive included that an increase in term could potentially result in increases in the costs to consumers, increased competition and innovation costs, and a significant reduction in the number of works entering the public domain (Helberger *et al.* 2008, p. 176; Hilty *et al.* 2009, pp. 590–1).

Parallels were also drawn with the passing of the Copyright Term Extension Act (CTEA) in the US in 1998, in which the term of protection of copyright was extended to life plus seventy years, and ninety-five years from the point of first publication for works of corporate authorship. For example, Gowers noted that one of the arguments he was presented with in his British Government-commissioned Review was that an increase in terms would result in equal levels of protection between the UK and US, and noted that comparing the two markets was not comparing like-with-like (Gowers 2006, sec. 4.23–4). Unlike the Term Extension Directive, which does not have retroactive effect and does not reapply protection to phonograms already in the public domain (Article 1(c) of the Directive), the CTEA retroactively took works that were in the public domain and rendered them subject to copyright protection. Patry argues that the this is damaging to the economy overall, increases the costs of producing new music and is not particularly beneficial to aritsts or performers (2011, chap. 8). Lessig refers to the corporate lobbying taking place prior to the CTEA being passed, stating that 'Congress knows that copyright owners will be willing to pay a great deal of money to see their copyright terms extended. And so Congress is quite happy to keep this gravy train running' (2004, p. 216). However, Lessig unequivocally states that this is not corruption or bribery in the sense of 'money in brown envelopes' in which money is explicitly given to members of Congress in return for specific policies, something exceedingly rare at the federal level (2012,

p. 8). Instead, much of the use of money in the US political system relates to running for election, or re-election. According to Lessig, the amount of money it took to run for congress in the US increased from \$56,000 to \$1.3 million from 1974 to 2008 (2012, p. 91). With regard to the money being spent by copyright owners, it is money donated to the campaigns to members of Congress that will be sympathetic to those specific business interests. There is no specific intent, Lessig argues, but a sense of 'gratitude' (2012, p. 115). When money is donated to a campaign, there is no discussion of specific policies, but after a campaign has been won, and a solicitation over a policy is made, 'it will be harder for you to say no' (2012, p. 115). It is submitted, however, that the European Commission is not Congress, and does not function in the same way. In particular, there is no need to secure funding for re-election. As shall be discussed in Chapter 4, if the Commission is susceptible to lobbying, it may well be for different reasons, relating to dominant discourses and perceptions of expertise.

The Enforcement Directive

The Enforcement Directive 2004/28/EC was passed on 23 April 2004, and entered into force in June of the same year. The Directive was passed unusually quickly for European legislation, with the process from the publication of the Proposal in January 2003 to the acceptance of the finalized Directive taking a mere one year and three months (Huniar 2004, p. 93). According to Kierkegaard, the Enforcement Directive was 'fast-tracked', being passed quickly after the first reading by the European Parliament, rather than being subject to a second reading (2005, p. 489). 'The hurry to pass the Directive . . . before the enlargement of the EU was to prevent the New Members from influencing the content of the controversial provisions' (Kierkegaard 2005, p. 489). This assessment is shared by Reinbothe (2010, sec. D.3) and Huniar (2004, p. 93), with Reinbothe stating that the Commission was concerned that the Accession states joining the EU in May 2004 constituted 'the harbour, if not the origin of counterfeiting and piracy, [meaning that] once the accession was achieved, the momentum for harmonizing the enforcement of intellectual property rights could have been lost for the foreseeable future' (2010, sec. D.3).

One of the justifications made for the creation of the Directive is found in a joint reading of its recitals. Recital 4 states that all Member States of the European Union have a duty to comply with the provisions of the TRIPS Agreement, while recital 7 notes that there were still disparities in the protection of intellectual property rights between Member States. As these disparities impact the functioning of the internal market, recital 8 claims, the objective therefore was to 'approximate legislative systems so as to ensure a high, equivalent and homogeneous level of protection in the internal market' (recital 10). The Directive was intended to cover infringements of all intellectual property rights (recital 13), where they take place on a commercial scale, defined as those acts 'carried out for direct or indirect economic or commercial advantage' (recital 14). With this in mind, Article 2 on the scope of the Directive is particularly broad, covering 'any infringement of intellectual property rights', meaning that the Directive is not limited to acts on a commercial scale (Reinbothe 2010, sec. B.2). This overly broad definition, and the vague definition of 'commercial scale' has been criticized as being vague and unhelpful (see for example Massa and Strowel 2004, p. 247), with Kierkegaard arguing that as a result of the wording, all acts of infringement could be considered as being on a commercial scale, as downloading music from a peer-to-peer service could constitute gaining an indirect economic advantage (2005, p. 491; see also Meller 2004). This is a concern that appears to have been realized in the case of *Promusicae*, which concerned the application of the Enforcement Directive to file-sharers on the internet (this case will be discussed in more detail in Chapter 7), and by the treatment of individual acts of infringement by way of file-sharing as constituting 'commercial scale' infringement in Germany (Schmitz and Ries 2012, p. 4; Benabou 2010, p. 169). A review of the Directive resulted in the Commission admitting that 'commercial scale' was not defined at all, with the effect that Member States would apply the principle differently (European Commission 2010, sec. 2.3.2).

The Enforcement Directive was specifically intended as being a TRIPS-plus legislative act, with the Commission stating that it intended to go beyond the minimum provisions provided for in the international agreement (European Commission 2003). The first of these TRIPS-plus provisions is Article 4. Whereas TRIPS states at Article 42 that owners of IP rights, and federations or associations having legal standing to assert such rights, should be able to do so, Article 4 extends the class of right-holders able to bring actions, permitting rights-holders, licensees, intellectual property collective rights-management bodies and professional defense bodies. Kierkegaard argues that this 'tilts' protection too far in the favour of right-holders to the detriment of consumers (2005, p. 491), whereas Reinbothe states that their 'added value is . . . disputable' (2010, sec. B.4). Article 6, pertaining to evidence, also contains TRIPS-plus elements. Whereas the first part of Article 6(1) is identical to Article 43(1) of the TRIPS Agreement, specifying that if a party brings reasonably available evidence sufficient to support its claims of infringement, then the opposing party can be ordered to provide any evidence in their control that the applying party has requested. However, it continues by providing that Member States may provide that in cases of large-scale infringement, a sample will be sufficient, going beyond what is required in TRIPS. In incidences of commercial infringement under 6(2), the opposing party can be required to disclose banking, financial or commercial documents ('clearly a "TRIPS plus" element' according to Reinbothe (2010, sec. B.6)), leading Kierkegaard to argue that the Article is broad enough to allow for 'fishing expeditions' by right-holders, raising significant privacy concerns (2005, p. 492). The right to information in Article 8, according to Reinbothe, constitutes the most important 'TRIPS plus' provision of the Directive, going 'in many respects beyond Article 47 of the TRIPS Agreement' (2010, sec. B.7). Much like the TRIPS provision, Article 8(1) states that judicial authorities may 'order that information on the origin and distribution networks of the goods or services which infringe an intellectual property right be provided' from an infringer. However, the scope of the right to information has been significantly broadened. The article covers those found to be in possession of goods infringing on a commercial scale; those found to be using the goods on a commercial scale; those found to be providing services on a commercial scale used for infringing; or any individual indicated by any of these people as being involved in the production, manufacture or distribution of the goods. According to Kur, this right to information was 'probably one of the core issues of the whole project' (2004, p. 826), and with respect to the internet, while Internet Service Providers (ISPs) do not face any liability or have an obligation to monitor usage of their services due to the safe harbor provisions of the E-Commerce Directive (as shall be discussed further in Chapter 5), they may nevertheless be obliged to provide information on subscribers to their service (Kur 2004, p. 826; Kierkegaard 2005, p. 493; Aguila 2012, sec. 9.2). Aguila argues that this Article is deliberately misleading, giving the impression it is only intended to apply to cases concerning infringement on a commercial scale, but the application to 'provided by the infringer and/or any other person' who operates on a commercial scale, means that it can also be applied in cases of individual infringement by individuals sharing infringing material on the internet, even in instances where this is not considered to be 'commercial' in nature (2012, sec. 9.2). Kierkegaard states that a similar provision in the Digital Millennium Copyright Act in the US has been used by the Recording Industry Association of America as a way of seeking information on thousands of alleged file-sharers (2005, p. 493). As shall be discussed in greater detail in Chapter 5, Article 11 of the Directive also provides for the granting of injunctions against intermediaries in order to prevent ongoing infringements, reiterating a duty that applies specifically to ISPs under Article 8(3) of the Information Society Directive.

Academic opinion on the Directive has been largely critical (Drexl *et al.* 2003; Kur 2004; Aguila 2012; Kierkegaard 2005; cf. Massa and Strowel 2004; Reinbothe 2010). Drexl *et al.* in 2003 argued that the Directive as proposed was hugely disproportionate (2003, p. 530), with an overly broad scope that appeared to go beyond what was necessary to achieve its objectives (2003, pp. 532–3). Kierkegaard, as has been discussed in this section, is highly critical of the Directive, stating that it 'goes beyond the scope of TRIPS and introduces provisions which strengthen the right holder's position and contain a number of rules that have the potential for abuse' (2005, pp. 494–5). Both Kur and Kierkegaard state that the harmonizing aims of the Directive are difficult to achieve due to the vague formulation of some of the terms (2004, p. 830; 2005, p. 495 respectively), and Aguila argues that harmonization has not been achieved under the Enforce-ment Directive (2012, sec. 9.5). Interestingly, despite representing an 'upwards harmonization' of EU law, and going beyond the protections afforded under TRIPS, right-holders were not satisfied with the implemented Directive, and demanded the EU work towards creating criminal sanctions for intellectual property infringement (EDRI 2005). Just one year after the entry into force of the Enforcement Directive, the Commission published a proposal for a Directive on criminal enforcement measures (European Commission 2005c), on the basis that additional provisions providing for criminal sanctions were necessary in order to supplement Directive 2004/48/EC (2005c, p. 2). The proposal stated in Article 3 that Member States must ensure that all intentional infringements of an intellectual property right on a commercial scale are treated as constituting criminal offences. An amended proposal released in 2006 went further, specifying the level of sanctions to be applied in a new Article 5, including maximum sentences of 'at least four years' (European Commission 2006, p. 10). The European Parliament approved this Directive on a first reading in 2007 (Official Journal of the European Union 2008, p. E526). However, the proposal was ultimately withdrawn by the European Commission in 2010 on the basis of uncertainties concerning the legal basis of the Directive, particularly after the entry into force of the TFEU (Official Journal of the European Union 2010, p. 9). However, the issue of criminal sanctions for copyright infringement has not been settled, and it remains to be seen whether a Directive imposing criminal sanctions for infringement will be proposed as part of the Commission's unfinished review of the Enforcement Directive.

The Recommendation on Collective Rights Management

While Commissioner for the Information Society in 2005, Viviane Reding made apparent the concern of some in the Commission that barriers to the cross-border sales of digital music were making it more difficult to develop online media services. The main obstacle to this is that copyright continues to be closely linked to national territories inside the EU. Acknowledging that some progress had been made towards harmonizing copyright law within the EU, Reding commented that a single market for digital content was far from being realized. The most significant obstacle, according to Reding, was that 'content is licensed still at national level, and not for the entire EU. That collecting societies stick close to national territories in their daily work, and that they also do so with regard to online licensing' (Reding 2005). As a means of attempting to combat the limiting of licensing agreements for digital music to individual territories, the Commission published a Communication on cross-border licensing. In this Communication, the Commission stated that while the Information Society Directive had harmonized the scope of economic rights, and made mention of the fact that these rights could be transferred or licensed, the EU up until that point did 'not address the conditions of rights management as such' (European Commission 2004, sec. 1.1.2). Reiterating that there is no 'European copyright' but instead harmonization of territorially exercised rights (2004, sec. 1.2.1), the Commission nevertheless stated that collecting rights-management organizations' differing standards of transparency and forms of governance in the Member States impacts upon the ability to license across borders (2004, sec. 1.2.3). The Commission determined that in order to promote cross-border licensing, it was necessary to take a legislative approach, stating that 'to rely on soft law, such as codes of conduct agreed upon by the market place, appears to be no appropriate option' (2004, p. 3.6). In a study released the following year, the Commission stated that it had three policy options: do nothing; eliminate territorial restrictions and discriminatory provisions in the reciprocal representation agreements concluded between collecting societies; or give right-holders the choice to authorize a collecting society of their choice to manage their works across the entire EU (European Commission 2005a, pp. 33–4). The Commission concluded that the third option was preferable, as it would give all right-holders across the EU the possibility to adhere to any collective rights manager of their choice for the EU-wide exploitation of their online rights, introducing competition to collective rights management (2005a, pp. 34–6).

Nevertheless, despite expressing the desire to legislate in this area, the Commission determined in its October 2005 Impact Assessment that a self-regulatory regime under a non-binding Recommendation was the best approach to promoting cross-border licensing, stating that Member States should screen their applicable national rules in order to avoid any provisions that would hinder EU-wide licenses being granted 'by any rights management entity for copyright and related rights for legitimate online music services, if that is what the market requires and right-holders want' (European Commission 2005b, sec. 7.2). This seems to directly contradict the approach stated in the 2004 Communication, in which it was stated that soft law such as a Recommendation was not an appropriate option. Recommendation 2005/737/EC on the collective cross-border management of copyright and related rights for legitimate online music services, made by the Commission in May 2005 and published in the Official Journal ten days after the Impact Assessment on 21 October 2005, 'invited' Member States to take action to promote the cross-border licensing of music for legitimate music services at para. 2. Paragraph 3 of the recommendation stated that right-holders should have the right to entrust the management of any of the 'online rights necessary to operate legitimate online music service, on a territorial scope of their choice'. The choice of approach by the Commission was heavily criticized by the European Parliament, who declared the Commission's choice of legislative instrument was contrary to principles of democracy and the duty to consult the Parliament (European Parliament 2007, sec. C). The Recommendation has also been criticized for failing to secure any meaningful change in licensing policies (Strowel and Vanbrabant 2013, p. 50).

In 2008, the Commission launched its Creative Content Online initiative, the intent of which was to 'support the development of innovative business models and the deployment of cross-border delivery of diverse online creative content services' (European Commission 2008, sec. 1.3). With regard to collective management, the Commission announced it would discuss the effectiveness of the Recommendation with interested stakeholders (2008, sec. 2.2), and work with the Parliament on a Recommendation that would (among other issues) cover innovative licensing regimes for audio-visual works (2008, sec. 3). However, despite announcing that the Recommendation would be published in mid-2008, ultimately the Creative Content Online agenda was rendered dormant in 2009, largely due to an inability to achieve consensus among collecting societies and right-holders regarding proposals for multi-territory licensing (Euractiv 2009). Euractiv reported Martin Selymar, who was Viviane Reding's spokesman, as saying 'there will be no recommendation. The Commission will only later present issue papers' (2009). In a Reflection Document released in October 2009, the Commission admitted that many of the creative content online proposals proved 'controversial' (European Commission 2009, p. 9), but that there was a need to promote cross-border or multi-territory licensing (2009, p. 10). The Commission suggested several possible approaches, ranging from a streamlined licensing process to mooting a possible European copyright code (2009, pp. 16–18), and opened discussions with stakeholders. Subsequently the Commission released a commissioned final report on multi-territory licensing in October 2010, that 'proposed to introduce a framework directive that promotes greater transparency and governance requirements' for collective rights management bodies' (KEA European Affairs and MINES ParisTech Cema 2010, p. 11). The report noted that 'recent EC-interventions in the field seem to disappoint both rights holders and users alike' (2010, p. 158) and that without the support of right-holders and collecting societies, 'it remains unclear how such a licensing system would operate' (2010, p. 160).

Ultimately, it appears that the Commission has settled on a system it refers to as a 'European Licensing Passport', in which collecting societies that wish to license online rights to musical works of a multi-territory basis must comply with conditions concerning efficient data handling and invoicing capabilities and transparency (European Commission 2012a, sec. 6.1). On this basis, the Commission published a Proposal for a Directive in July 2012, with the intent on providing a framework in which musical works could be licensed on a multi-territory basis, in part through ensuring 'better governance' and competition between collecting societies (European Commission 2012b, p. 2). In the proposed Directive, multi-territory licensing is covered in Articles 21–33, and covers issues such as the need to demonstrate adequate capacity to process multi-territory licenses (Article 22); the assurance of transparency (Article 23); the need for accurate and timely invoicing (Article 25) and payment (Article 26) to right-holders; agreements between collecting societies for multi-territory licensing (Article 28); and obligations to represent other collecting societies in multi-territory licensing (Article 29). Quintais notes that this Directive is one of the longest and most complex on copyright law that the EU has produced (2013, p. 65), and that while the proposed Directive may facilitate multi-territory licensing, it does little to impose it (2013, p. 70). Quintais also states suspicions that very heavy lobbying may lead to significant alteration, or even watering down of the multi-territory licensing proposals (Quintais 2013, p. 72). This concern has been expressed by Neelie Kroes, currently Commissioner for the Digital Agenda. While stating that the proposed Directive was a positive step, she went on to state that 'our proposal needs to be agreed by the European Parliament and Council. Some previous attempts by us to modernise copyright rules – like our relatively modest proposal on orphan works – were significantly watered down by the legislator' (Kroes 2012). It would appear then that Kroes also has concerns that intense lobbying may impact the ability of the Commission to effectively legislate in this area. At the time of writing, the proposed Directive is still waiting for assessment by the European Parliament, and as such, it is difficult to determine what the fate of the Directive may be. Suffice it to say, efforts to harmonize the law relating to cross-border licensing thus far have been far from successful.

Concluding remarks

The development of European copyright law as an approximation rather than unification of laws has been marred by criticisms regarding the territoriality of those resulting laws, the seemingly limited harmonization those laws bring, and the processes by which those laws have been produced. Aspects of copyright law that have been successfully legislated upon, such as the scope, duration and enforcement of copyright, have been harmonized in such a way as to draw considerable criticism not only in the effectiveness of such harmonization, but also with regard to the legitimacy and intent of those acts. As such, a growing consensus among many academics in the field of copyright law is that 'in today's copyright culture, more than ever, legislators are no longer the primary arbiters of public policy. Instead, they are hostages of strong lobby groups whose interests usually prevail over those of the general public' (Zemer 2006, p. 137). As is evidenced by the preceding sections, where the studied Directives have successfully entered into force, many of the comments by academics have focused upon the role of industry representatives in the process, and the 'lobbying' that took place. Where the EU has experienced difficulty in harmonizing law is in the territorial nature of licenses for copyrighted works, particularly in the field of online music distribution. It would appear that there is a certain reticence among right-holders and right administrators to change the way in which these licenses operate, and not only have several initiatives of the Commission in the field of cross-border collective rights managements and licensing failed, but there appears to be a certain skepticism, even among European Commissioners, that the draft Directive will be more successful. It may be that 'heavy lobbying' during the Directive's passage through the European Parliament may result in the finalized text either being significantly changed, or even placed on hiatus.

Yet an important point to make is that lobbying is the act of attempting to influence a government or legislative body to adopt, or refrain from adopting, a particular course of action. This ultimately means that actors seeking to make their opinions known on a particular piece of legislation, or provide advice on how that legislation should be worded (for example) are involved in those lobbying processes. This does not only apply to 'big businesses' entertainment industry representatives, but as shall be demonstrated, civil society organizations, other business sector industry representatives and academics. For this reason, it is submitted that the question that should be asked is not 'why do institutions such as the European Commission bow to industry pressures?', but 'why are some lobbyists more successful than others in having their preferences accepted?'. This shall be discussed in much more depth in Chapters 4, 5 and 6. Prior to engaging in this analysis however, Chapter 3 will seek to expand upon the market practices in the online music distribution market, demonstrating the fragmented nature of this market, and the seeming inability of the CJEU to rectify this fragmentation through non-legislative means.

Bibliography

Aguila, P.C., 2012. 'Enforcement of IPRs'. In T.H. Synodinou, ed., *Codification of European copyright law: Challenges and perspectives.* Alphen aan den Rijn: Kluwer Law International.

Akester, P., 2010. 'The new challenges of striking the right balance between copyright protection and access to knowledge, information and culture'. *European Intellectual Property Review*, 32(8), pp. 372–81.

Benabou, V.L., 2010. 'The Chase: The French insight into the "three strikes" system'. In I.A. Stamatoudi, ed., *Copyright enforcement and the Internet.* Alphen aan den Rijn, The Netherlands; Frederick, MD: Kluwer Law International.

Bently, L. and Sherman, B., 2004. *Intellectual Property Law*, 2nd edn. Oxford: Oxford University Press.

Boyle, J., 2008. *The public domain: Enclosing the commons of the mind.* New Haven, CT: Yale University Press.

Case C-192/04 *Lagardère Active Broadcast v Société pour la perception de la rémunération équitable (SPRE)* [2005] ECR I-7199.

Commission Recommendation of 18 May 2005 on collective cross-border management of copyright and related rights for legitimate online music services (2005/737/EC).

Cook, T. and Derclaye, E., 2011. 'An EU copyright code: What and how, if ever?' *Intellectual Property Quarterly*, 3, p. 259.

Council Directive 91/250/EEC on the legal protection of computer programs [1991] OJ L122/42.

Council Directive 93/98/EEC of 23 October 1993 harmonising the term of protection of copyright and certain related rights [1993] OJ L209/0.

Council Decision 94/800 of 22 December 1994 concerning the conclusion on behalf of the European Community, as regarding matters within its competence, of the agreements reached in the Uruguay round of multilateral negotiations, [1994] OJ L336/1.

Deazley, R., 2004. *On the origin of the right to copy: Charting the movement of copyright law in eighteenth-century Britain (1695–1775).* Oxford: Hart.

DeLong, J.V., 2002. 'Defending intellectual property'. In W. Crews, ed., *Copy fights: The future of intellectual property in the information age.* Washington, DC: Cato Institute.

Directive 92/100/EEC on rental rights and lending right and on certain rights related to copyright in the field of intellectual property [1992] OJ L346/61.

Directive 96/9/EC on the legal protection of databases.

Directive 2001/29/EC of the European Parliament and of the Council of 22 May 2001 on the harmonisation of certain aspects of copyright and related rights in the information society.

Directive 2004/48 on the enforcement of intellectual property rights [2004] OJ L195/16.

Directive 2006/115/EC of the European Parliament and of the Council of 12 December 2006 on rental right and lending right and on certain rights related to copyright in the field of intellectual property.

Directive 2006/116/EC of the European Parliament and of the Council of 12 December 2006 on the term of protection of copyright and certain related rights.

Directive 2011/77/EU of the European Parliament and of the Council of amending Directive 2006/116/EC on the term of protection of copyright and certain related rights.

Drahos, P. and Braithwaite, J., 2002. *Information feudalism: Who owns the knowledge economy?* London: Earthscan.

Drexl, J., Hilty, R.M. and Kur, A., 2003. 'Proposal for a Directive on measures and procedures to ensure the enforcement of intellectual property rights: A first statement'. *International Review of Intellectual Property and Competition Law*, 34(5), pp. 530–5.

Dusollier, S., 1999. 'Electrifying the fence: The legal protection of technological measures for protecting copyright'. *European Intellectual Property Review*, 21(6), p. 285.

Editorial, 2008. 'Creativity stifled? A joint academic statement on the proposed copyright term extension for sound recordings'. *European Intellectual Property Review*, 30(9), pp. 341–7.

EDRI, 2005. 'New Commission directive proposal on IPR'. *EDRI*. Available at: www.edri.org/edrigram/number3.14/IPR [Accessed 26 July 2013].

Eechoud, M. van, Hugenholtz, P.B., Guibault, L., Gompel, S. van, Helberger, N., 2009. *Harmonizing European copyright law: The challenges of better lawmaking*. Alphen aan den Rijn: Wolters Kluwer Law & Business.

Epstein, R.A., 2009. 'Disintegration of intellectual property: A classical liberal response to a premature obituary'. *Stanford Law Review*, 62, p. 455.

Euractiv, 2009. Commission shelves plans to curb online piracy. *Euractiv*. Available at: www.euractiv.com/infosociety/commission-shelves-plans-curb-on-news-221283 [Accessed 26 July 2013].

European Commission, 1988. *Green Paper on copyright and the challenge of technology: Copyright issues requiring immediate action*. Brussels: European Commission.

European Commission, 1991. *Follow-up to the Green Paper: Working programme of the Commission in the field of copyright and neighbouring rights*. Brussels: European Commission.

European Commission, 2003. *Intellectual property: Commission proposes Directive to bolster the fight against piracy and counterfeiting*. Brussels: European Commission.

European Commission, 2004. *Communication: The management of copyright and related rights in the internal market*. Brussels: European Commission.

European Commission, 2005a. *Commission staff working document: Study on a Community initiative on the cross-border collective management of copyright*. Brussels: European Commission.

European Commission, 2005b. *Impact assessment reforming cross-border collective management of copyright and related rights for legitimate online music services*. Brussels: European Commission.

European Commission, 2005c. *Proposal for a European Parliament and Council Directive on criminal measures aimed at ensuring the enforcement of intellectual property rights.* Brussels: European Commission.

European Commission, 2006. *Amended proposal for a Directive of the European Parliament and of the Council on criminal measures aimed at ensuring the enforcement of intellectual property rights.* Brussels: European Commission.

European Commission, 2008. *Communication from the Commission to the European Parliament, the Council, the European Economic and Social Committee and the Committee of the Regions on creative content online in the single market.* Brussels: European Commission.

European Commission, 2009. *Creative content in a European digital single market: Challenges for the future: A reflection document of DG INFSO and DG MARKT.* Brussels: European Commission.

European Commission, 2010. *Application of Directive 2004/48/EC of the European Parliament and the Council of 29 April 2004 on the enforcement of intellectual property rights.* Brussels: European Commission.

European Commission, 2011. *A single market for intellectual property rights: Boosting creativity and innovation to provide economic growth, high quality jobs and first class products and services in Europe.* Brussels: European Commission.

European Commission, 2012a. *Commission staff working document: Executive summary of the impact assessment.* Brussels: European Commission.

European Commission, 2012b. *Proposal for a Directive of the European Parliament and of the Council on collective management of copyright and related rights and multi-territorial licensing of rights in musical works for online uses in the internal market.* Brussels: European Commission.

European Parliament, 2007. *Resolution of 13 March 2007 on the Commission recommendation of 18 October 2005 on collective cross-border management of copyright and related rights for legitimate online music services.* Brussels: European Parliament.

Farrand, B., 2012. 'Too much is never enough? The 2011 Copyright in Sound Recordings Extension Directive'. *European Intellectual Property Review, 34*(5), pp. 297–304.

Favale, M., 2008. 'Fine-tuning European copyright law to strike a balance between the rights of owners and users'. *European Law Review, 33*(5), pp. 687–708.

Foged, T., 2002. 'US v EU anti circumvention legislation: Preserving the public's privileges in the digital age?' *European Intellectual Property Review, 24*(11), pp. 525–42.

Geiger, C., 2009. 'The extension of the term of copyright and certain neighbouring rights: A never-ending story?' *International Review of Intellectual Property and Competition Law, 40*(1), pp. 78–82.

Georgopoulos, T., 2012. 'The legal foundations of European copyright law'. In T.-H. Synodinou, ed., *Codification of European copyright law: Challenges and perspectives.* Alphen aan den Rijn: Kluwer Law International.

Ginsburg, J.C., 2011. 'European copyright code: Back to first principles'. *Journal of the Copyright Society of the USA, 58*(3), p. 265.

Gowers, A., 2006. *The Gowers review of intellectual property.* London: HM Treasury.

Grosheide, W., 2009. 'Moral rights'. In E. Derclaye, ed., *Research handbook on the future of EU copyright.* Cheltenham: Edward Elgar.

Haque, H., 2008. 'Is the time ripe for another exclusive right? A proposal'. *European Intellectual Property Review, 30*(9), pp. 371–8.

Hart, M., 2002. 'The copyright in the Information Society Directive: An overview'. *European Intellectual Property Review*, *24*(2), pp. 58–64.

Heide, T., 1999. 'The Berne three-step test and the proposed copyright Directive'. *European Intellectual Property Review*, *21*(3), p. 105.

Helberger, N., Dufft, N., Gompel, S. van, Hugenholtz, P.B., 2008. 'Never forever: Why extending the term of protection for sound recordings is a bad idea'. *European Intellectual Property Review*, *5*, pp. 174–81.

Hilty, R.M., 2012. 'Reflections on a European copyright codification'. In T.-H. Synodinou, ed., *Codification of European copyright law: Challenges and perspectives*. Alphen aan den Rijn: Kluwer Law International.

Hilty, R.M., Kur, A., Klass, N., Geiger, C., Peukert, A., Drexl, J., Katzenberger, P., 2009. 'Comment by the Max-Planck Institute on the Commission's proposal for a Directive to amend Directive 2006/116 concerning the term of protection for copyright and related rights'. *European Intellectual Property Review*, *31*(2), pp. 59–72.

House of Lords European Committee, 2008. *The Treaty of Lisbon: An impact assessment*. Westminster: House of Lords.

Hugenholtz, P.B., 2000. 'Why the copyright Directive is unimportant, and possibly invalid'. *European Intellectual Property Review*, *11*, pp. 501–2.

Hugenholtz, P.B., 2009. 'Copyright without frontiers: The problem of territoriality in European copyright law'. In E. Derclaye, ed., *Research handbook on the future of EU copyright*. Cheltenham: Edward Elgar.

Hugenholtz, P.B., 2012. 'Harmonisation or unification of European union copyright law'. *Monash University Law Review*, *38*(1), p. 4.

Huniar, K., 2004. 'The enforcement directive: Its effects on UK law'. *European Intellectual Property Review*, *28*(2), pp. 92–9.

Jehoram, H.C., 2005. 'Restrictions on copyright and their abuse'. *European Intellectual Property Review*, *27*(10), p. 359.

Johns, A., 2011. *Piracy: The intellectual property wars from Gutenberg to Gates*. Chicago, IL: University of Chicago Press.

KEA European Affairs and MINES ParisTech Cema, 2010. *Multi-Territory licensing of audiovisual works in the European Union: Final report prepared for the European Commission, DG Information Society and Media*. Brussels: European Commission.

Keplinger, K.S., 2003. 'The role of the US in world-wide copyright protection'. In F. Gotzen, Katholieke Universiteit te Leuven and Centrum voor Intellectuele Rechten, eds., *The future of intellectual property in the global market of the information society: Who is going to shape the IPR system in the new millennium?* Brussels: Bruylant.

Kierkegaard, S., 2005. Taking a sledge-hammer to crack the nut: The EU Enforcement Directive. *Computer Law and Security Report*, *21*(5), p. 488.

Koelman, K.J., 2000. 'A hard nut to crack: The protection of technological measures'. *European Intellectual Property Review*, *22*(6), p. 272.

Koelman, K.J., 2006. 'Fixing the three-step test'. *European Intellectual Property Review*, *28*(8), p. 407.

Kretschmer, M., 2003. 'Digital copyright: The end of an era'. *European Intellectual Property Review*, *25*(8), pp. 333–41.

Kroes, N., 2012. 'Reforming copyright for the digital age: The Commission takes an important step forward'. *Blog of Neelie Kroes, Vice-President of the European Commission*. Available at: http://blogs.ec.europa.eu/neelie-kroes/copyright-licensing-reform/ [Accessed 26 July 2013].

Kur, A., 2004. 'The Enforcement Directive: Rough start, happy landing?' *International Review of Intellectual Property and Competition Law, 35*(7), pp. 821–30.

Lessig, L., 2004. *Free culture: The nature and future of creativity.* New York: Penguin Press.

Lessig, L., 2012. *Republic, lost: How money corrupts congress and a plan to stop it.* New York: Twelve.

Locke, J., 2010. *Two treaties of Government.* New York: Classic Books International.

Lucchi, N., 2006. *Digital media and intellectual property management of rights and consumer protection in a comparative analysis.* Berlin: Springer.

McCreevy, C., 2008. *Performing artists: No longer be the 'poor cousins of the music business'* Brussels: European Commission.

McIntosh, N., 2001. 'Napster faces the music'. *The Guardian.* Available at: www.guardian.co.uk/technology/2001/sep/25/digitalmusic.news [Accessed 27 June 2013].

Massa, C.H. and Strowel, A., 2004. The scope of the proposed IP Enforcement Directive: Torn between the desire to harmonise remedies and the need to combat piracy. *European Intellectual Property Review, 26*(6), pp. 244–53.

Mazziotti, G., 2008. *EU digital copyright law and the end-user.* Berlin: Springer.

Meller, P., 2004. 'EU backs deal on copyright piracy'. *International Herald Tribune.*

Moncayo von Hase, A., 2008. 'The application and interpretation of the agreement on trade-related aspects of intellectual property rights'. In C.M. Correa and A. Yusuf, eds, *Intellectual property and international trade: the TRIPs agreement.* Alphen aan den Rijn: Kluwer Law International.

Official Journal of the European Union, 2008. *European Parliament legislative resolution of 25 April 2007 on the amended proposal for a directive of the European Parliament and of the Council on criminal measures aimed at ensuring the enforcement of intellectual property rights.*

Official Journal of the European Union, 2010. *Withdrawal of obsolete Commission Proposals.*

Ohly, A., 2009. 'Economic rights'. In E. Derclaye, ed., *Research handbook on the future of EU copyright.* Cheltenham: Edward Elgar.

Patry, W.F., 2011. *How to fix copyright.* Oxford: Oxford University Press.

Peukert, A., 2011. 'Intellectual property as an end in itself'. *European Intellectual Property Review, 33*(2), p. 67.

Quintais, J.P., 2013. 'Proposal for a Directive on collective rights management and (some) multi-territorial licensing'. *European Intellectual Property Review, 35*(2), pp. 65–73.

Reding, V., 2005. *Why broadband needs content.* Montpellier: IDATE 27th International conference.

Reinbothe, J., 2010. 'The EU Enforcement Directive 2004/48/EC as a tool for copyright enforcement'. In I.A. Stamatoudi, ed., *Copyright enforcement and the Internet.* Alphen aan den Rijn, The Netherlands; Frederick, MD: Kluwer Law International.

Schloetter, A.L., 2012. 'The Acquis Communautaire in the area of copyright and related rights: Economic rights'. In T.-H. Synodinou, ed., *Codification of European copyright law: Challenges and perspectives.* Alphen aan den Rijn: Kluwer Law International.

Schmitz, S. and Ries, T., 2012. 'Three songs and you are disconnected from cyberspace? Not in Germany where the industry may "turn piracy into profit"'. *European Journal of Law and Technology, 3*(1), pp. 1–14.

Seville, C., 2010. 'Nineteeth-century Anglo-US copyright relations: The language of piracy versus the moral high ground'. In L. Bently, J. Davis and J.C. Ginsburg, eds,

Copyright and piracy: An interdisciplinary critique. Cambridge; New York: Cambridge University Press.

Spinello, R.A. and Bottis, M., 2009. *A defence of intellectual property rights.* Cheltenham: E. Elgar.

Spitzlinger, R., 2011. 'On the idea of owning ideas: Applying Locke's labor appropriation theory to intellectual goods'. *Masaryk University Journal of Law and Technology*, 5, p. 273.

Stokes, S., 2009. *Digital copyright: law and practice.* Oxford; Portland, OR: Hart.

Strowel, A., 1994. 'Droit d'auteur and copyright: Between history and nature'. In B. Sherman and A. Strowel, eds, *Of authors and origins: Essays on copyright law.* Oxford; New York: Clarendon Press; Oxford University Press.

Strowel, A. and Vanbrabant, B., 2013. 'Copyright licensing: A European view'. In J. de Werra, ed., *Research handbook on intellectual property licensing.* Cheltenham: Edward Elgar.

Sun, H., 2005. 'Copyright law under siege: An inquiry into the legitimacy of copyright protection in the context of the global digital divide'. *International Review of Intellectual Property and Competition Law*, 36(2), pp. 192–213.

The Wittem Group, 2011. 'European copyright code'. *European Intellectual Property Review*, 33(2), p. 76.

Topham, G., 2000. 'Napster'. *The Guardian.* Available at: www.guardian.co.uk/world/2000/jul/27/qanda.cybercinema [Accessed 27 June 2013].

Torremans, P., 2010. *Holyoak and Torremans intellectual property law.* Oxford; New York: Oxford University Press.

Tritton, G. and Davis, R., 2008. *Intellectual property in Europe.* London: Sweet & Maxwell.

Westkamp, G., 2007. *The implementation of Directive 2001/29/EC in the Member States, Part II.* London: Queen Mary Intellectual Property Research Institute.

Zemer, L., 2006. 'Rethinking copyright alternatives'. *International Journal of Law and Information Technology*, 14, p. 137.

Zemer, L., 2007. *The idea of authorship in copyright.* Aldershot: Ashgate.

Chapter 3

One market, divided?

The fragmented state of the market for digital music distribution in the European Union, and judicial approaches to territorial restrictions

> Every kingdom divided against itself is brought to desolation; and every city
> or house divided against itself shall not stand.
>
> (Matthew 12:25)

As we have seen in the previous chapter, territoriality is one of the predominant issues of contemporary European Union copyright law. However, as this chapter shall demonstrate, it is not only intellectual property law itself that is ultimately national in character; the same may be said for the provision of digital music services. Where harmonization of copyright law in the EU has been achieved it has been of an 'upwards approximation' nature, becoming increasingly restrictive. Where it has failed, it has meant that copyright retains its national character. The combination of these two phenomena has been perceived as having the potential to create barriers to the development of digital music services. Where legislation has been unsuccessful, it may be that the Court of Justice of the European Union (CJEU) may be able to offer limited support in facilitating the realization of a single market for digital music distribution, rather than one that is territorially restricted. However, as this chapter will demonstrate, there is still a significant level of uncertainty in whether the CJEU has the will and ability to effectively remove territorial restrictions in the digital music market. While recent case law indicates that the CJEU is at least aware of the difficulties in establishing a cohesive single market for digital music, the impact of its decisions in the area of intellectual property and territorial restrictions is by no means conclusive.

The outline of this chapter is as follows. The first section provides a brief overview of legal digital music download services in the EU, focusing in particular on iTunes due to its significant share of the market. This chapter will demonstrate that although music services appear to be gradually rolling out service in the majority of Member States, it appears that at this point in time, iTunes is one of the few services offered in every Member State. However, the analysis will also demonstrate the territorially restricted nature of these services – even if iTunes is accessible in every Member State, it is as a 'national' store, which is restricted to users in that Member State. The analysis of CJEU jurisprudence applicable to this will begin by assessing the free movement of services under Article 56 TFEU, in order to determine whether territorially restricted digital music services are in breach of this provision. Identifying the CJEU's consideration of the importance of 'transfrontier' services, the sections of this chapter concerning Article 56 TFEU will demonstrate the difficulty in applying Article 56 TFEU directly to a service provider such as Apple, and the uncertainty of the applicability of this article to territorial restrictions intended (or claimed to) protect intellectual property rights in the digital environment. The subsequent sections of this chapter will consider the issue of territorial restrictions through the lens of competition law, seeking to determine whether any potential agreement between music providing services and record labels that has the effect or result of partitioning the digital music market is contrary to competition law. The predominant focus of these sections will be on the Commission investigation into Apple and the recent *CISAC* decision, demonstrating the difficulty the CJEU and General Court have had in applying competition law to territorial restrictions on the basis of intellectual property protection. It must also be stated that while collecting societies will be briefly mentioned in this chapter, the focus of the chapter will be on the relationship between service providers and end-users. The role of collecting societies will be the subject of in-depth analysis in Chapter 6. Finally, the chapter will conclude by assessing the impact of the *Premier League* case, demonstrating how the case may be read in ways that both support and detract from the argument that Article 56 TFEU and EU competition law can be used as a means of defeating territorial restrictions in the digital music market as a general principle.

The state of the digital music market

At the time of writing, it has been ten years since the iTunes Store first opened for digital business. As of 6 February 2013, the iTunes Store has sold 25 billion songs worldwide (Apple 2013a), and a reported 64 per cent share of the market for digital music (Archer 2012). Following the success of the US iTunes Store, Apple opened three stores in the UK, France and Germany in June 2004. Stores in Austria, Belgium, Finland, Greece, Italy, Luxembourg, the Netherlands, Portugal and Spain were subsequently opened in October 2004. Stores in Denmark, Sweden and Ireland opened in 2005, and by September 2011 in the rest of the EU area. At the time of writing, the iTunes Store is now accessible in twenty-seven Member States, with new Member State Croatia being the exception (Apple 2013b), and offers over 25 million songs (Apple 2012a). This includes music from the 'big three' record labels, Universal Music Group, Sony Music Entertainment and Warner Music Group. Other digital music stores exist, although none are nearly as successful as Apple's iTunes Store, nor as accessible. 7digital, for example, began operating in the UK in 2004, and would appear to be Apple's biggest rival for popular music in Europe, having digital stores based in Austria, Belgium, Denmark, Finland, France, Germany, Ireland, Italy, Luxembourg, the Netherlands, Portugal, Spain and the United Kingdom.

However, as with iTunes, a disparity can be seen. 7digital does not yet have stores in Greece or any of the post-2004 Accession Member States. This information is readily available on 7digital's website. On its 'Help' page under the heading 'Can I shop at 7digital from outside of the UK?', it is stated that 'we operate download sites in an increasing number of countries. To see if we have a store in your country, please scroll to the bottom of the page to view the links to our current international services' (7Digital 2013). 7Digital currently offers 24 million songs for download including music of the three major labels, according to its main website at www.7digital.com, one million less than Apple makes available. Amazon, the world's largest internet-based retailer has also offered digital music downloads since September 2007, offering US-based consumers the ability to buy DRM-free music from their store. In Europe, Amazon extended its service onto the Amazon.co.uk service in December 2008. A second European service was begun on the Amazon.de retail site early in 2009, and a third in France in June 2009. As of February 2013, Amazon's MP3 store is only available in six EU Member States, namely the UK, France, Germany, Spain, Italy, and Austria through the German MP3 store (Amazon 2013). Amazon currently offers 20 million songs for download, including from the three major labels.

The consumer market for the legal purchase and download of digital music in the EU is highly fragmented (Leurdijk and Nieuwenhuis 2012; Farrand 2009; Edwards 2007; Eechoud et al. 2009; Anderson 2008). In fact, it would be safe to say that the market for digital music downloads is so fragmented that it is difficult to talk of a single market for digital media distribution existing within the EU. Neither Apple, 7digital or Amazon, which effectively constitute the three largest retailers of digital music in the EU, operate a pan-European service in which all content is accessible by all consumers in all Member States without borders or technical restrictions. For example, instead of having one service for the entirety of the EU, Apple's iTunes Store consists of twenty-seven independent services, each operating individually within a Member State. As Edwards states, 'pursuant to agreements between Apple and each record company, consumers can only buy music from the iTunes' online store in their country of residence. iTunes verifies consumers' country of residence through their credit card details' (Edwards 2007, p. N81). Therefore, each iTunes user will be restricted to using the iTunes service of the country with which his credit card is registered. By way of example, an English consumer will only be able to use the UK service, whereas a German consumer may only use the services based in Germany (Farrand 2009, p. 508). According to the UK iTunes Store terms and conditions, the service is 'available to you only in the United Kingdom. You agree not to use or attempt to use the Stores from outside this location. iTunes may use technologies to verify your compliance' (Apple 2012b). The terms and conditions for the other EU-based stores contain the same stipulation, albeit in the official languages of that country. This type of prohibition is not limited to iTunes, however, as purchasers of digital music may well be aware. 7digital states at para. 12.2 of its terms and conditions that:

Content may be restricted by territory. Where required, to conclude the purchase of any such restricted products, you will be required to provide a billing address in the relevant territory. You agree not circumvent any territorial restrictions in place on the Services or provide false billing information.

(7digital UK 2012)

Amazon similarly restricts content by national territory, stating at para. 2.2 of its terms and conditions, 'As required by our Music Content providers, Music Content is available only to customers located in the United Kingdom' (Amazon UK 2012). It would appear, then, that within the EU's internal market there is significant fragmentation of the market for digital music downloads as the result of territorial restrictions placed upon the operation of these services. In the remainder of this chapter, the laws and CJEU jurisprudence applicable to the free movement of services and competition law will be expanded upon, and their applicability to the territorial restrictions in this market will be assessed.

Do territorial restrictions on the provision of services constitute a hindrance to the single market?

When dealing with the digital transfer of data between Member States (which ultimately, digital music is, no matter how indistinguishable from music in analogue form), there is the question of whether the law applying to the free movement of goods, or the freedom to provide services, should apply. Although Articles 34–6 TFEU make mention of goods, the first definition came in the case of *Commission v Italy*, where goods were defined as products which 'can be valued in money and which are capable, as such, of forming the subject of commercial transactions' (1968, paras 428–9). As can be seen by the success of the digital media distribution services, and the pricing models detailed therein, digital data can without doubt be valued in money, and 6 billion sales testify to the possibility of digital music forming the subject of a commercial transaction. While Advocate General Fennelly stated in *Jägerskiöld* that goods must 'possess tangible physical characteristics' (1999, para. 20), it has been determined that an intangible such as electricity can constitute a good (*Almelo* 1994, para. 28). Therefore, if digital data were to be considered by either Community Law or national laws to be a good, then the law relating to the free movement of goods would apply. However, this is not the case. Directive 98/34/EC was implemented in order to ensure that technical standards and regulations throughout the Community were established in a transparent manner. While this Directive did not expand on the consideration of digital services, a second Directive quickly followed, Amendment Directive 98/48/EC. The Amendment Directive specifically addresses the changes and possibilities brought by widespread use of the internet, and the development of the 'Information Society'. Article 1(2) of the Amending Directive states that Directive 98/34/EC should be amended so that under Article 1 'services', shall mean any Information Society service, or in other words, any service normally provided for remuneration, at a distance, by electronic means and at the individual request of a recipient of services is to be treated as a service and not a good. Radio and television broadcast services were specifically excluded as they are universally transmitted for simultaneous access by unlimited users by Annex V section 3.

Based on this definition, digital media distribution such as the selling of MP3 downloads by Apple constitutes an Information Society service governed by Articles 56 and 57 of the TFEU. The service is commercial, provided at a distance by electronic means, and at the individual request of a consumer. A user sitting at a computer at home accesses the iTunes server electronically, chooses which specific track or album he would like to download, and then pays for the download with a credit card. Therefore, by the definition provided by the Amending Directive, what the consumer is paying for is not the digital file itself, but the service Apple provides by making available a particular music file, and then transferring it to the consumer. The issue at hand regarding territoriality does not concern the single digital file, but the access to that file through a particular service. The E-Commerce Directive 2000/31/EC followed these Directives two years later, passed with the intention of 'contributing to the proper functioning of the internal market by ensuring the free movement of information society services between the Member States' (2000, Article 1). In order to achieve this, Article 3 of the E-Commerce Directive dictates that the Member States should ensure that such services provided by companies established within its territory comply with the national provisions applicable in the Member State in question, and based on a principle of mutual recognition, Member States should not therefore restrict within their territory the freedom to provide services of companies based in other Member States.

For the purpose of determining who may rely upon Article 56, it is worth considering the wording of Article 56 TFEU in its entirety. The Article states that:

> within the framework of the provisions set out below, restrictions on freedom to provide services within the Community shall be prohibited in respect of nationals of Member States who are established in a State of the Community other than that of the person for whom the services are intended.

As can be seen from the wording, the Article is specifically designed to protect the providers of services. Indeed, much of the case law in this field focuses specifically on these types of restrictions – the case of *Van Binsbergen* (1974) is a key example (Barnard 2007, p. 356), dealing with a restriction in Dutch law preventing legal representatives from representing clients in Dutch courts if not established in that country. When an advocate for Van Binsbergen moved to Belgium during proceedings and was subsequently prevented from representing his client any further, the ECJ found that this was a breach of Article 56 TFEU.

Unfortunately, in the case of consumers unable to use a digital media distribution service such as Apple's iTunes or 7digital, it is not as straightforward a situation. In such an instance it is not a service provider who may potentially seek to claim that there is a restriction on the provision of services, but the recipient of said service. Are they too able to claim the breach of EU law? In the view of Barnard, although a strict interpretation of Article 56 only grants rights to service providers, 'if service providers can travel to the state of the recipient, then logic suggests that the recipient should also be able to travel to the state of the provider' (Barnard 2007, p. 357). In the joint cases of *Luisi and Carbone* (1984), two Italian nationals who were travelling to other Member States as tourists in order to receive medical treatment were fined for taking out more money from Italy than was permitted under the then-existing currency regulations. In the opinion of the CJEU in this case, the freedom of users of a service to move is the necessary corollary of the right to move to provide a service, 'which fulfils the objective of liberalising all gainful activity not covered by the free movement of goods, persons and capital' (1984, para. 10). The right of citizens of the EU to travel in order to receive a service was considered as being as valid a right as that of service providers to travel in order to offer those services.

A logical extension of this principle is to the provision of services where neither the provider nor the recipient physically crosses a border, as in the case of a cross-border music download. This extension was made initially in the case of *Alpine Investments* (1995), a case dealing with a prohibition by the Dutch government on 'cold-calling' – a business practice whereby Alpine Investments was calling potential investors without prior consent to offer various financial services. Alpine Investments was not just calling clients in the Netherlands where the company was based, but also in other Member States. A Dutch law prohibited the practice of 'cold-calling' in order to offer investment services on public policy grounds. Alpine Investments protested, on the grounds that such a prohibition on offering services in other Member States constituted a restriction on the provision of services contrary to Article 56. In reviewing the case, the ECJ determined that although it was not disproportionate to prohibit cold-calling in order to ensure investor confidence in the market (and therefore achieving a recognized public policy goal), that 'on a proper construction, Article 56 TFEU covers services which the provider offers by telephone to potential recipients established in other Member States and provides without moving from the Member State in which he is established' (1995, para. 22). This was reaffirmed in the case of *Bond* where the CJEU made specific reference to the service provided as a 'transfrontier service for the purposes of Article 56 of the Treaty' (1988, para. 15). Applied specifically to information society services, the recent case of *Piergiorgio Gambelli* (2003) confirmed that the 'transfrontier' principle would also apply in situations concerning the provision of services over the internet. Gambelli concerned criminal proceedings brought against several defendants for their involvement in agencies linked by the internet to Stanley International Betting Ltd, a bookmaker established in the UK. They were accused of collaborating with bookmakers abroad in the activity of collecting bets, normally reserved by law to the State in Italy, in contravention of Italian criminal law. The defendants claimed that such a law ran contrary to the provisions for the freedom to provide services under Article 56 TFEU. The CJEU determined that such a law did in fact restrict the freedom to provide services, although it stated that whether such restrictions were proportionate in order to achieve their aims was a matter for the national courts. The CJEU stated in its reasoning that the principle that the freedom to enjoy a service offered in another Member State without being subjected to restrictions applied equally and specifically to internet-based services in which neither the provider nor the user of the service moves (2003, paras 54–5).

Based on this principle, it is safe to therefore conclude that although Article 56 TFEU was written with the intention of granting rights to service providers who moved from one Member State to another in order to provide services, subsequent case law has shown that the law will also apply in situations where neither provider nor recipient move, yet the service is cross-border in nature. Furthermore, both a consumer and a provider of a service can rely upon this principle. For these reasons, a consumer who feels that his right to access internet-based services available in another Member State is restricted may potentially bring an action based on Article 56 TFEU. After all, neither the consumer nor the service provider moves across a border. The consumer will access the service from a personal computer, based (usually) in the Member State in which they are residing. In the case of a consumer wishing to access the iTunes service based in that Member State, should any issue of restrictions arise, said restrictions will not constitute restrictions under Article 56 TFEU, as there is no cross-border element. However, the fact that users are trying to access the iTunes service in another Member State means that in theory any restriction, should one be found, will be both subject and contrary to Article 56 TFEU. As the Treaty and secondary legislation makes provision for the provision of cross-border internet services in the interest of the harmonization and integration of an internal market for 'Information Society' services, it therefore must stand to reason that Article 56 TFEU, which regulates cross-border services, may catch such transactions. However, when the restriction is in place due to a license agreement between commercial parties, and is the result of a technical restriction put in place by a private rather than state entity, can Article 56 TFEU apply?

The application of Article 56 TFEU to territorial restrictions in the digital music market

It has been generally accepted since the case of *Van Gend en Loos* (1963) that Treaty provisions can have vertical direct effect and subsequently be invoked against the State by individuals. The Courts have specifically stated that Article 56 TFEU has direct effect in a number of cases. In the previously cited *Van Binsbergen* case, the issue of the direct applicability of Article 56 and whether an individual could bring a claim against a Member State was addressed, with the

CJEU stating that the intent of Article 56 was to abolish restrictions on freedom to provide services, in particular abolishing all discrimination against a person providing that service (and in the light of new case law, those receiving said service) by reason of his nationality or the fact that he is established in a Member State other than that in which the service is to be provided. For this reason, Article 56 has direct effect and can be relied upon by individuals bringing actions against Member States (paras 26–7). However, in this instance, we are not dealing with a decision, practice or policy operative at the Member State level but a restriction on a service put in place by a corporation.

In the pivotal case of *Walrave and Koch*, which dealt with sporting bodies' discriminatory regulations concerning nationality, it was suggested by the CJEU that the Treaty provisions on the free movement of workers and the freedom of services should be interpreted in a broad manner, and that 'the rule on non-discrimination applies in judging all legal relationships' (1974, para. 28). While this would appear to include the contractual stipulations concerning territory of an online music provider, the decision states specifically that this principle applies to bodies involved in 'collective' regulation (1974, para. 17). This has been taken to mean regulatory bodies with a quasi-public function, such as football associations. The CJEU reaffirmed this in *Dona v Mantero*, stating that Article 56 would be applied to rules aimed at collective regulation, and that rules or a national practice, even if adopted by a sporting organization, could infringe this provision, and an action successfully brought against the sporting organization in question (1976, para. 19). However, the CJEU did not specifically state whether this applied to all organizations, or merely those exercising a quasi-public regulatory function. The situation did not improve with the controversial cases of *Laval* (2007) and *Viking* (2007). *Laval* dealt with a situation where the CJEU had to determine whether the actions of a trade union regulating collective agreements could breach Article 56 TFEU where it imposed restrictions on the ability of posted workers to work in another Member State. In *Laval*, Swedish trade unions took strike action against a Latvian construction firm, on the grounds that the firm refused to sign a collective agreement that would benefit the Latvian workers posted in Sweden, as well as preventing a form of social dumping. One of the questions posed to the CJEU was whether the strike action taken by the unions could constitute a hindrance of the freedom to provide services under Article 56. *Viking* had similar facts, but concerned freedom of establishment under Article 49 TFEU.

The *Laval* and *Viking* cases have generated a significant amount of legal debate, not only in consideration of the issue of the horizontality of the free movement provisions, but also of certain employment and social issues outside of the remit of this book. In particular, as the CJEU found that the rules applying to the freedom to provide services would apply to trade unions, which it did not consider to be public bodies (*Laval* 2007, para. 84), it thereby gave Article 56 what appears to be a genuine horizontal effect. The CJEU in *Viking* went further, stating that 'there is no indication in [the preceding] case-law that could validly support the view that it applies only to associations or organisations exercising a regulatory task or having quasi-legislative powers' (*Viking* 2007, para. 65). However, it appears that the question of the extent of this horizontal effect has remained unanswered. As Davies states, 'it remains to be seen whether the ECJ will confine the horizontal effect of Article 56 to situations of this type (i.e., those with a regulatory nature)' (Davies 2008, p. 137). Snell has argued that even before *Laval* the scope of Article 56 is too wide, and that actions against individual regulatory bodies or companies is more effectively handled through competition law (2002, pp. 144–5). However, Prechal and De Vries have argued the opposite, stating that the intention behind the free movement rules and competition law was to provide a 'seamless web of judicial protection' for the internal market (2009, p. 6). Whereas the traditional viewpoint has largely been that free movement provisions applied to Member States, and the competition rules under Articles 101 and 102 TFEU to private undertakings, Prechal and De Vries contend that 'a strict separation between the free movement provisions and competition rules is increasingly becoming less apparent, parallel to the dilution of the traditional public-private divide' (2009, p. 6). This is a view supported by Azoulai, who argues that given the economic integration goals of the writers of the European Treaties, 'the pre-eminence of the Treaty rules whose aim was to break open the national markets was self-evident' (2008, p. 1340), and by Ronnmar (2010, pp. 281–2). Nevertheless, other authors are sceptical as to the extent that *Laval* and *Viking* cases have enshrined a principle of horizontal direct effect with regard to Article 56, such as Trstenjak and Beysen, who say it is more accurate to discuss a 'limited horizontal direct effect' that has not been expressly expanded beyond trade unions since the *Laval* and *Viking* decisions (2013, p. 315), and Apps, who states that the CJEU specifically avoided creating a 'general' principle of horizontal direct effect, instead expanding the principle to trade unions by referring to them as 'non-excluded' agencies (2009, pp. 142–5). Furthermore, while Article 45 on the free movement of workers was explicitly given horizontal direct effect in *Angonese* (2000) and then reaffirmed in *Raccanneli* (2008), Apps notes that this was not done in the case of *Viking*, which did not mention *Angonese* at all, and has not been applied in any cases relating to services (2009, p. 147). For this reason, it is difficult to state with any certainty whether Article 56 TFEU could be applied directly to a service such as iTunes.

Nevertheless, there is the possibility that a territorial restriction in the provision of a service, such as that applied to digital music distribution services, could be challenged on the basis that the intellectual property right it seeks to protect is a national law. The basis for such a claim can be found in the cases of *Coditel I* (1980) and the recent *Premier League* (2011) cases. In *Coditel I*, a license for exclusive distribution was granted to Cine Vog, a Belgian company, to show the film 'Le Boucher' in Belgian cinemas. At the same time, Coditel, a Belgian cable television distribution service, picked up a transmission of the film being broadcast legitimately in Germany on German television. Coditel transmitted the film on its cable network. The contract Cine Vog had with the French right-holders of the film stated that the right to transmit the film on television could not be exercised until forty months after the first showing of the film in Belgium – at this point, the film had only been showing for seven months. As a result, Cine Vog sued Coditel for infringement of copyright (Tritton and Davis 2008, sec. 7–90). Ultimately, the ECJ in *Coditel* found that Article 56 TFEU does not prohibit the imposition of a geographical limitation of a license to broadcast, where the limitation serves an objective purpose, so long as the measures do not go any further than is required to fulfill that objective (*Commission v Germany* 1986; *Sager* 1991, para. 15) and is applied in a non-discriminatory manner (*Gebhard* 1995; *Haim* 2000). In so doing, the CJEU distinguished the application of the free movement of goods rules relating to intellectual property from those of the movement of services. While it was held that territorial exclusion of goods could not be justified by a contract dictating the rights of a copyright holder as in the case of *Dansk Supermarked* (1981), this did not hold true for broadcasts of movies by a cable network. The reasoning of the CJEU was that with goods subject to copyright, such as books and CDs, the financial reward to right-holders is assured through the physical sale, corresponding to the number of products sold. With television broadcasts on the other hand, this is not possible, as they make available to the public copyrighted work on a broadcast basis, making it difficult to determine the royalties to be paid (*Coditel I* 1980, para. 13). However, the *Premier League* case was explicitly distinguished from *Coditel I* by the CJEU (2011, para. 119). The *Premier League* case was initiated in the UK in *Murphy v Media Protection Services Ltd* (2008), a case dealing with an English publican who used a Greek satellite-decoding card in order to broadcast Premier League football games. Murphy chose to do this as purchasing and using a Greek decoder meant that pay-per-view games could be viewed for a much lower fee than that offered by BSkyB's UK-based service. When Murphy was caught using a Greek decoder by agents acting on behalf of the Football Association Premier League Association Ltd (FAPL), Murphy argued that the prohibition on the use of foreign decoders was a territorial restriction in breach of competition law and the free movement of services (see *Premier League* 2011, paras 50–6). Referring to *Coditel I*, the CJEU argued that in that instance, the use of the copyrighted material was without authorization, whereas in this instance, the use was authorized, albeit in a different Member State (2011, paras 118–20). The CJEU stated that on this basis, any legislation that prevented the importation and use of a decoder card legally sold in another Member State is in breach of Article 56 TFEU (2011, paras 89, 125). This case leaves open the possibility that a territorial restriction that prevents a user from using an otherwise authorized and legal digital music service accessible in another Member State could be found to be in breach of Article 56 TFEU. However, the potential impact of this case is subject to debate. As this case was also heard by the CJEU with regard to FAPL's agreements being incompatible with competition law in addition to Article 56 TFEU, the significance of the case will be discussed subsequent to the sections of this chapter concerning competition law analysis of the fragmented digital music market.

Competition Law I: the (non) evidence of price-fixing

The purpose of EU competition law is 'to intervene in the marketplace when there is some problem with the competitive process or when there is a "market failure"' (Rodger and MacCulloch 2009, p. 1). As is stated Article 3(3) of the Treaty on the Functioning of the European Union (TFEU), 'The Union shall establish an internal market. It shall work for the sustainable development of Europe based on balanced economic growth and price stability . . . [and] a highly competitive social market economy'. This is to be achieved, according to Article 3 TFEU, by establishing competition rules necessary for the functioning of the internal market. According to a UK Government White Paper:

> The importance of competition in an increasingly innovative and globalised economy is clear. Vigorous competition between firms is the lifeblood of strong and effective markets. Competition helps consumers get a good deal . . . competition is a central driver for productivity and growth in the economy.
>
> (Department for Trade and Industry 2001, s.1.1)

Competition law seeks to achieve two goals, which are very closely related (and, to an extent, interdependent). First, competition law seeks to ensure that markets remain as competitive as possible in order to ensure high economic efficiency, based on discourse that a multitude of effective actors and undertakings in competition are able to bring down costs, improve production, and ensure that the wheels of commerce continue to turn. Competition law also ostensibly seeks to protect consumers, by both preventing abusive conduct undertaken by single businesses, and ensuring that cartels cannot artificially raise prices, limit production, or restrict consumer choice.

The formation of cartels, or the agreement to cooperate made by rival competitors in a market, is perceived as one of the most serious forms of anti-competitive practice, and is the one that is dealt with most severely. Neelie Kroes, then the European Commissioner for Competition, stated at a conference in 2005 that:

> Cartel behaviour is illegal, unjustified and unjustifiable – whatever the size, nature or scope of the business affected. Cartels attack free markets at their very hearts. They don't just mess up the grass on a level playing field – they blow great holes out of the surface. And it is consumers who are asked over and over again to pay the price of replacing the turf. The long-term

eradication of cartels is therefore essential if we are to deliver the fair competitive environment needed to allow growth and job-creation to flourish in Europe.

(Kroes 2005)

However, by their very nature cartels are secretive agreements, and with few exceptions, are unlikely to leave an easy-to-find, detailed paper trail of their movements inviting prosecution – although there are some notable exceptions such as the case of *Hasbro, Argos and Littlewoods* (2003), in which an amusing email exchange regarding price fixing stated that nothing should ever be put in writing as it was 'highly illegal and it could bite you right in the arse!!!' (2003 para. 53). For this reason, Article 101(1) TFEU states that as well as applying to agreements between undertakings, the competition provisions will also consider illegal 'concerted practices'. One of the first significant concerted practices cases was *Dyestuffs* (1972), which concerned a series of uniform price increases of dyes based on Analine between January 1964 and October 1967. In a subsequent Commission investigation and ECJ decision, it was found that although there was no formal agreement between the firms to increase their prices, nevertheless there was evidence of concerted practice between several firms in the dyestuff market, with each company subsequently following the price increases of the other firms. In its decision, the ECJ stated that although a firm was free to change its prices in response to market forces 'nevertheless it is contrary to the rules on competition . . . for a producer to cooperate with his competitors, in any way whatsoever, in order to determine a coordinated course of action relating to a price increase' (*Dyestuffs* 1972 para. 118). This reasoning was expanded upon in the case of *Suiker Unie* (1975), with the CJEU stating that a concerted practice refers to coordination between undertakings that although not resulting in a formalized agreement, nevertheless are the result of knowing collusion (paragraphs 26–7).

While it may be difficult to determine whether actions taken by firms constitute an anti-competitive agreement or a concerted practice, it has been stated by Advocate General Reischl that it is not absolutely essential to a finding of conduct contrary to Article 101, due to both types of conduct being equally illegal and any distinction is ultimately a matter of unimportant classification (*Van Landewyck* 1980 p. 3310). There is no legal distinction made between the types of behaviour; all that matters is that the conduct was collusive (Whish and Bailey 2012, p. 102). Indeed, in the *PVC* case the Commission determined that the parties to the anti-competitive conduct had participated in an 'agreement and or concerted practice' indicating that no real distinction is made in practice (1994, paragraphs 30–1).

The way in which digital music retailers operate is to sign agreements with the record labels whose music they wish to distribute. In the case of the iTunes, 7digital, Amazon *et al.*, the biggest of these agreements are those made with the major record labels mentioned previously, and with smaller agreements being made with 'independent' record labels. According to a report released by the IFPI in 2009 and reproduced by Wikström, the then 'big four' (including the now defunct EMI) as these record labels are known, accounted for approximately 71 per cent of record sales internationally, with each having a market share of 11 per cent, 14 per cent, 20 per cent and 26 per cent respectively (2009, pp. 73–7). With the insolvency of EMI, however, and the absorption of its recorded music catalogue by Universal (and subsequent sale by Universal of EMI's European labels to Warner), the market for music has become even more concentrated (Pfanner 2013). While the Competition DG of the European Commission expressed concern at the level of concentration in the market, they nevertheless permitted the acquisition of EMI by Universal following a market investigation (European Commission 2012). In comparison, independent labels have a comparatively small market share of approximately 30 per cent, despite the high number of independent labels. For example, the Association of Independent Music in the UK purports to represent over 800 member companies, including both independent labels and individual artists (Association of Independent Music 2012). Given the high market share held by three major labels, this indicates that the market for records is a highly concentrated, oligopolistic one.

Could there be concerted practice between in the EU's digital music market that competition law could address? Article 101(1) lays out a list of types of agreement that have the potential to be anti-competitive. These agreements have as their object or effect the prevention, restriction or distortion of competition, and in particular can include price fixing, limiting or controlling production, markets or share markets. Horizontal price fixing is possibly the most obvious form of anti-competitive agreement, and the most straightforward. Cases such as *British Sugar* (1999) show that the Article 101 prohibition covers not only situations where a price has been actually fixed in a formal way (1999, paragraphs 91–2), but even where parties to an agreement could rely upon the other participants to pursue collaborative strategies of higher pricing in 'an atmosphere of mutual certainty' (European Commission 1999, pp. 138–40). In the present case, there are indications that could lead to an allegation of price fixing – tracks offered by each of the major record labels on European services is charged at £0.99 in the UK and 1.29€ in Eurozone countries, indicating that there is little in the way of price competition between the record labels. Indeed, there appears to be little in the way of price competition between the services themselves, with the exception of Amazon – by way of example, 'American Idiot' by Green Day costs £0.99/1.29€ on iTunes and 7digital, but £0.89/0.99€ on Amazon. This could perhaps indicate collusion between the services themselves, and Article 101 explicitly covers distributors as well as suppliers according to the *Musique Diffusion* case (1983). Nevertheless, it is somewhat unlikely that any collusion is at the level of the digital music platforms. In the past, Apple has explicitly stated that its prices are largely dictated by the major record labels and collecting societies and in 2008 threatened to close the service when confronted with a potential hike in costs as a result of faltering negotiations concerning royalty rates

(Shiels 2008). This would appear to indicate that any attempt to resolve the potential competition issue relating to pricing in the EU would have to focus upon relations between suppliers of music, i.e., record labels and digital distributors such as the iTunes Store.

The Commission considers agreements between suppliers and distributors as constituting 'vertical agreements'. Vertical agreements have been regarded as being potentially anti-competitive since the case of *Consten and Grundig* (1966). However, certain types of agreement that may have been considered as anti-competitive have been exempted under the Vertical Agreement Block Exemption Regulation. The 1999 Regulation was replaced by the 2010 Regulation in April 2010, with the most significant change being that Article 3, concerning the market share cap, was made applicable to the purchaser (i.e., the distributor) as well as the seller (i.e., the supplier). Article 3 specifies a maximum market share of 30 per cent for the exemption to apply, meaning that any agreement with Apple's iTunes Store cannot be exempted due to its 64 per cent market share, and therefore must be assessed under Article 101 TFEU. The European Commission has expressed concern over digital music pricing in the EU in the past (Farrand 2009; Siragusa 2008). In particular (and largely due to Apple's significant market share), the focus of such concern has been on the iTunes Store's uniform pricing (Farrand 2009; Shiller and Waldfogel 2009; Kokkoris and Katona 2010). In September 2004, the Office of Fair Trading (OFT), a British Governmental department, which among other regulatory functions is charged with investigating competition issues within the UK, announced in December 2004 that it would be referring the matter directly to the European Commission after the media and consumer protection groups raised awareness of price differentials between British, French and German versions of the iTunes Store (Farrand 2009, p. 508). In a statement made by the OFT on 6 December 2004, it was stated that the European Commission would be 'better placed to consider this matter, in particular as Apple iTunes operates in more than three EC Member States' (Pinsent Masons 2004). The Commission began investigating in April 2007, and announced that it had sent a Statement of Objections not only to Apple, but also to major record companies. The Statement related to 'agreements between each record company and Apple that restrict music sales . . . consumers are restricted in their choice of where to buy music, and consequently what music is available, and at what price.' (European Commission 2007b). It is worth noting this statement could equally apply to all the services offering music by the major record labels within the EU area. Writing at the time that the Commission was investigating, Siragusa commented that the case could potentially break new ground 'in attempting to transpose on-line distribution principles on cross-border trade that were developed for physical distribution' (2008, p. 102). In applying territorial restrictions on the access of iTunes Stores through locking access to the territory in which a credit card was registered, consumers are locked into both the price and locally available repertoire. In other words, consumers were not able to access music that may be cheaper in another Member State, nor music not available in their own store (Farrand 2009, p. 509; Siragusa 2008, pp. 103–4). Yet before the investigation was concluded, Apple announced to the Commission in June 2007 and then publicly on 9 January 2008 that it would be reducing its UK prices to be in line with those in the rest of Europe. The Commission welcomed this decision, closing its investigation, releasing a statement that said that it had concluded that the structure of Apple's iTunes Stores was not the result of agreements between Apple and the major record labels (Farrand 2009, p. 509; European Commission 2008a).

How could this be the case, given the uniformity of pricing identified by authors such as Shiller and Waldfogel (2009)? The answer, it appears, may be found in another competition decision released by the Commission prior to the Apple decision. In October 2007, the Commission announced that it was allowing the joint venture between Sony and Bertelsmann for the creation of Sony BMG (that later became Sony Music Entertainment), following an investigation into the potential anti-competitive effects of such a venture in both digital and physical markets for recorded music (European Commission 2007c). In particular, the Commission noted that while the significant market concentration apparent in having five (and now three) firms with a market share of above 70 per cent could give rise to a situation of collective dominance, the pricing structure within the EU area was not the result of collusion between record labels. Instead, the Commission found that labels were most likely to attempt to maximize revenue through the use of 'different prices, different pricing structures and [the] use [of] different business models' (European Commission 2007a, para. 102), including significant variation in wholesale prices charged to Apple (2007a, para. 115). Furthermore, the Commission stated, the existence of a uniform price on iTunes was more likely the result of Apple's '"one price fits all" pricing policy' (European Commission 2007a, para. 116). Yet focusing on comparative prices between the UK and Eurozone countries does not appear to be an effective means of remedying the problems with the digital music distribution market in the EU. In July 2008 Apple announced that it was abandoning its UK price cut, claiming that due to the changes in the world economy the action was no longer necessary. Quoted in an article by BBC News, a representative of the company stated that 'the announcement was that we would match the UK price to that of the lower priced European countries . . . this is no longer necessary as exchange rates have effectively done this for us' (Youngs 2008). Ironically, given the original cause of the action, at the time of writing in July 2013 the Pound has depreciated in value compared to the Euro (with £1 having a value of €1.16, compared to €1.52 in June 2004). As exchange rates will always be in a state of flux (unless of course the UK joins the Euro), then price alone is not an effective means of assessing anti-competitive effects in digital music distribution. Instead, the focus should be on territorial restrictions.

Competition Law II: licensing and territorial restrictions

The landmark case of *Consten and Grundig* (1966) mentioned earlier concerned the imposition of territorial restrictions between a supplier and distributor heard by the CJEU. Grundig entered into an exclusive distribution agreement with French firm Establissements Consten. One term of this agreement was that Consten would be the sole seller of Grundig products in France (but would not be permitted to sell those goods outside of France), and in return, Grundig would not sell those goods in France except through Consten. This clause was considered as constituting a hard-core restriction of competition, and therefore infringed (now) Article 101 TFEU (1966, pp. 343–4). For this type of agreement, parties cannot rely upon the Vertical Agreement Block Exemption Regulations, as they state at Article 4(b) that 'any restriction of the territory into which, or of the customers to whom, the buyer may sell the contract goods or services' will be considered as being in breach of Article 101(1).

It is difficult to determine whether a successful action could be brought against Apple's iTunes and its suppliers (or indeed, any of the other music distribution platforms) on the basis of territorial restrictions. In theory at least, agreements that serve to partition the internal market would constitute hard-core anti-competitive agreements. However, when concerning licensing agreements for the distribution of digital music, the situation is not so clear. The starting point for considering the application of competition law in this area is the *Coditel II* (1982) case. *Coditel II* perhaps unsurprisingly followed the *Coditel I* (1980) case, as described earlier in this chapter. *Coditel II* could be considered as being an addendum to *Coditel I*, in which Cine Vog sought to determine whether the agreement in question could be considered anti-competitive, even if it did not fall foul of Article 56 TFEU. Reasoning that there were objective justifications for the exclusivity and territorial restriction, relating to subtitling/dubbing and the financing of film in Europe (1980, para. 16), the CJEU in *Coditel II* stated that in this particular instance, the agreement was not in breach of competition law (1980, para. 20). In particular, the need to be able to effectively calculate royalty payments was a determinant factor in this case, as in *Coditel I*. While the possibility exists that there may be a breach of competition law in an exclusivity agreement of this nature depending on the terms of that agreement, in general content licensing will be considered as falling outside the usual competition rules regarding territorial exclusivity (Kraatz 1990, p. E91; Batchelor 2007, p. 221; Aitman and Jones 2004, pp. 143–4).

One recent case that brings this into question however is *Premier League* (2011), as discussed earlier. With regard to the arguments raised regarding competition law, the CJEU began by reaffirming the validity of *Coditel II*, stating that the granting of an exclusive license to broadcast copyright-protected subject matter is not in itself anti-competitive (2011, para. 137). However, the CJEU distinguished *Premier League* from *Coditel II*, arguing that, in this instance, the license agreement was specifically designed to partition the market so that FAPL could charge different fees in different Member States. Furthermore, FAPL took action to prevent consumers from otherwise legally purchasing decoders from other Member States, eliminating competition between broadcasters (2011, paras 140–2). The CJEU found that FAPL was not able to provide any legal or economic justification for dividing the market in such a way, stating that there was no other choice but to find that the license agreements between FAPL and broadcasters infringed Article 101 TFEU (2011, paras 143–6).

Until very recently, it appeared that recent decisions concerning collecting societies supported the consideration of restrictive agreements of this nature being contrary to competition law. Collecting societies, and their important role in both protecting intellectual property rights and contributing to the fragmentation of the single market, are considered in much more detail in Chapter 6 of this book. For the purposes of the analysis in this section, however, a very brief overview of their functioning will be provided. Collecting societies are organizations that administer the rights of copyright holders, typically the authors, artists and/or producers of the copyright work, whether it be in the form of a book, movie or sound recording (Batchelor 2007, p. 217). These societies monitor the use of music and collect royalty payments from individuals such as bar proprietors, or collective groups. One such example is the collecting society 'PRS for Music' in the UK (this society is the combination of the Performing Rights Society and the Mechanical Copyright Protection Society). The PRS for Music collecting society tracks the number of CDs, music DVDs and internet sales of music made, as well as issuing licenses for the performing of music in live venues. On the basis of this monitoring, PRS for Music makes calculations of the royalty payments that should be made to artists as a percentage of profits made from sales and uses of copyrighted works. Collecting societies are usually organized as single national organizations operating within one particular sector (for example, music or book licensing), which operate as de facto monopolies, with the justification that such a system provides maximum protection for artists as revenue can be calculated more accurately by one body. This justification has been explicitly recognized by the CJEU in *BRT v SABAM* (1974), and it is for this reason that licensing content for exploitation on a restricted national basis has been considered as legal, despite the fact that this would ordinarily be considered as being a 'hard-core' restriction of trade between Member States (*Coditel II*, paras 14–17).

The Commission has made it clear that it holds reservations when applying this policy to digital services, however. In the *Simulcasting* Commission investigation, several collecting societies agreed to a reciprocal arrangement allowing individual members to grant pan-European licenses (as opposed to the previous national-enforcement agreements of old) for broadcasting creative content held by any of the participating collecting societies. This agreement was found to be in breach of Article 101(1) on the grounds that there was no splitting of administrative costs and royalty payments, meaning there would be little encouragement for consumers to shop-around (due to a lack of transparency that would allow consumers to determine which collecting societies were more efficient and offering a more cost-effective service) and little reason for the collecting societies to compete with each other. Furthermore, the fixing of fees based on the aggregate of national rates of the Member States was found to be a form of anti-competitive price-fixing contrary to Article 101 as it did not allow individual collecting societies to set lower licensing fees to compete with other societies. Nevertheless, the agreement was allowed to stand for three reasons: first, IFPI was willing to amend the agreement so that administrative costs and royalty payments were split, allowing for collecting societies to compete by reducing their administrative costs; second, the fixing of fees was entitled to exemption under Article 101(3) on the grounds that this was indispensable to the agreement, and ultimately benefited consumers by facilitating a broadcasting service, 'as the guarantee of a certain level of remuneration ensured that collecting societies joined the licence scheme and prevented individual societies undermining the rate' (Batchelor 2007, p. 220). Third, the exemption was given a limited duration – from 22 May 2002 to 31 December 2004, on the grounds that the agreement was to run for an experimental period, after which it would be reviewed.

In the Commission investigation into *CISAC* (2006), it appeared that this line of reasoning would be followed. In 2006, the Commission issued a Statement of Objections regarding an agreement between collecting societies represented by CISAC. CISAC is, according to the Commission, an umbrella organization that represents twenty-four collecting societies in the EEA area (European Commission 2008c, paras 7–8). According to the complaint, the CISAC Model Agreement contained three clauses that prevented collecting societies party to the Agreement from issuing multi-territory licenses outside of their own territory. The first was a membership clause, and the second and third were a pair of territorial clauses. Considering that these clauses would have a negative impact on competition and the development of an effective market for digital music in the EU, the Commission issued the CISAC parties with a Statement of Objectives; however, it made clear that the Statement referred not to traditional bilateral agreements such as the monitoring of performing rights in each territory (such as ensuring nightclubs have licenses to play musical works), but only 'certain relatively new forms of copyright exploitation: internet, satellite transmission and cable retransmission of music' (Dehin 2010, p. 227). Concluding its investigation, the Commission determined that the practice of dividing the market by territory by CISAC members amounted to a concerted practice, as they were strictly defined terms of the CISAC Model Agreement and as such 'cannot simply be explained by autonomous behaviour prompted by market forces' (*CISAC* 2008, para. 72). CISAC appealed this decision to the General Court, which reversed in part the Commission's decision (*CISAC* 2013). In particular, the General Court stated that the territorial restrictions could be objectively justified on the grounds that they were necessary in order to combat the unlawful use of copyrighted works (2013, paras 152–7). With regard to the Commission's view that the offline monopolies held by collecting societies were not justifiable in the online environment, the General Court stated that the 'arrival of new information technologies allowing the exploitation of works online does not mean that those structures are suddenly obsolete or that the economic operators concerned should immediately demonstrate their intent to compete' (2013, para. 130). For this reason, it is difficult to determine the exact position of territorial restrictions in licensing agreements in the digital environment. While in the *Premier League* case, such restrictions were deemed to be anti-competitive, in *CISAC*, they were deemed to be necessary. In the next section, the impact of *Premier League* will be considered in more detail, and some conclusions on the ability of Article 56 TFEU and competition law to remove territorial restrictions on the use of digital music platforms such as iTunes.

Premier League, CISAC and territorial restrictions: where do we go from here?

Some commentators have argued that the decision in *Premier League* fits within the general approach of Article 56 TFEU and competition law, and does not represent a radical departure from CJEU jurisprudence (Blackshaw 2011, p. 27; Smith and Maxwell 2012, p. 35; Prinsley and Sproul 2012, p. 360), while others argue that it could have significant impact on the ability of intellectual property right-holders to apply territorial restrictions (Smith and Silver 2011, p. 401; Anderson 2011; Hugenholtz 2012, p. 12; Clark 2013). One indication that this decision could have potentially far-reaching consequences can be found in the reasoning of Advocate General Kokott. At para. 175 of the Advocate General's Opinion, Kokott stated that:

> This impairment of freedom to provide services is particularly intensive as the rights in question not only render the exercise of freedom to provide services more difficult, but also have the effect of partitioning the internal market into quite separate national markets. Similar problems exist with regard to access to other services, for example the sale of computer software, musical works, e-books or films via the internet.

Clark argues that this statement must be read in the context of the wider debate on the EU's internal market, and the concern over the ability of intellectual property rights to create barriers within that market to the detriment of the consumer (2013, p. 463). Similarly, Hugenholtz refers to the decision as 'ground-breaking . . . [and] militates against licensing contracts that confer absolute territorial exclusivity' (2012, p. 12). Ward and Amor state that there is no reason why this decision may be limited to cases involving sporting rights (2012, p. 89), and Hyland argues that the effect of the decision is likely to extend 'well beyond the narrow realm of football broadcasting' (2012, p. 12). One part of the Opinion and CJEU decisions that have the potential to be useful in a challenge to the territorial restrictions in the digital music download market relates to 'authorized' services. In this case, consumers were attempting to make use of a service that was authorized for use in another Member State. The CJEU reasoned that even if the use of the foreign decoder was not authorized by the right-holder, it nevertheless constituted a lawful use, and the authorization *was* granted in the Member State from which the decoder card was acquired (2011, paras 118–120). Similar reasoning could be applied to the use of 7digital in a different Member State; the service is authorized and licensed to sell music to end-users, and if a consumer chose to purchase the music in that second Member State, it would nevertheless constitute a lawful use, in which no copyright had been infringed. Instead, it would be an act prohibited by a term within a contractual agreement, albeit one regarded as being void due to its infringement on the principles of free movement and competition. Furthermore, if Advocate General Kokott's reasoning is followed, the contractual stipulation cannot be used against third-party consumers who are not part of the contractual agreement – 'such contractual rules can have effect only between the contracting parties' (2011, para. 173). If the CJEU decides future cases in this way, then it may be that a substantial barrier to the functioning of the internal market and the pan-European access to digital music download services may be guaranteed by way of CJEU jurisprudence.

However, it is also possible that the decision will not have a significant impact on territorial restrictions on digital music distribution services. The decoder card was of particular importance to the case as decided. In the Advocate General Opinion, Kokott paid significant attention to the definition of 'illicit device' given in Article 2 of the Conditional Access Directive (Directive 98/94). Article 4 of the Directive prohibits the 'manufacture, import, distribution, sale, rental or possession for commercial purposes of illicit devices' intended to circumvent protections on services provided on a conditional access basis (such as pay-per-view sporting events), and FAPL maintained that the purchase of a decoder card legally available in one Member State became an illicit device once used in another Member State against the will of the undertaking broadcasting the protected service. According to Kokott, the CJEU should give short thrift to an argument that is so 'clearly wrong' (2011, para. 50). Article 2(e) of Directive 98/94 states that an illicit device is 'any equipment or software designed or adapted to give access to a protected service in an intelligible form without the authorisation of the service provider'. Kokott reasoned that in no way was a licit card sold in one Member State adapted by being transferred to and used in another Member State, even if this was without the authorization of the service provider. To decide otherwise, and prevent the use of a decoder card from one Member State in another would have the effect of prohibiting cross-border services (2011, para. 174) and allowing restrictions on parallel exports, effectively permitting a breach of competition law (2011, para. 247). While a consumer could potentially access iTunes in another Member State by having a credit card in that country, it is not particularly realistic that a UK resident would go to the effort of registering a credit card in France so as to use the French iTunes. Where a service is locked by means of territorial restriction by IP address, this is a form of Digital Rights Management (DRM). According to Article 6(4) of Directive 2001/29/EC,

Member States are obliged to provide adequate legal protection against the circumvention of any effective technological measures, which the person concerned carries out in the knowledge, or with reasonable grounds to know, that he or she is pursuing that objective. In other words, even if the act itself is not unlawful, the breaching of the DRM in order to access that service is unlawful, meaning that the use of a proxy server to access content available in a different Member State may still constitute an offence (Kirk 2006, pp. 162–3; Favale 2008, p. 696; Booton and MacCulloch 2012, pp. 170–4; Synodinou 2013, pp. 225–6). The Commission has also made it clear that DRM systems fall under the scope of the Conditional Access Directive, where those systems guarantee territorial restrictions in order to protect intellectual property rights (European Commission 2008b, para. 3.4). If this is the case, then the circumvention of DRM technology imposing a territorial restriction could constitute the use of an illicit device (in this instance, software), meaning that whereas the use of an authorized decoder in *Premier League* was permitted, circumvention in order to use a digital music service in another Member State may not be permitted (see also Massey 2009, p. 102).

Furthermore, while the Advocate General did express that similar problems existed with regard to other services, such as music provision (2011, para. 175), neither the Advocate General nor the CJEU specifically included other services in either the Opinion or the decision, appearing to restrict the decision to satellite broadcasts and the use of decoders. While Ward and Amor state that there is no reason the principles espoused by the CJEU could not apply to other forms of distributed content (2012, p. 89), the *CISAC* case decided after *Premier League* has demonstrated that the EU's courts will still uphold certain types of territorial exclusion agreement, and as CISAC is a organization representing collecting societies acting in the area of music rights, a decision relating to digital music services may be decided similarly. Alternatively, as the decision in CISAC appears to hang on the monitoring of unauthorized rather than authorized uses (2013, para. 144), the two cases may be distinguished. There are some other specificities of the *Premier League* case that may not apply to digital music services. In particular, the CJEU decision specifically discussed the limited copyrights in *Premier League*, reiterating that there was no copyright over the football game itself and only over aspects of the broadcast such as musical themes and graphics (2011, paras 98–9). When concerning a digital music track, which is covered by copyright in its entirety, the CJEU may decide differently. Finally, particular attention was paid to the issue of remuneration. The CJEU was concerned that the main reason for its territorial restrictions was to maintain artificial prices differences (2011, para. 115), allowing FAPL to receive remuneration that went beyond 'appropriate' to 'highest possible' in a way that was only achievable through maintaining territorial restrictions (2011, para. 108; Hugenholtz 2012, p. 12). As we have seen earlier in this chapter, however, with regard to the agreements between Apple and record labels, the Commission found that there was no indication that the pricing of music was the result of concerted practices, nor that there were radical differences in prices between Member States. It must be stated that due to the number of variables at play in these cases, the impact of *Premier League* on music download services ultimately remains uncertain, and may not be clarified unless or until the CJEU specifically rules on such a case.

Concluding remarks

The question of whether consumers can claim against private organizations for rules or practices that appear to run contrary to the principles of the internal market is a complex one that does not appear to have a clear answer. While the case law seems to indicate that such a finding is at least possible, this is by no means conclusive, due to the unsettled nature of the case law in this field. With case law such as *Premier League* being described by some influential scholars in the field of European intellectual property law as a ground-breaking case, there appears to be substantial support for the view that the *Premier League* case provides for a general principle that territorial restrictions in the provision of a service such as iTunes can constitute an infringement of Article 56. Furthermore, such a view appears to be supported by statements made by Kokott in her Advocat General's Opinion on the case, and that a contrary finding would appear to defeat the purposes laid down by the E-Commerce Directive, the intent of which was to ensure that the internal market principles would be applied consistently not only in the market for physical goods and services, but also internet-based services. However, the facts of *Premier League* are sufficiently distinguishable from the facts concerning music services such as iTunes or 7digital that it is difficult to determine whether *Premier League* would be followed in a case concerning these services. While *Coditel* and *Coditel II* were distinguished from *Premier League*, these cases were not overruled, indicating that intellectual property protection could still function as an overriding objective justification for territorial restrictions. The *CISAC* case is also likely to cause considerable consternation for this reason. Ultimately, it is difficult to determine whether a general principle exists concerning fragmentation and territorial restrictions on digital media services in the internal market, and this uncertainty is likely to remain until such time as the CJEU hears a case concerning these services specifically.

That the internal market for the distribution of digital music has been geographically partitioned is indisputable. The evidence presented thus far in this book has demonstrated that territoriality has been problematized by European institutions, and is considered a significant hurdle to be overcome, both with regards to the territoriality of law that institutions such as the Commission have had limited success in combatting, and with regard to the territorial restrictions functioning within the internal market that the CJEU does not appear to have been able to overcome. It would therefore appear to be the case that harmonization (or at the very least, approximation) appears to be have been successful where the harmonization leads to either an expansion in the scope or duration of copyright, or where it leads to stronger enforcement mechanisms, but significantly harder to achieve if such harmonization would lead to a relaxing of these provisions or results that could be perceived as threatening to strong intellectual property protections.

The analysis of the digital music market and difficulties faced by the European Courts concludes the first section of the book, which has sought to provide greater context for the discussion to follow. The first chapter has discussed some of the theoretical underpinnings of the broader analysis of networks of power, and the grounded theoretical approach that will be used to assess the role of quiet politics in intellectual property policy development. Chapter 2 has provided context for the development of intellectual property laws, demonstrating the tensions in theoretical justifications for intellectual property protection, justifications for intellectual property law-making, and the difficulties identified in harmonizing law and ending territoriality in the EU. Chapter 3 has demonstrated the impact of this territoriality on the functioning of a digital single market for digital music, and the difficulty that the European Courts have had in addressing this perceived problem. The next section of this book will address the politics behind the legislation, and the networks of power that pervade policy development in intellectual property law in the EU. Asking the question 'does business always get what business wants?', these chapters will focus on different aspects of copyright development in order to determine the basis for legal development, the dominant discourses within those developments, and the role of experts and perceived expertise in those processes. Attention will also be paid to how the media presented those processes, if in fact the media paid any attention to those processes at all. In other words, the next three sections will also seek to demonstrate the relatively low level of political salience that intellectual property law and policy has possessed until recently.

In Chapter 4, networks of power and the role of discourse will be assessed with regard to the development of law and policies concerning the scope and subject matter of intellectual property laws pertaining to the internet, and the importance of 'economics' in those discourses. In Chapter 5, the focus will be on digital copyright enforcement, the discourses surrounding infringement more generally, and the linking of digital copyright infringement to other areas of policy development by institutional actors. In particular, the genealogy of a discourse of 'threat' as a policy tool will be examined. In Chapter 6, particular focus will be given to issues of territoriality and the role of collecting societies, demonstrating how discourses concerning intellectual property protection and competition identified in this chapter appear to have contributed towards the perception that the partitioning of the digital market constitutes the result of collecting society organization.

Bibliography

7Digital, 2013. 'Help'. *7Digital*. Available at: www.7digital.com/help [Accessed 3 July 2013].

7digital UK, 2012. 'Terms and conditions of use'. *7digital.* Available at: www.7digital. com/termsandconditions [Accessed 3 July 2013].

Aitman, D. and Jones, A., 2004. 'Competition law and copyright: Has the copyright owner lost the ability to control his copyright?' *European Intellectual Property Review, 26*(3), pp. 137–47.

Amazon, 2013. 'Amazon MP3 music downloads frequently asked questions'. *Amazon MP3 Store Germany.* Available at: www.amazon.de/gp/help/customer/display.html?nodeId= 200319960#intl [Accessed 3 July 2013].

Amazon UK, 2012. 'Amazon MP3 store: Terms of use'. *Amazon MP3 Store UK.* Available at: www.amazon.co.uk/gp/help/customer/display.html/ref=hp_left_cn?ie=UTF8& nodeId=200285010 [Accessed 3 July 2013].

Anderson, J., 2011. 'The curious case of the Portsmouth publican: Challenging the territorial exclusivity of TV rights in European professional sport'. *International Sports Law Review,* 3, pp. 53–60.

Anderson, N., 2008. 'Fragmented European market hurting digital music sales'. *Ars Technica.* Available at: http://arstechnica.com/uncategorized/2008/02/fragmented-european-market-hurting-digital-music-sales/ [Accessed 31 May 2013].

Apple, 2012a. 'Apple unveils new iTunes'. *Apple Press Info.* Available at: www.apple.com/ pr/library/2012/09/12Apple-Unveils-New-iTunes.html [Accessed 3 July 2013].

Apple, 2012b. 'Terms and conditions'. *Apple iTunes Store.* Available at: www.apple.com/ legal/internet-services/itunes/uk/terms.html#SALE [Accessed 5 July 2013].

Apple, 2013a. 'iTunes Store sets new record with 25 billion songs sold'. *Apple Press Info.* Available at: www.apple.com/pr/library/2013/02/06iTunes-Store-Sets-New-Record-with-25-Billion-Songs-Sold.html [Accessed 3 July 2013].

Apple, 2013b. 'Legal – internet services – iTunes store terms and conditions'. *Legal.* Available at: www.apple.com/legal/internet-services/itunes/ww/#europe [Accessed 3 July 2013].

Apps, K., 2009. 'Damages claims against trade unions after Viking and Laval'. *European Law Review, 34*(1), p. 141.

Archer, R., 2012. 'iTunes dominates download market and streaming audio grows'. *CEPro.* Available at: www.cepro.com/article/itunes_dominates_download_market_ streaming_audio_grows [Accessed 3 July 2013].

Association of Independent Music, 2012. 'About AIM: The Association of Independent Music'. *Association of Independent Music.* Available at: www.musicindie.com/about [Accessed 4 July 2013].

Azoulai, L., 2008. 'The Court of Justice and the social market economy: The emergence of an ideal and the conditions for its realisation'. *Common Market Law Review,* 45, p. 1335.

Barnard, C., 2007. *The substantive law of the EU: The four freedoms.* Oxford: Oxford University Press.

Batchelor, B., 2007. 'Antitrust challenges to cross-border content licensing: The European Commission investigations of collecting societies and iTunes'. *Computer and Tele-communications Law Review, 13*(8), pp. 217–22.

Blackshaw, I., 2011. 'One–nil to the publican'. *European Lawyer,* 110, pp. 25–7.

Booton, D. and MacCulloch, A., 2012. 'Liability for the circumvention of technological protection measures applied to videogames: Lessons from the United Kingdom's experience'. *Journal of Business Law,* 3, pp. 165–89.

CA98/8/2003, Agreements between *Hasbro U.K. Ltd, Argos Ltd and Littlewoods Ltd* fixing the price of Hasbro toys and games (19 February 2003).

Case 26/62 *Van Gend en Loos* [1963] ECR 13.

Cases 56, 58/64 *Establissements Consten Sarl and Grundig-Verkaufs-GmbH v Commission*, OJ [1966] ECR Special edition 0299.

Case 7/68 *Commission v Italy* [1968] ECR 423.

Case 48-69 *Imperial Chemical Industries Ltd. v Commission (Dyestuffs)* [1972] ECR 619.

Cases 40–8/73, 50/73, 54–6/73, 111/73, 113–14/73 *Cooperatieve Vereniging 'Suiker Unie' UA v Commission* [1975] ECR 1663.

Case 127/73 *BRT v SABAM* [1974] ECR 313.

Case 33/74 *JHM van Binsbergen v Bestuur van de Bedrijfsvereniging voor de Metaalnijverheid* [1974] ECR 1299.

Case 36/74 *Walrave and Koch v Association Union cycliste internationale, Koninklijke Nederlandsche Wielren Unie and Federación Española Ciclismo* [1974] ECR 1405.

Case 13/76 *Gaetano Dona v Mario Mantero* [1976] ECR 1333.

Case 209/78 *Van Landewyck v Commission* [1980] ECR 3125.

Case 72/79 *Coditel I v Cine Vog Films* [1980] ECR 881.

Case 58/80 *Dansk Supermarked A/S v A/S Imerco* [1981] ECR 0181.

Cases 100–3/80 *Musique Diffusion Francaise SA v Commission* [1983] ECR 1825.

Case 262/81 *Coditel II v Cine Vog Films* [1982] ECR 3381.

Cases 286/82 and 26/83 *Luisi and Carbone v Ministero del Tesoro* [1984] ECR 377.

Case C-205/84 *Commission v Germany* [1986] ECR 3755.

Case 352/85 *Bond van Adverteerders and others v Netherlands* [1988] ECR 2085.

Case C-76/90 *Sager* [1991] ECR I-4221.

Case C-393/92 *Almelo v NV Energibedriff Ijsselmij* [1994] ECR I-1477.

Case C-384/93 *Alpine Investments BV v Minister van Financiën* [1995] ECR I-1141.

Case C-55/94 *Gebhard* [1995] ECR I-4165.

Case C-424/97 *Haim* [2000] ECR I 0000.

Case C-97/98 *Jägerskiöld v Gustafsson* [1999] ECR I-7319.

Case C-281/98 *Angonese v Cassa di Risparmio di Bolzano* [2000] ECR I-4139.

Case C-243/01 *Criminal Proceedings against Piergiorgio Gambelli and others* [2003] ECR I-13031.

Case C-341/05 *Laval un Partneri Ltd v Svenska Byggnadsarbetareforbundet and others* [2007] ECR I-11767.

Case C-438/05 *International Transport Workers' Federation and Finnish Seamen's Union v Viking Line ABP and OU Viking Line Eesti* [2007] ECR I-10779.

Case C-94/07 *Andrea Raccanelli v Max-Planck-Gesellschaft zur Forederung der Wissenschaften eV* [2008] ECR I–5939.

Case CO/7295/07 *Karen Murphy v Media Protection Services Ltd* [2008] EWHC 1666.

Cases C-429/08 and 403/08, *Football Association Premier League Ltd and Others v QC Leisure and Others* and *Karen Murphy v Media Protection Services Ltd*, 4 October 2011.

Case T-442/08 *CISAC v European Commission* (12 April 2013).

Clark, R., 2013. 'Exhaustion, geographical licensing restrictions and transfer prohibitions: Two surprising decisions' *Journal of Intellectual Property Law & Practice*, 8(6), pp. 460–9.

Commission Decision of 14 October 1998 relating to a proceeding pursuant to Article 81 of the EC Treaty British Sugar, OJ [1999] L 76/1.

Davies, A.C.L., 2008. 'One step forwards, two steps back? The Viking and Laval Cases in the ECJ'. *Industry Law Journal, 37*, p. 126.

Dehin, V., 2010. 'The future of online music services in the European Union: A review of the EU Commission's recent initiatives in cross-border copyright management'. *European Intellectual Property Review, 32*(5), p. 220.

Department for Trade and Industry, 2001. *Productivity and enterprise: A world class competition regime.* (Cm 5233). London: Her Majesty's Stationery Office.

Edwards, P., 2007. 'Commission objects to territorial music restrictions'. *Entertainment Law Review, 18*(6), pp. N8–81.

Eechoud, M. van, Hugenholtz, P.B., Guibault, L., Gompel, S. van, Helberger, N., 2009. *Harmonizing European copyright law: The challenges of better lawmaking.* Alphen aan den Rijn: Wolters Kluwer Law & Business.

European Commission, 1999. *28th report on competition policy 1998.* Brussels, Luxembourg: Office for Official Publications of the European Communities.

European Commission, 2006. *Commission sends Statement of Objections to the International Confederation of Societies of Authors and Composers (CISAC) and its EEA Members,* Brussels: European Commission.

European Commission, 2007a. *Commission Decision of 03/X/2007 declaring a concentration to be compatible with the common market and the EEA Agreement (Case No COMP/M.3333 – Sony/ BMG).* Brussels.

European Commission, 2007b. 'Competition: European Commission confirms sending a Statement of Objections against alleged territorial restrictions in on-line music sales to major record companies and Apple'. *Europa.* Available at: http://europa.eu/rapid/press-release_MEMO-07–126_en.htm?locale=en [Accessed 4 July 2013].

European Commission, 2007c. 'Mergers: Commission confirms approval of recorded music joint venture between Sony and Bertelsmann after re-assessment subsequent to Court decision'. *Europa.* Available at: http://europa.eu/rapid/press-release_IP-07–1437_en.htm [Accessed 4 July 2013].

European Commission, 2008a. 'Antitrust: European Commission welcomes Apple's announcement to equalise prices for music downloads from iTunes in Europe'. *Europa.* Available at: http://europa.eu/rapid/press-release_IP-08-22_en.htm?locale=en [Accessed 4 July 2013].

European Commission, 2008b. *Second report on the implementation of Directive 98/84/EC of the European Parliament and of the Council of 20 November 1998 on the legal protection of services based on, or consisting of, conditional access.* Brussels.

European Commission, 2008c. *Commission Decision of 16/07/2008 relating to a proceeding under Article 81 of the EC Treaty and Article 53 of the EEA Agreement (Case COMP/C2/38.698 – CISAC),* Brussels: European Commission.

European Commission, 2012. 'Mergers: Commission clears Universal's acquisition of EMI's recorded music business, subject to conditions'. *Europa.* Available at: http://europa.eu/rapid/press-release_IP-12–999_en.htm#PR_metaPressRelease_bottom [Accessed 4 July 2013].

Farrand, B., 2009. 'The case that never was: An analysis of the Apple iTunes case presented by the Commission and potential future issues'. *European Intellectual Property Review, 31*(10), pp. 508–13.

Favale, M., 2008. 'Fine-tuning European copyright law to strike a balance between the rights of owners and users'. *European Law Review, 33*(5), pp. 687–708.

Hugenholtz, P.B., 2012. 'Harmonisation or unification of European union copyright law'. *Monash University Law Review*, *38*(1), p. 4.

Hyland, M., 2012. 'The Football Association Premier League ruling: The Bosman of exclusive broadcasting rights?' *Communications Law*, *17*(1), pp. 7–13.

IFPI 'Simulcasting' [2003] OJ L107/58.

Kirk, E., 2006. 'Apple's iTunes digital rights management: "Fairplay" under the essential facilities doctrine'. *Communications Law*, *11*(5), pp. 161–6.

Kokkoris, I. and Katona, K., 2010. 'Critical analysis of the ECMR reform'. In I. Kokkoris and I. Lianos, eds, *The reform of EC competition law: New challenges*. Alphen aan den Rijn: Wolters Kluwer Law & Business.

Kraatz, K.-J., 1990. 'EC Commission – competition – audiovisual works'. *Entertainment Law Review*, *1*(5), pp. E90–91.

Kroes, N., 2005. *The first hundred days: 40th anniversary of the Studienvereinigung Kartellrecht 1965–2005, International Forum on European Competition Law*. Brussels: European Commission.

Leurdijk, A. and Nieuwenhuis, O., 2012. *Statistical, ecosystems and competitiveness analysis of the media and content industries: The music industry*. Spain: Joint Research Centre, European Commission.

Massey, R., 2009. 'Conditional access and sports rights in Europe: Good and bad news'. *Entertainment Law Review*, *20*(3), pp. 100–2.

Pfanner, E., 2013. 'Universal unloads European labels bought from EMI'. *The New York Times*. Available at: www.nytimes.com/2013/02/08/technology/universal-unloads-european-labels-bought-from-emi.html [Accessed 4 July 2013].

Pinsent Masons, 2004. 'Apple iTunes referred to European Commission'. *Out-Law*. Available at: www.out-law.com/page-5131 [Accessed 4 July 2013].

Prechal, S. and De Vries, S., 2009. 'The seamless web of judicial protection in the internal market'. *European Law Review*, *34*(1), p. 5.

Prinsley, M. and Sproul, G., 2012. 'Premier League copyright infringed but High Court calls time on anti-competitive contracts and overturns Portsmouth publican's criminal convictions for copyright infringement'. *International Business Law Journal*, *3*, pp. 357–62.

PVC OJ [1994] L 239/14.

Rodger, B.J. and MacCulloch, A., 2009. *Competition law and policy in the EC and UK*. London: Routledge-Cavendish.

Ronnmar, M., 2010. 'Laval returns to Sweden: The final judgment of the Swedish Labour Court and Swedish legislative reforms'. *Industrial Law Journal*, *39*(3), pp. 280–7.

Shiels, M., 2008. 'iTunes store shutdown feared'. *BBC News*. Available at: http://news.bbc.co.uk/2/hi/technology/7645537.stm [Accessed 4 July 2013].

Shiller, B. and Waldfogel, J., 2009. *Music for a song: An empirical look at uniform song pricing and its alternatives*. National Bureau of Economic Research. Available at: www.nber.org/papers/w15390 [Accessed 4 July 2013].

Siragusa, M., 2008. 'Is there an independent/additional (European, International) open-market criterion for determining abuse?' In I. Govaere and H. Ullrich, eds, *Intellectual property, market power and the public interest*. Brussels: P.I.E. Peter Lang. Available at: http://search.ebscohost.com/login.aspx?direct=true&scope=site&db=nlebk&db=nlabk&AN=486106 [Accessed 4 July 2013].

Smith, J. and Silver, J., 2011. 'FA Premier League down at half-time in European Championship: Advocate General finds that territorial exclusivity agreements relating to the transmission of football matches are contrary to EU law'. *European Intellectual Property Review*, *33*(6), pp. 399–401.

Smith, S. and Maxwell, A., 2012. 'Premier League football cases: Linguistic tactics, non-naked match feeds and the away goals rule'. *Computer and Telecommunications Law Review*, *18*(2), pp. 33–6.

Snell, J., 2002. *Goods and services in EC law: A study of the relationship between the freedoms.* Oxford: Oxford University Press.

Synodinou, T.-E., 2013. 'E-books, a new page in the history of copyright law?' *European Intellectual Property Review*, *35*(4), pp. 220–7.

Tritton, G. and Davis, R., 2008. *Intellectual property in Europe.* London: Sweet & Maxwell.

Trstenjak, V. and Beysen, E., 2013. 'The growing overlap of fundamental freedoms and fundamental rights in the case-law of the CJEU'. *European Law Review*, *38*(3), p. 293.

Ward, C. and Amor, D., 2012. 'Significant change to the European media rights landscape?' *Computer and Telecommunications Law Review*, *18*(3), pp. 86–90.

Whish, R. and Bailey, D., 2012. *Competition law.* Oxford: Oxford University Press.

Wikström, P., 2009. *The music industry: Music in the cloud.* Cambridge: Polity.

Youngs, I., 2008. 'UK iTunes shelves music price cut'. *BBC News.* Available at: http://news.bbc.co.uk/2/hi/entertainment/7507100.stm [Accessed 5 July 2013].

Chapter 4

Networks of power I

The role of industry representatives in framing policies regarding the scope and duration of copyright

> Governments of the Industrial World, you weary giants of flesh and steel, I
> come from Cyberspace, the new home of Mind . . . Our world is different . . .
> Your legal concepts of property, expression, identity, movement, and context
> do not apply to us. They are all based on matter, and there is no matter here.
>
> (John Perry Barlow 1998)

As was discussed in Chapter 2 of this book, one trend that has become apparent
in copyright law development in the EU is that of 'upwards harmonization',
namely harmonization that seeks to ensure the strongest possible protections for
intellectual property rights, irrespective of any perceived impact on user rights.
While these changes are often referred to as being the result of lobbying on the
part of creative/entertainment industries, the possible reasons and theoretical
explanations for the success of these lobbying processes have not been discussed
in detail. The purpose of the first of the three chapters on networks of power
and quiet politics is to apply these theories to the development of laws regarding
the scope and duration of copyright in light of digital media. The chapter will
begin by assessing the dominant discourses of the radical changes brought about
by the wide-scale adoption of the internet, and the concept of the 'knowledge
economy' or 'information society', and why industry discourses considering the
need for changes to law in light of these radical changes were well received. The
chapter will continue with discussion of the role of economics in the discourse
of intellectual property protection, and why entertainment industry representatives
are well placed to use this discourse in support of their legislative preferences.
The fact that copyright reform has traditionally been perceived as being a high-
complexity, low-salience issue also helps to explain why industry representatives
are able to secure legislation that appears favourable to their interests. This
analysis will then be applied to the Term Extension Directive, demonstrating
that within a dominant discourse of creator protection/incentivization, arguments
made in favour of increasing protection of those creators are much more likely
to be positively received and become dominant discourses within the legislative
process than those arguments against increasing protections, which fall outside
of the bounds of accepted discourse. This may in turn help to explain why industry

statistics were preferred over academic studies on the impact of term extension, combined with the perceived expertise of entertainment industry representatives and their apparent ability to frame media discourse on legislative changes.

The Information Society Directive: the rationale of the knowledge economy

Described as being part of the 'second phase' of harmonization of copyright in the EU (Hugenholtz 2009, p. 13; Tritton and Davis 2008, p. 531) and being indicative of what Boyle refers to as the 'second enclosure movement' (2008, chap. 3), the implementation of the Information Society Directive (2001/29/EC) can be interpreted in light of the dominant discourses of the late 1990s. As seen in John Perry Barlow's *Declaration of the Independence of Cyberspace* (1998), a general trend in discourse in the 1990s was that 'the Internet changed everything' and we now live in the 'Information Age' (see for example Elkin-Koren and Salzberger 2013, p. 3). As early as 1993, the European Commission stated that Europe was seeing 'the forging of a link of unprecedented magnitude and significance between the technological innovation process and economic and social organization . . . [and that] a new "information society" is emerging'. (European Commission 1993, p. 92). In light of the perceived radical changes in the way in which economies would function and the disruptions that would be caused by this new technology, this theme of the changes wrought by the 'information society' continued in a 1995 Commission Green Paper. Referring to the information society as being a 'reality' of world-wide concern (European Commission 1995, para. 19), the Commission stated that law must adapt in light of technological change in order to 'maintain the balance between the imperatives of the protection of authors and the dissemination of their works' (1995, para. 28), with protection of copyright and its related rights being 'absolutely vital' (1995, para. 10).

One of the first uses of the term 'knowledge economy' appears in a work by Drucker (1969), in which the changing nature of economic activity in the US was discussed. Drucker discussed how during World War II it was the semi-skilled machine operators, or in other words, the factory workers making munitions and other military supplies, that were the centre of the American workforce. By the late 1960s, however, it was the 'information worker', the people who processed, manipulated and used technical knowledge that became the basis of the US economy (Drucker 1992, p. 264). The term 'knowledge economy', analogous to the Commission's use of 'information society', has been defined as comprising 'production and services based on knowledge-intensive activities . . . The Key component of a knowledge economy is a greater reliance on intellectual capabilities than on physical inputs or natural resources' (Powell and Snellman 2004, p. 201). According to Powell and Snellman, one of the predominant aspects of discourse concerning the knowledge economy is that it represents something fundamentally different to everything that had come before it (2004, p. 200).

In comparison, Webster argues that while many scholars may disagree as to what exactly is meant by the terms knowledge economy and information society, there is nevertheless 'something special about "information"' (2006, p. 2). Schiller, for example, takes a Marxist-structuralist view of the information society, considering it to represent nothing more than the production, processing and transmission of large amounts of data in order to meet the needs of large corporations, national governments and the military-industrial complex, reinforcing pre-existing social conditions (1981, p. 25). In comparison, Castells takes a somewhat more positive view of what the information society can represent, referring to the information age resulting in a 'new society' in which 'the action of knowledge upon knowledge itself [is] the main source of productivity' (1996, p. 17). Bell refers instead to the concept of the 'post-industrial society', a concept that according to Webster has been highly influential among scholars and the media (2006, p. 32). According to Bell, 'the post industrial society is an information society' (1976, p. 467), in which society is based on services, and the ability to use information (1976, p. 127). Webster states that this view maintains that in a 'service/post-industrial society the material of work for the majority is information' (2006, p. 41). The view of information, and the internet, as having changed everything appears to continue. Benkler states that it is reasonable to discuss the 'Internet Revolution', as 'the change brought about by the networked information environment is deep. It is structural. It goes to the very foundations of how liberal markets and liberal democracies have coevolved.' (2006, p. 2). This is not to say that all scholars hold the view that the internet and the information society have changed everything, and indeed, there are those who are sceptical of such a claim, or indeed how verifiable such a claim can be (Powell and Snellman 2004; Webster 2006, chap. 2; Kochan and Barley 1999). Nevertheless, the view that 'the internet has changed everything' pervaded media reporting in the late 1990s. Examples include *The Independent* asking 'Who's ready for the revolution?' quoting Bill Gates as saying 'the Internet changes everything' (Koenig 1999), and *The Economist* stating that the internet 'has the capacity to change everything' with the potential to turn business upside down (Special Report 1999). Writing in *Foreign Policy* about his resignation as managing director of the IMF in 1999, Camdessus discussed that his position was in his opinion untenable given the radical changes in the world, revolutionary transformations including 'the Internet [which] changed everything' (Camdessus and Naím 2000, p. 32). DiMaggio *et al.* drily noted in 2001 that 'most observers allege the Internet is changing society. Perhaps not surprisingly, given the novelty of the new digital media, there is little agreement about what those changes are' (2001, p. 308). While there may have been little agreement as to how the internet was changing things, the fact that the internet acts as a catalyst for change was very much the dominant discourse in the mid-to-late 1990s. It was within this discourse that the Commission was initiating its policies with regard to copyright on the internet. From a Foucauldian perspective, the fact that the internet had changed and would continue to change everything became a constructed truth, the commonly accepted vision of observed reality. For this reason, discourses that fit into this conceptualization of the internet-enabled world, or information society, would be more likely to be accepted as 'true' and reaffirmed than those that challenged such a conception.

Market failures, copyright economics and digital distribution: the framework for the property discourse

Returning to the Green Paper, the Commission considered that the protection of copyright and related rights in the digital environment was absolutely essential in order to ensure the functioning of the internal market (1995, para. 11–12), to promote Europe's cultural heritage (while acknowledging the commercial value of that heritage) (1995, para. 13–15), to achieve economic goals relating to the dissemination of works that would only be achieved through providing incentives in the form of copyright protection (1995, para. 16–17), and the social dimension in terms of fostering job creation (1995, para. 18). According to Burrell and Coleman, the Commission was largely influenced by arguments concerning market failure, balance and the proprietary conceptualization of copyright (2005, pp. 198–200). For this reason, it would be useful to consider the dominant discourses at play concerning the economics of copyright before then assessing the networks of power functioning with respect to how the Information Society Directive was implemented.

Elkin-Koren and Salzberger have argued that with the perceived role that information and information goods have in the economy, 'creative works and inventions are claimed to be the single most important factor driving growth' in developed and some developing countries (2013, p. 3). As a result, the study of intellectual property economics has generated much more interest (2013, p. 3). The result, and what we will see in later sections of this chapter, is that 'the economic discourse of intellectual property dominates law-making processes and policy debates related to the regulation of the information environment' (2013, p. 4). However, where economists have been largely sceptical of the role of intellectual property rights in ensuring growth and incentivizing future creation/invention, law and economics as a discipline has been dominated by voices that largely support the view that stronger protections are more likely to lead to growth and are therefore desirable (2013, p. 5). One particular aspect of this argument in favour of strong protection relates to the conceptualization of a market failure that must be avoided when considering works protected by copyright. Copyrightable works such as music have a value to society, and without copyright protection, the traditional argument runs, the production of such works would fail to occur at an optimal level. For example, recording an album involves considerable costs, including the recording itself in a studio, production, distribution and advertising. If that work was to then be copied at little cost to the copier, and then redistributed on a mass scale in such a way as the original would not be bought, these costs could not be recouped. This becomes particularly pertinent given the ease at which music can be digitally copied and distributed through the internet. The legal protection given by copyright is intended to rectify this 'market failure' by providing incentives that encourage the production and dissemination of works '[providing] a legal means by which those who invest time and labour in producing . . . goods can be confident that they will not only be able to recoup that investment, but also reap a profit proportional to the popularity of their work' (Bently and Sherman 2004, p. 36). This line of reasoning presupposes that:

> When intellectual property rights are effectively enforced, the owner of a new computer chip or novel can use the power of exclusion to extract a price from other users. The price rewards the creator, which results in more innovations and faster growth – a form of 'dynamic efficiency'.
>
> (Cooter and Ulen 2008, p. 124)

Cooter and Ulen state that in the absence of strong intellectual property rights, innovators may keep ideas secret in order to profit from them. For example, Renaissance playwrights active before copyright protection existed would carefully hide their manuscripts in order to ensure that only their actors could perform their plays. Intellectual property laws allow instead for playwrights to license their plays to theatre companies, so that they receive royalty payments or enter into contractual agreements to their economic benefit. In doing so, secrecy is replaced by a 'property' right, which allows for an author to have greater control over his work. This allows for increased dissemination of a work, resulting in 'static efficiency' (2008, p. 125). For mainstream law and economics scholars, the treatment of intellectual property as a form of property is necessary due to the fact that in itself, intellectual property take the form of a public good, insofar as it is non-rivalrous and non-excludable (Perelman 2004, p. 165; Cooter and Ulen 2008, pp. 120–6; Landes and Posner 2003, pp. 12–15). In other words, the use of this information does not diminish the amount of information accessible by others. For example, reading Lewis Carroll's *Through the looking glass* does not prevent others from being able to read that story. In comparison with real property, by drinking all the water in a glass, the drinker has deprived others from drinking that water. In this way, real property in tangibles is rivalrous, in that consumers are in competition for those resources. Information, in comparison, cannot be exhausted in this manner. Information is also non-excludable. Non-excludable goods are those that it is (theoretically) impossible to prevent others from having access to. Using the example of *Through the looking glass* once again, it is highly unlikely that should someone wish to read this story, that someone else would be able to prevent them from doing so. Although a particularly obstinate individual may refuse to allow the interested party to read his copy, he may find this information elsewhere. He may buy a copy from his local bookstore, or alternatively use the online digital book depository Project

Gutenberg to read the full text online. Although an individual may be prevented access to the real property of his bad-tempered friend's book, he cannot be prevented from accessing the information that the book contains from another source. However, Landes and Posner argue that copyrighted works are excludable, and should be treated as such in order to prevent free riding and ensure that there is still an incentive to create (2003, pp. 21–4). With rival, excludable goods, the price is determined by scarcity. If there is a surplus of goods, then prices will be lowered until there is market equilibrium and those goods are consumed. Conversely, where goods are scarce, prices will rise as consumers compete for those goods. However, with provision of public goods there is inefficiency, as price (and by extension, compensation) cannot be determined by scarcity, as the goods are not depleted, nor can they be made successfully exclusive. The quantity of available goods cannot, this line of reasoning goes, work as an effective market mechanism when dealing with public goods (Cooter and Ulen 2008, p. 125). When dealing with information, we are dealing with a 'good' with no marginal costs. Marginal costs are the change in total costs that arise when the quantity of produced goods increases by one unit. Information, once created, does not have additional costs. According to Benkler:

> Once a scientist has established a fact, or once Tolstoy has written 'War and Peace', neither the scientist nor Tolstoy need spend a single second on producing additional 'War and Peace' manuscripts or studies for the one hundredth, one thousandth or one millionth user of what they wrote. The physical paper for the book or journal costs something, but the information only need be created once.
>
> (2006, p. 36)

If information-based goods were priced at their marginal cost, it is argued within this discourse that there would be no incentive to innovate – furthermore, if there were no way for producers to gain reimbursement for their fixed costs, they too would be unlikely to help produce and distribute works. Towse argues that these features make it 'unlikely that private for-profit firms will produce public goods, because "free-riding" by consumers makes it impossible for producers to charge for them' (2010, p. 28). If it is assumed (as is the case with mainstream law and economics literature) that the prospect of reward is the main driver behind invention and innovation, and that without this prospect of reward on a reasonable scale, the inducement to invent will be weakened, resulting in less cultural output from artists (Andersen 2007, p. 136). In this way, in order to avoid a perceived market failure, information is treated as a form of quasi-property, which can be made excludable through copyright protection. Intellectual property rights are capable of allowing such goods to be marketed at a price considerably above marginal costs (Perelman 2004, p. 167).

This reflects what the Commission saw as the balance struck between access and incentivization. The Green Paper states that for 'the potential of the information society to be realised to the full, it will be necessary to maintain a balance between the interests of the parties concerned (right-holders, manu-facturers, distributors and users of services as well as network operators)' (European Commission 1995, para. 6). The emphasis on 'maintaining' and 'preserving' this balance can be seen throughout the Green Paper, with reference to the need to 'preserve the balance between the rights accorded to holders . . . and the interests of users' (1995, para. 35) and adapting law to new circumstances so as to 'maintain the balance between the imperatives of the protection of authors and the dissemination of their works' (1995, para. 28). The Commission Follow-Up used similar language, stating that 'Europe's traditionally high level of protection must be maintained and further developed' (1996, p. 2). Burrell and Coleman state that the use of this language is indicative of the fact that the Commission believed that this balance had already been struck in the analogue environment, and 'at no point did the Commission attempt to justify its con-clusion that the level at which rights and exceptions had been set was appropriate' (2005, p. 199). This may be because within the frame set by law and economics discourse in the field of copyright law, the Commission held as an accepted truth that this balance had been struck. It did not need to be justified, because it had already been justified. In the Proposal for the Information Society Directive, this view was reiterated when the Commission stated:

> The proposal aims at maintaining the traditionally advanced level of copyright protection . . . while safeguarding . . . a fair balance of rights . . . it is the environment in which works and other subject matter are being created and exploited which has changed – not the basic copyright concepts.
>
> (1997, para. 6)

Returning then to the theme that the internet changes everything, we must consider what exactly it is that has changed. The first, and most fundamental, is that the perceived market failures with regard to marginal costs and intellectual property were remedied somewhat by being able to charge for tangible goods, such as books. Information in digital form, in comparison, is intangible and can be reproduced instantly, with total accuracy and little effort (Akester and Lima 2005, p. 71; Samuelson 1990; Stokes 2009). Take the book previously discussed; as was stated, the information in the book is non-rivalrous and non-exclusionary, and thus represents a public good. The book, however, is a physical product that has rivalrous and exclusionary properties. A digital book, on the other hand, more closely represents a 'pure' public good – once the book's text is compiled into written code, the intangible nature of that code means that it once again becomes non-rivalrous, and theoretically non-exclusionary. Furthermore, identical copies can be created quickly, easily, and at little to no cost. In the market for physical products, production, reproduction and distribution can take a considerable amount of time and money. After an album is recorded and put onto a master CD, this master must then be used to write the CDs of an initial run. Assume a run of 10,000 CDs – all these CDs must have the images burnt onto the disc. These discs must then be packaged in CD slipcases with accompanying booklets. The slipcases must then be boxed, and then delivered to the various destinations for sale. This implies having supply chains, which depending on the scale of the operation, could be national or international. This all requires a significant investment, in terms of cost of materials, cost of shipments, and the time taken for these tasks to be performed. In comparison, once that master is compiled into code, that album can then be reproduced 10,000 times near instantaneously, and is not limited by access to materials. In this respect, it has been argued that traditional distribution cannot compete with the digital dissemination of works (Akester and Lima 2005, p. 78). Elkin-Koren and Salzberger state that the costs of communication on digital networks are relatively low, since digital bits travel in small packets and transmission does not require dedicating any communication channel for exclusive use (2004, p. 56). Towse refers to this as being a 'problem', reinforcing the earlier state view of Elkin-Koren and Salzberger that law and economics approaches to copyright generally see stronger protections as favourable. According to Towse, digitalization has given rise to a situation in which 'information goods' are effectively public goods once they are on the internet (2010, p. 28). In such a view, the Technologic Prevention Measures, or TPMs, legislated for in the WIPO Treaties and Article 6 of Directive 2001/29/EC are a necessity, so as to ensure that digital locks fulfill the role that physical goods previously played, namely to ensure the 'scarcity' and exclusionary nature of digital versions of creative works. Whereas Ku (2002) and Benkler (2004) do not see this as a problem but a way of democratizing and spreading cultural works by removing a barrier to access, it is arguably the view of Towse that is dominant in the discourse concerning the changes brought by the internet. This may help to explain why, in Burrell and Coleman's words, the question the Commission always asked was 'are rights sufficiently protected in the online environment?' rather than 'are the rights in the digital environment too strong?' (2005, p. 200). If the starting point that the Commission worked from in terms of an accepted discourse was that there is a suitable balance between interests in the offline environment, this balance is upset by internet-induced changes, and due to proprietary concerns and a need for incentivization strong protections are necessary, then the idea that greater protection needs to be afforded in the online environment would therefore seem logical. It would also help to explain why the exceptions and limitations to copyright under Article 5 of Directive 2001/29/EC were considered to be part of an exhaustive, closed list of limitations, rather than being examples of possible exceptions and limitations within an open list.

Networks of power and quiet politics in the information society

Yet, as Foucault would argue, such ideas do not exist in a vacuum. Or to put it differently, the knowledge produced stating that there is a problem, which must be addressed, comes from an actor exercising power. With regard to the development of the Information Society Directive, this power was exercised in a network in which industry representatives can influence the timbre of the legislation. Prior to the Commission Green Paper, a report known as the Bangemann Report (1994) was completed by a working group formed by the Commission. Repeating the theme that the internet changed everything, through discussion of how 'information and communication technologies are generating a new industrial revolution already as significant and far-reaching as those of the past' (1994, p. 10), the Report explicitly stated that 'there is information that is proprietary and needs protection via intellectual property rights. IPRs are an important factor in developing a competitive European industry . . . across a wide range of industrial and commercial sectors' (1994, p. 21). The statement of this proprietary interest in the advisory report may help to explain the proprietary arguments made within the Green Paper. Furthermore, the Report went on to state that 'Europe has a vested interest in ensuring that protection of IPRs receives full attention and that a high level of protection is maintained (1994, p. 21). As was previously stated, the Green Paper made reference to 'maintaining' and 'preserving' balances and a high level of protection, helping to explain why the Commission's preferred approach with the Directive was to harmonize to a higher standard. Most interesting was the make-up of the working group. As well as including representatives of national governments, the working group comprised representatives of the chemical industry, automobile manufacturers, book publishers, entertainment conglomerates and electronics companies, in addition to other industrial sectors (see European Commission and Bangemann Group 1994, p. 6 for a list of attendees). This can be explained by Culpepper's quiet politics theory – as was mentioned in Chapter 1, one way in which businesses can influence policies to their benefit is through participation in working groups and steering committees. 'The power of managers in this context is to set the terms of the debate in an environment that is established with an explicit eye to protecting their interests' (Culpepper 2011, p. 9). In participating in this working group, and being described by the Commission as 'prominent persons' (European Commission and Bangemann Group 1994, p. 6), corporate representatives are presented as experts, and are able to exert influence in the role of 'expert' so as to shape the acceptable limits of discourse through the knowledge produced. In this instance, corporate representatives were not only able to lobby for their vision of the Directive after the policy was initiated by the Commission but, through sitting on the working group prior to the Green Paper, they were able to influence the framework in which that lobbying took place. Here we see the multilateral way in which power is exercised – the working groups, as experts, provide the Commission with the frame for which copyright law is to be reformed. In turn, by labelling the working group as 'prominent persons', power is exercised that adds legitimacy to the actions of that working group. Knowledge is produced both about the importance of copyright protection, but also about the expertise of the working group members that influenced the Commission's approach to the Green Paper. It is also worth noting that Lewinski argues that the WIPO Treaties referred to in Chapter 2 of this book, which the Information Society Directive was also ostensibly intended to implement, were significantly influenced by the then-EC, with the provisions being in accordance with the earlier published Green Paper (1999, p. 768). This is again indicative of the usefulness of perceiving power in the sense of something that is exercised in a network, rather than hierarchically.

As articles by prominent scholars indicate, the lobbying process did not end with the working group but continued after the Proposal for the Directive was completed (Hugenholtz 2000; Samuelson 1996, p. 134; Burrell and Coleman 2005, p. 207). When the Proposal was sent to the European Parliament, lobbyists representing the interests of users such as public libraries found themselves outmatched by representatives of the entertainment industries. Lewinski found that rather than moderating the position taken by the Commission on protection, the European Parliament strengthened the protections afforded (1999, p. 778). For example, in the fifty-eight amendments proposed by the Parliament in its first Resolution, one amendment changed recital 3 of the proposed Directive to include the words 'providing for a high level of protection for intellectual property' (1999), which remained in the finalized Directive as recital 4. Another example of this strengthening can be seen in the Parliament's Recommendation for a second reading of the Proposal, in which references to exceptions for non-commercial use were modified to read 'neither directly nor indirectly commercial' (2001, p. 8). According to one interview reproduced by Burrell and Coleman, a lobbyist who believed that MEPs from the socialist bloc that 'ought to have been natural allies of user groups' (2005, p. 208) seemed loathe to be involved with those groups. In fact, the interviewee continued, those MEPs seemed 'to regard copyright as an esoteric subject with which they need not concern themselves' (2005, p. 209). This statement is particularly interesting, as it fits effectively with the framework provided by quiet politics. Culpepper specifically mentions that in areas of low political salience, policy is not determined by political allegiance or government partisanship, but from the preferences of managerial organizations (2011, p. 3). While with regard to copyright reform the actors involved are entertainment industry representatives rather than managerial organizations per se, it would appear that the results are similar. It is also of note that copyright was perceived by MEPs as being a complicated area that they need not familiarize themselves with. This also fits effectively within the quiet politics framework, in which highly complex issues that are not politically salient are left to perceived 'experts' to manage. Entertainment industry representatives are perceived as being best placed to assess the needs and threats to their businesses, helping to explain why so many were involved in the production of the Bangemann Report. Knowledge plays an important part in this process – according to one interviewee, representative groups such as IFPI, Vivendi and Disney are much more 'expert' in lobbying, understanding the processes to a greater extent than user groups (Burrell and Coleman 2005, p. 209). Because of this perception of industry expertise, statements made by entertainment industry representatives are more likely to be accepted as true, particularly if they fit within the framework constructed by the dominant discourse.

MEP responses would appear to indicate that the issue of digital copyright reform was not particularly salient to European voters. With regard to media reporting, online searches of newspaper websites in the UK indicate relatively few news stories during the legislative process. The BBC News archives hold two news stories from between February 1999 and the passing of the Directive, and four stories after the adoption of the Directive. Of those published beforehand, one makes reference to the lobbying between the music industry and other lobbying groups regarding caching (Nuttall 1999a), but the other indicates elements of framing by industry groups. The story refers to 'legislation against Internet piracy' and provides a summary of the intended changes (Nuttall 1999b). *The Guardian* only has two stories directly relating to the Directive prior to its passing, one of which is specifically about the need for stronger IP protection, with statements from industry representatives such as IFPI (Osborn 2000), and the other about net piracy costing 'billions', necessitating stronger protections (Hall 2000). No stories pertaining to the Directive could be found in the archives for the *Daily Mail*, *The Sun* or the *Telegraph*. As Guber and Bosso stated, and was discussed in Chapter 1, media framing can be important in determining public reaction to a particular issue, particularly where the public has little knowledge or understanding of an issue (2007, p. 43). This allowed the issue to be framed as one of protection, the threat posed by piracy and the artists that would be affected by it (a theme that shall be returned to in Chapter 5). That this issue was not of high political salience can be seen by the statement by Burrell and Coleman's interviewee, who stated 'the lack of interest in copyright matters is also shared by many consumer organizations, perhaps because they believe it is too difficult to translate concerns about copyright into the issues consumers actually care about' (2005, p. 209). This lack of interest may also be explained by the role of the media. Understanding of copyright policy is asymmetrical, with entertainment industry representatives comprehending the law and the potential impact of law much more effectively than the general public. Baum and Potter argue that in these situations, the media can play a 'crucial role of collecting, framing and distributing information' (2008, p. 49). If the public does not understand an issue, particularly one that is complex and not particularly salient, then private business is much more effectively able to frame that issue positively. That consumers had little interest in the reforms happening at the European level, combined with little media coverage of the developments (and that media coverage appearing favourable to the reforms), indicates that this was not an issue of political salience for MEPs. In turn, this helps to explain why the European Parliament seemed more favourably disposed to lobbying efforts from the entertainment industry, and 'hostile ... towards the user view' (Burrell and Coleman 2005, p. 209). The user view, in this instance, did not effectively fit within the dominant discourse concerning the fact that the internet 'changed everything', requiring stronger protections for content. In comparison, 'experts' with knowledge of copyright were able to influence not only the legislative process, but also the framing of the issue of copyright in the digital environment. Through exercising power within this network, ranging from participation in working groups and direct lobbying of the European Parliament, in an environment of apparent low voter interest and therefore low political salience, the entertainment industry was able to secure its preferred form of copyright regulation.

Term extension: the rationales of author protection and incentivization

The development of legislation concerning the duration of copyright must also be assessed within the framework of dominant discourse in order to understand the role of industry representatives as policymakers in the field of copyright law. The increases to the duration of protection for copyrighted works began in the 'first phase' of copyright development at the EU level, beginning with the Green Paper on copyright and the challenge of technology (European Commission 1988). While the majority of the discussion relating to term of protection specifically dealt with computer programs (1988, chap. 5) and databases (1988, chap. 6), it was mentioned that the appropriate duration of protection should be discussed (1988, sec. 1.3.5). In the follow-up Communication, however, a much stronger language of protection was introduced. According to the Commission, 'copyright provides a basis for Intellectual creation. To protect copyright is to ensure that creativity is sustained and developed, in the interest of authors, the cultural industries, consumers, and ultimately of society as a whole' (1991, sec. 1.3). Furthermore, neighbouring rights protection 'underpin these objectives in various ways, particularly by guaranteeing a proper return to performing artists and those who invest in the provision of these cultural goods and services' (1991, sec. 1.3). For this reason, copyright protection must be strengthened (1991, sec. 1.4). Stating a need to ensure harmonization of copyright terms in order to ensure the functioning of the internal market (see also Chapter 2 of this book), the Commission reasoned that there were four principles that would guide their proposal: namely, that the harmonization should be total, that the terms should provide 'a high level of protection' with a minimum term higher than that provided for in international agreements, that terms higher than that in any future Directive would be permitted, and that a 'balance' would be achieved between copyright and neighbouring rights (1991, sec. 8.2.5). As was discussed in Chapter 2, this resulted in Directive 93/98/EEC harmonizing the term of protection for copyright and related rights (replaced by Directive 2006/116/EC), harmonizing the term of protection as life plus seventy years for copyrighted works, and fifty years from the date of first publication in the case of phonograms, films and performances. The language of the Communication was retained, and can be seen in recital 11 of the 2006 Directive, which states that:

> The level of protection of copyright and related rights should be high, since those rights are fundamental to intellectual creation. Their protection ensures the maintenance and development of creativity in the interest of authors, cultural industries, consumers and society as a whole.

In the Proposal for an extension to the term of protection for sound recordings, the discourse of protection of creative people continues. The grounds for the Proposal, according to the Commission, was to 'improve the social situation of performers, and in particular sessions musicians, taking into account that performers are increasingly outliving the existing 50 year period of protection for their performances' (2008d, p. 2).

The protection and incentivization of authors/creators, for perhaps obvious reasons, is a dominant discourse within copyright law and policy. Whether we are discussing copyright in the Anglo-American tradition or the continental *droit d'auteur*, protection in order to reward/incentivize as the basis for granting copyright protection is hegemonic – it is the accepted truth within copyright discourse (but that this is an accepted truth by policy actors does not mean that it is uncontested, as will be demonstrated later in this chapter). Some of the economic reasoning has been provided earlier in this chapter, regarding the necessity of protection as a means of providing incentives for creation – absent the provision of suitable economic recompense, a creator will have no inclination to create. Ohly considers the granting of economic rights to creators as 'the least controversial aspect' of copyright (2009, p. 213). 'The field of economic rights is the area on which copyright systems and author's rights systems largely agree that every legal system that stops short of outright abolition of copyright will have to confer economic benefits on the author' (2009, p. 213). In other words, the acceptable limits of discourse are those that permit a copyright system to exist, in which it is accepted that there must be an economic benefit to a creator. Debate thereby centers on the means of best ensuring this economic benefit, rather on whether it should be ensured at all. That creators should benefit is accepted within both the utilitarian and labour theory conceptualizations of copyright. The utilitarian argument runs, if we wish to see more creation to the benefit of society, we must provide economic incentives in order to ensure that creators continue to produce (Tussey 2011, pp. 45–6; Landes and Posner 2003; Elkin-Koren and Salzberger 2013; Cooter and Ulen 2008). Alternatively, if we approach the issue from the labour theory view, copyright protection is based on the right of authors to benefit from labour they invest in works (Tussey 2011, p. 42; Spitzlinger 2011; Spinello and Bottis 2009; Epstein 2009; DeLong 2002). Irrespective of which approach is taken, however, one principle remains constant – a creator must be recompensed for their work.

Conflict between experts and the establishment of a dominant discourse on optimal terms for sound recordings

Directive 2011/77/EU on the protection of sound recordings was particularly contentious among informed parties. Highly critical articles were written by prominent intellectual property scholars (Helberger *et al.* 2008; Hilty *et al.* 2009), and a petition was started by a coalition of user interest groups including the Open Rights Group, La Quadrature du Net and the Electronic Frontier Foundation. P. Bernt Hugenholtz at the University of Amsterdam went as far as to send a letter to Manuel Barroso (President of the European Commission), as well as to Charlie McCreevy (then Commissioner for the Internal Market), the European Parliament and the Council of the EU (Hugenholtz 2008). These concerned parties were reacting to the Proposal to extend the term of protection for sound recordings from fifty years to ninety-five years, almost doubling the term of protection (European Commission 2008d, p. 6). These academics and user groups opposed an extension of the term of protection for sound recordings, stating that there was no economic evidence that appeared to support such an extension. However, the frame for debate in which this discourse took place was not whether a greater economic return would be justified in order to provide incentives, but whether it would in fact create the incentive desired. In other words, the debate was conducted in such a way that the fact that performers should be protected was accepted, but the success of such measures in achieving that aim (and indeed, the genuine intent of those measures) was contested.

A discourse has become increasingly prevalent in copyright scholarship that considers that copyright law does not treat creators particularly well, 'especially when one examines both international and national laws pertaining to moral rights, ownership . . . and assignment' (Suthersanen 2007, p. 120). Whereas 'pre-modern' copyright until the Statute of Anne was largely based on principles of state and religious censorship, and in England the provision of a monopoly right for the Stationers' Guild (Cotter 2003; Patterson 1968; Samuelson 2002; Netanel 2008), the Statute of Anne sought to break the Stationers' Guild's monopoly over printing, by allowing an author to have a right of copy for up to fourteen years. Interestingly, even in the early eighteenth century, the protection of authors was a significant discourse used by book publishers who were seeing those monopolies broken. In arguing for a greater term of protection, publishers did so on the basis of protecting the authors that they had previously purchased manuscripts from, often at a very low rate of pay. Patterson described these arguments by book publishers as duplicitous – 'the publishers . . . had as much concern for authors as a cattle rancher has for cattle' (1968, p. 167). Such arguments are based in a suspicion of the role of corporate or business interests in protecting pre-existing positions through the user of creators as a rhetorical device. Or, to put it in Foucauldian terms, creators become an object of discourse, an object in this instance to be protected. Another way of putting it is that the concept of the author is 'instrumentalized' – using Patterson's example of cattle, a cattle rancher's concern for the cattle is not for the well-being of an individual cow for its own intrinsic worth. The concern is based on the potential return from those cows, usually in the form of the purchase price of meat. In this sense, the interest of the book publisher or music producer is not in protecting artists for artists' sakes, but for the potential return from the commodification of their work.

It is in this frame that arguments against term extension were made. In particular, the Gowers Review (Gowers 2006), conducted in the UK at the behest of the British Government, and the Institute for Information Law (IViR) study commissioned by the European Commission (IViR 2006) were both very sceptical of the likelihood of the extension resulting in increased remuneration for performers. Gowers contended that the 'net present value of a prospective change in term would be 1 per cent or lower for performers' (Gowers 2006, sec. 4.29), and IViR stated on analysis of the data that 'the median individual payment for performers in the UK averaged a meager GBP 75 per year' (IViR 2006, p. 107). This is largely due to a relatively small percentage of top-selling artists dominating the music market, the vast majority of artists receive little to no compensation from royalty payments, earning less than the minimum distributable amount (Farrand 2012). Furthermore, it was argued by academics, the term extension could result in a redistribution of revenues from living to dead artists, as works of popular but deceased musicians such as Jimi Hendrix remain popular and sell more than many current artists (Helberger et al. 2008; Farrand 2012; Kretschmer 2011). Receiving evidence from performing artists, the Gowers Review found that it was unlikely that an artist would decide not to record a song because it would lose copyright protection in 'only' fifty years time (2006, sec. 4.3.2). Another reason that performers were unlikely to see much in the way of revenue from such changes, the reasoning went, was because of the fact that the economic rights of copyright are often assigned to record labels. As a result, the money collected in royalties goes directly to those record labels to then apportion (Toynbee 2004, p. 134; Greenfield and Osborn 2004, p. 97). In this respect, academics reasoned that the proposed term extension would result in a windfall for producers, rather than for performers (Hilty et al. 2009, p. 71). Similar reasoning was used by academics in the wake of the Copyright Term Extension Act in the US, ranging from arguments that the extension of copyright protection to life plus seventy years (and ninety-five years from publication in the case of works of corporate authorship) would not benefit artists but would increase corporate control over creative works (Lessig 2004; Heald 2007) and would not incentivize the creation of new works (Boldrin and Levine 2008, p. 100). However, such arguments were largely unsuccessful, and in the case of *Eldred v Aschroft* (2003) the changes to copyright were deemed constitutional, and the extension in the interest of creators.

In comparison, the study relied on most heavily by the Commission in its Impact Assessment was that produced by Price Waterhouse Cooper (PWC) on behalf of the British Phonographic Industry (BPI) (Hugenholtz 2008). While not publicly accessible at the time of deliberations, extracts located in the Impact Assessment provide insight into the record industry's arguments. Needless to say, the PWC study did not agree with Gowers' or IViR's findings. The study found that term extension would be beneficial, generating between €44 million and €843 million, resulting in an additional €46 to €737 per performer per year (European Commission 2008a, sec. 7.3.1). Furthermore, it was argued that the extension would increase the revenue available to the publishers, that could then 'fund new talent . . . record companies state that they often use the income derived from older recordings to produce and market new recordings.' (2008a, sec. 7.3.6). This was contested both in the Gowers Review where it was determined that 'monies earned so far in the future fail to impact on current spending decisions' (2006, sec. 4.3.1), and IViR stating that the overall effect of a term extension on investment would be limited, as the largest part of revenues primarily finances the running cost of phonogram producers (2006, p. 115). It would be safe to conclude then, that irrespective of the merits of the arguments presented, there was significant difference between the arguments raised by studies presented by those in favour of term extension and those against. As shall be demonstrated in the next section, the Commission appeared to give those that were against term extension short thrift.

Networks of power and quiet politics in the term extension debate

The passing of Directive 2011/77/EU is strongly indicative of the networked nature of power in policy processes. After the Gowers Review rejected the idea of extending the term of copyright protection, the British Phonographic Industry made a statement in which they stated 'if the UK government decides not to support copyright equalization then the music industry will have to continue its campaign in Europe. There the signs are encouraging.' (BBC News 2006). Furthermore, despite having commissioned the Gowers Review, the British Government appeared to reject the findings of Gowers, instead urging the EU to take up the issue of term extension (Eechoud et al. 2009, p. 182). This reinforces that power is not only exercised hierarchically, but multilaterally. Upon analysis of documents released by the European institutions during the legislative process for Directive 2011/77/EU on term extension, it becomes readily apparent that the discourse of extension was without doubt the dominant one. As is noted by Pisuke, the process of extending the term of protection for sound recordings pre-dates the Commission Proposal, and indeed, was already being referred to in a Working Document attached to a Communication on Creative Content Online in a way that made the position of the European Commission quite clear (2012, sec. 8.4). Interestingly, the Communication (2008c) itself does not mention term extension in any way. However, in the Working Document, it is stated that the:

recording industry argues that the term of protection for sound recordings should be extended within Europe from 50 to 95 years to match the term in the U.S. In an online global market, performers and producers in the EU are at a substantial disadvantage compared with the US and many other trading partners. They argue that consistent longer terms of protection will facilitate the dissemination of works into a larger number of markets and provide an incentive for the development of new ways of getting back catalogue, specialised genres and niche music to consumers.

(2008b, sec. 3.2.6)

It is worth reproducing this quotation in full for two reasons. The first is to compare it to the paragraph dedicated to contrary opinion. Immediately afterwards, the Commission states that 'taking a contrary position, the Gowers Review of Intellectual Property, December 2006, includes a recommendation to retain the protection period of 50 years for sound recordings and performers' rights' (2008b, sec. 3.2.6). While the position of the record labels is expanded upon with justifications, the Gowers Review is relegated to a secondary position. The reasoning of Gowers is not expanded upon, only the conclusion given. Rhetorically, the Gowers Review is in a weaker position than that of the record labels, a statement on the fringes of the acceptable discourse, if not outside it. The position of the record labels did not appear to be questioned in any way, suggesting that their position had been accepted, and the need for extension of the term considered as truth (in the Foucauldian sense of the word). Prior to the Communication being released, the Commission ran a consultative exercise from 28 July until 13 October 2006 that received 175 responses (2008b, sec. 1.2), the vast majority of which were from entertainment industry representatives and collecting societies. In the IFPI response to the Commission, IFPI makes clear the need for term extension. In fact, the wording of the IFPI statement is functionally identical to the later published Working Document (IFPI 2006, p. 6). Bertelsmann's response is also very similar (2006, p. 2). This would suggest that prior to the Proposal, the accepted truth on the part of the Commission was that term extension was necessary. As with the previously discussed Information Society Directive legislative process, the fact that entertainment industry 'experts' were involved in the initial stages of the process through the provision of knowledge/information means that they were more effectively able to frame the debate. The very short duration of the consultation is also an indication of this. As with the Green Paper released prior to the publication of the Proposal on the Information Society Directive, the short timescale for responses to be prepared 'made it almost inevitable that [only those who] were already geared-up to respond would provide input' (Burrell and Coleman 2005, p. 209). This assists in reinforcing the perception that these entertainment industry representatives are experts that understand their business needs better than policymakers, and are best suited to determine the way in which their businesses should be run (Culpepper 2011, p. 9; Bernhagen and Bräuninger 2005, p. 5). Individual firms accumulate knowledge about relevant policy issues in the course of performing their everyday activities, and international organizations such as IFPI, are excellently placed to be able to collate and present this information (Bernhagen and Bräuninger 2005, p. 5).

When tracing the development of the legislation through policy documents, it is possible to determine that industry discourses remained dominant throughout, to the detriment of non-industry discourses. The executive summary of the Impact Assessment provided with the Proposal makes clear that the arguments of the entertainment industry were accepted as true; the Commission refers to the need to ensure that performers are protected in their later years, as sound recordings made when a performer was twenty lose protection when they are in their seventies, depriving them of royalty income (2008a, p. 2). 'A term extension would ensure that these income sources do not cease during the performer's lifetime' (2008a, p. 4). In the previously mentioned letter by P. Bernt Hugenholtz, it is stated that the study performed by IViR was mentioned only once in the Impact Assessment, and out of context (2008, pp. 1–2). With regard to the Gowers Review, the Impact Assessment predominantly used the Review to provide counterpoints to industry arguments. Furthermore, when used in this manner, the Commission would then clarify why the Gowers Review was considered incorrect (2008a, sec. 7.2.3). In comparison, industry figures, such as those provided by PWC, were used throughout the Impact Assessment in order to justify the decision to extend the term of protection. As Hugenholtz states, it becomes obvious that 'several conclusions of the IViR studies do not agree with the policy choices underlying the Commission's proposals' (2008, p. 2). Indeed, the Impact Assessment indicates that the IViR and Gowers studies fell outside of the accepted discourse, and for this reason, were either ignored, or actively argued against. While the Proposal's explanatory memorandum stated that no external expertise was necessary in order to develop the legislative policy (2008d, p. 6), this is not strictly true. External expertise was sought, and that which fit within the narrative constructed were incorporated into the main text of the Impact Assessment and memorandum, and those that did not fit within the narrative were not included. The European Parliament's Report on the Proposal was equally supportive of the move to increase the term of protection, with the Legal Affairs Committee stating that the increased term would help to protect performers, producers and the cultural diversity of the EU (2009b, p. 19). The Committee on Industry, Research and Energy was also in support, advocating the extension of the proposal to other types of performer (2009b, p. 28), as was the Committees on the Internal Market and Consumer Protection (2009b, p. 38) and on Culture and Education (2009b, p. 48). As with the Impact Assessment, no indication was given in the Report that there were competing views that challenged the need for a term extension – such views fell outside of the frame of the discourse. After moving to reduce the extension from forty-five years to twenty, in April 2009, the European Parliament announced that it had voted in favour of the Directive, with 377 votes in favour, 178 against and 37 abstentions. The European Parliament's reduction of the term from ninety-five years to the seventy enshrined in Directive 2011/77/EU does not appear to be down to the concerns expressed in academic reports, but in a desire to have the legislation passed by a Council unable to agree on protection lasting for ninety-five years (Pinsent Masons 2009; European Parliament 2009a). While Belgium, the Czech Republic, Luxembourg, the Netherlands, Romania, Slovakia, Slovenia and Sweden voted against adopting the Directive, indicating they at least were not convinced of the 'truth' of the dominant discourse, the Directive was nevertheless passed in September 2011. In recital 4 of the Directive, the dominant discourse was further reaffirmed and embedded. The creative input of performers is highly important, and this 'should be reflected in a level of protection that acknowledges their creative and artistic contribution'.

Finally, was this an issue in which quiet politics was at play? Media reporting on the term extension suggests it was. The BBC wrote thirteen stories concerning the term extension between 2007 and 2011, the majority of which contained many of the arguments made by IFPI and the pro-extension studies, suggesting that entertainment industry representatives were able to frame the discourse used in those stories. Certain stories also made reference to particular artists, such as Cliff Richard, who claimed that without the royalties from extended terms, older performers would suffer (BBC News 2007), or Dame Vera losing the right to songs over fifty years old that were used against her wishes by far-right groups (Joyce 2009). One story does discuss the creation of the Featured Artists Coalition (FAC), who were not in favour of the music industry's proposals, instead wanting the rights to revert to performers (BBC News 2009). However, this does not suggest that the FAC was against term extension, only the way in which term extension would function. The *Guardian* similarly has two related stories in 2007, three in 2009, and two after the passing of the Directive. Of those prior to the Directive's passing, four of the five are positive towards term extension, providing stories of elderly performers struggling due to a lack of royalties (Pidgeon 2009), or using language very similar to that of IFPI (Tran 2009; Hencke and correspondent 2009; Allen and correspondent 2007). Particularly when compared to the volume of reporting on ACTA (as will be discussed in Chapter 8), the relative paucity of news coverage, and the tone of that coverage, suggests that term extension was an issue of low political salience to the general public, irrespective of its salience to user groups and academics. That the issue was of low political salience can also be inferred through the lack of any reference by the European Parliament to user concerns over term extension. As with the Information Society Directive, it may have been the case that the issue of optimal sound recording terms was considered too complex to study in significant detail, with the result that knowledge produced and disseminated by perceived experts formed the basis of the European Parliament's decision.

Concluding remarks

While academics in the field of intellectual property law have frequently made reference to the impact of lobbying upon the development of laws and policies at the level of the EU, there has been comparatively little attention paid to the theories that may help to explain the success of these lobbying practices. This chapter has sought to explain the success of lobbying through the use of the networks of power conceptualization of relations between institutional and non-institutional actors and reference to the theory of quiet politics as an explanation for reliance on entertainment industry data. One primary finding of this chapter is that one potential explanation for the success of industry lobbyists comes from the fact that these representatives are both able to effectively frame the limits of acceptable discourse in the legislative debate, or alternatively make arguments that fit effectively within a pre-existing dominant discourse. For example, when in the late 1990s the hegemonic discourse concerned the fact that the internet had changed everything, and we were living in the midst of the digital revolution, arguments in favour of altering or modifying laws because of these radical changes are able to gain more traction than arguments that urge policymakers to refrain from taking action. As the dominant discourse within copyright law is that creators should be economically rewarded/incentivized, and as such, high levels of protection are necessary, arguments that the term of copyright protection should be extended, thereby raising the level of protection, fit within accepted discourses. In comparison, those arguments made against raising the level of protection do not fall within the bounds of accepted discourse, challenging an accepted 'truth'. The fact that industry representatives are well-equipped to engage in these debates, having the ability to respond to calls for evidence quickly and understand the European legislative processes only adds to their success. The flexibility of these groups is also key to their success; when, for example, moves to increase the term of protection failed at the national level in the UK, the recording industry appeared to be able to successfully bring the issue to the European level, indicating the multilateral nature of power relations operating in this area of law.

Part of this success is also due to perceptions of expertise – that industries are best placed to understand the needs of their industries, and as such appear on working groups and as evidence providers. In some respects, the power/knowledge apparatus works in a circular manner – because of the perceived expertise of these representatives, they are able to sit on working group meetings that discuss pre-legislative initiatives. Because they appear on these working groups, the perception of their expertise grows. As copyright law appears to be perceived as a complex area, that (at least, in 2000–1) was not considered by the European Parliament as worth investing time in studying or understanding, indications are that copyright reform is not considered politically salient. In other words, national politicians or MEPs were unlikely to lose seats on the basis of copyright policies. For this reason, when dealing with extensions to the scope and duration of copyright, MEPs were willing to defer to music industry expertise. In the next chapter, this analysis shall be applied to developments regarding the enforcement of copyright, to determine whether there is evidence that this legislation too was enacted within a domain of quiet politics.

Bibliography

Akester, P. and Lima, F., 2005. 'The economic dimension of the digital challenge: A copyright perspective'. *Intellectual Property Quarterly*, *1*, pp. 69–81.

Allen, K. and correspondent, 2007. 'Musicians' copyright pleas fall on deaf ears'. *The Guardian*. Available at: www.guardian.co.uk/media/2007/jul/24/citynews.music news?INTCMP=SRCH [Accessed 14 July 2013].

Andersen, B., 2007. 'How technology changes the scope, strength and usefulness of copyright: Revisiting the "Economic Rationales"'. In F. Macmillan, ed., *New directions in copyright law, volume 5.* Cheltenham: Edward Elgar.

Barlow, J.P., 1998. *Declaration of the independence of cyberspace.* Electronic Frontier Foundation. Available at https://projects.eff.org/~barlow/Declaration-Final.html [Accessed 2 August 2013].

Baum, M.A. and Potter, P.B.K., 2008. 'The relationships between mass media, public opinion, and foreign policy: Toward a theoretical synthesis'. *Annual Review of Political Science*, *11*(1), pp. 39–65.

BBC News, 2006. 'Musical copyright terms "to stay"'. *BBC*. Available at: http://news.bbc.co.uk/2/hi/entertainment/6186436.stm [Accessed 14 July 2013].

BBC News, 2007. 'Music stars "must keep copyright"'. *BBC*. Available at: http://news.bbc.co.uk/2/hi/entertainment/6661283.stm [Accessed 14 July 2013].

BBC News, 2009. 'Artists battle over music rights'. *BBC*. Available at: http://news.bbc.co.uk/2/hi/entertainment/7974727.stm [Accessed 14 July 2013].

Bell, D., 1976. *The coming of post-industrial society: A venture in social forecasting.* New York: Basic Books.

Benkler, Y., 2004. 'Sharing nicely: On shareable goods and the emergence of sharing as a modality of economic production'. *Yale Law Review*, *114*, pp. 273–358.

Benkler, Y., 2006. *The wealth of networks: How social production transforms markets and freedom.* New Haven, CT: Yale University Press.

Bently, L. and Sherman, B., 2004. *Intellectual property law.* 2nd edn, Oxford: Oxford University Press.

Bernhagen, P. and Bräuninger, T., 2005. 'Structural power and public policy: A signaling model of business lobbying in democratic capitalism'. *Political Studies*, *53*(1), pp. 43–64.

Bertelsmann A.G., 2006. 'Response to the Commission Public Consultation on Content Online in the Single Market'. Available at: http://ec.europa.eu/avpolicy/docs/other_actions/contributions/bertelsmann_col_en.pdf [Accessed 14 July 2013].

Boldrin, M. and Levine, D.K., 2008. *Against intellectual monopoly.* New York: Cambridge University Press.

Boyle, J., 2008. *The public domain: Enclosing the commons of the mind.* New Haven, CT: Yale University Press.

Burrell, R. and Coleman, A., 2005. *Copyright exceptions in Europe: The digital impact.* London: Cambridge University Press.

Camdessus, M. and Naím, M., 2000. 'A talk with Michel Camdessus about God, globalization, and his years running the IMF'. *Foreign Policy*, *120*, pp. 32–45.

Castells, M., 1996. *The rise of the network society: Economy, society, and culture.* Oxford: Blackwell.

Cooter, R. and Ulen, T., 2008. *Law and economics.* Boston, MA: Pearson/Addison Wesley.

Cotter, T.F., 2003. 'Gutenberg's legacy: Copyright, censorship and religious pluralism'. *California Law Review*, 91(2), pp. 323–94.

Culpepper, P.D., 2011. *Quiet politics and business power: Corporate control in Europe and Japan.* Cambridge: Cambridge University Press.

DeLong, J.V., 2002. 'Defending intellectual property'. In W. Crews, ed., *Copyfights: The future of intellectual property in the information age.* Washington, DC: Cato Institute.

DiMaggio, P., Hargittai, E., Newman, W.R., Robinson, J.P., 2001. 'Social implications of the internet'. *Annual Review of Sociology*, 27, pp. 307–36.

Directive 2001/29/EC of the European Parliament and of the Council of 22 May 2001 on the harmonisation of certain aspects of copyright and related rights in the information society.

Directive 2011/77/EU of the European Parliament and of the Council of amending Directive 2006/116/EC on the term of protection of copyright and certain related rights.

Drucker, P.F., 1969. *The age of discontinuity: Guidelines to our changing society*, 1st edn. New Brunswick, NJ: HarperCollins.

Drucker, P.F., 1992. *The age of discontinuity: Guidelines to our changing society.* New Brunswick, NJ: Transaction.

Eechoud, M. van, Hugenholtz, P.B., Guibault, L., Gompel, S. van, Helberger, N., 2009. *Harmonizing European copyright law: The challenges of better lawmaking.* Alphen aan den Rijn: Wolters Kluwer Law & Business.

Elkin-Koren, N. and Salzberger, E.M., 2004. *Law, economics and cyberspace: The effects of cyberspace on the economic analysis of law.* Cheltenham: Edward Elgar.

Elkin-Koren, N. and Salzberger, E.M., 2013. *The law and economics of intellectual property in the digital age: The limits of analysis.* London: Routledge.

Epstein, R.A., 2009. 'Disintegration of intellectual property: A classical liberal response to a premature obituary. *Stanford Law Review*, 62, p. 455.

European Commission, 1988. *Green Paper on copyright and the challenge of technology: Copyright issues requiring immediate action.* Brussels: European Commission.

European Commission, 1991. *Follow-up to the Green Paper: Working programme of the Commission in the field of copyright and neighbouring rights.* Brussels: European Commission.

European Commission, 1993. *Growth, competitiveness, employment: The challenges and ways forward into the 21st century: White Paper.* Brussels, Luxembourg: Office for Official Publications of the European Communities.

European Commission, 1995. *Green Paper: Copyright and related rights in the information society.* Brussels: European Commission.

European Commission, 1996. *Communication from the Commission: Follow-up to the Green Paper on copyright and related rights in the information society.* Brussels: European Commission.

European Commission, 1997. *Proposal for a European Parliament and Council Directive on the harmonisation of certain aspects of copyright and related rights in the information society.* Brussels: European Commission.

European Commission, 2008a. *Commission Staff Working Document accompanying the Proposal for a Council Directive amending Council Directive 2006/116/EC as regards the term of protection of copyright and related rights: Impact Assessment on the legal and economic situation of performers and record producers in the European Union.* Brussels: European Commission.

European Commission, 2008b. *Commission Staff Working Document: Document accompanying the Communication from the Commission to the European Parliament, the Council, the European Economic and Social Committee and the Committee of the Regions on creative content online in the Single Market.* Brussels: European Commission.

European Commission, 2008c. *Communication from the Commission to the European Parliament, the Council, the European Economic and Social Committee and the Committee of the Regions on creative content online in the Single Market.* Brussels: European Commission.

European Commission, 2008d. *Proposal for a European Parliament and Council Directive amending Directive 2006/116/EC of the European Parliament and of the Council on the term of protection of copyright and related rights.* Brussels: European Commission.

European Commission and Bangemann Group, 1994. *Europe and the global information society: Recommendations of the high-level group on the information society to the Corfu European Council.* Brussels: European Commission.

European Parliament, 1999. *Legislative resolution embodying Parliament's opinion on the proposal for a European Parliament and Council Directive on the harmonisation of certain aspects of copyright and related rights in the Information Society.* Brussels: European Commission.

European Parliament, 2009a. 'Music copyright to be extended to 70 years for performers'. *Europarl.* Available at: www.europarl.europa.eu/sides/getDoc.do?language=en&type=IM-PRESS&reference=20090422IPR54191 [Accessed 15 July 2013].

European Parliament, 2009b. *Report on the proposal for a directive of the European Parliament and of the Council amending Directive 2006/116/EC of the European Parliament and of the Council on the term of protection of copyright and related rights.* Brussels: European Parliament.

European Parliament and Committee on Legal Affairs and the Internal Market, 2001. *Recommendation for second reading on the Council common position for adopting a European Parliament and Council directive on the harmonisation of certain aspects of copyright and related rights in the Information Society.* Brussels: European Parliament.

Farrand, B., 2012. 'Too much is never enough? The 2011 Copyright in Sound Recordings Extension Directive'. *European Intellectual Property Review*, 34(5), pp. 297–304.

Gowers, A., 2006. *The Gowers Review of Intellectual Property.* London: HM Treasury.

Greenfield, S. and Osborn, G., 2004. 'Copyright law and power in the music industry'. In S. Frith and L. Marshall, eds, *Music and copyright.* Edinburgh: Edinburgh University Press.

Guber, D.L. and Bosso, C., 2007. 'Framing ANWR: Citizens, consumers, and the privileged position of business'. In M.E. Kraft and S. Kamieniecki, eds, *Business and environmental policy corporate interests in the American political system.* Cambridge, MA: MIT Press.

Hall, S., 2000. 'Net record pirates "will cost billions"'. *The Guardian.* Available at: www.guardian.co.uk/uk/2000/jun/15/sarahhall?INTCMP=SRCH [Accessed 13 July 2013].

Heald, P., 2007. 'Losing to Disney: The complex lesson of Eldred v Ashcroft and the corporate control of copyright'. In F. Macmillan, ed., *New directions in copyright law, volume 2.* Cheltenham: Edward Elgar.

Helberger, N., Dufft, N., Gompel, S. van and Hugenholtz, P.B., 2008. 'Never forever: Why extending the term of protection for sound recordings is a bad idea'. *European Intellectual Property Review*, 5, pp. 174–81.

Hencke, D. and correspondent, W., 2009. 'Motown stars told: Reach out: Royalties may soon be there'. *The Guardian*. Available at: www.guardian.co.uk/business/2009/mar/16/music-industry-law-motown?INTCMP=SRCH [Accessed 14 July 2013].

Hilty, R.M., Kur, A., Klass, N., Geiger, C., Peukert, A., Drexl, J., and Katzenberger, P., 2009. 'Comment by the Max-Planck Institute on the Commission's proposal for a Directive to amend Directive 2006/116 concerning the term of protection for copyright and related rights'. *European Intellectual Property Review*, 31(2), pp. 59–72.

Hugenholtz, P.B., 2000. 'Why the Copyright Directive is unimportant, and possibly invalid'. *European Intellectual Property Review*, 11, pp. 501–2.

Hugenholtz, P.B., 2008. 'Open letter concerning European Commission's "intellectual property package"'. Available at: www.ivir.nl//news/Open_Letter_EC.pdf [Accessed 14 July 2013].

Hugenholtz, P.B., 2009. 'Copyright without frontiers: The problem of territoriality in European copyright law'. In E. Derclaye, ed., *Research handbook on the future of EU copyright*. Cheltenham: Edward Elgar.

IFPI (International Federation of the Phonographic Industry), 2006. 'IFPI repsonse to the Commission questionnaire "Content Online"'. Available at: http://ec.europa.eu/avpolicy/docs/other_actions/contributions/ifpi_col_en.pdf [Accessed 14 July 2013].

Institute for Information Law, 2006. *The recasting of copyright and related rights for the knowledge economy*. Amsterdam: University of Amsterdam.

Joyce, J., 2009. 'Dame Vera loses out on old songs'. *BBC*. Available at: http://news.bbc.co.uk/2/hi/entertainment/7899602.stm [Accessed 14 July 2013].

Kochan, T.A. and Barley, S.R. eds, 1999. *The changing nature of work and its implications for occupational analysis*. Washington, DC: National Research Council.

Koenig, P., 1999. 'Who's ready for the revolution?' *The Independent*. Available at: www.independent.co.uk/news/business/whos-ready-for-the-revolution-1083465.html [Accessed 12 July 2013].

Kretschmer, M., 2011. 'Comment of copyright term extension'. *Centre for Intellectual Property Policy and Management Blog*. Available at: www.cippm.org.uk/copyright_term.html [Accessed 14 July 2013].

Ku, R., 2002. 'The creative destruction of copyright: Napster and the new economics of digital technology'. *University of Chicago Law Review*, 69(1), pp. 262–324.

Landes, W.M. and Posner, R.A., 2003. *The economic structure of intellectual property law*. Cambridge, MA: Harvard University Press.

Lessig, L., 2004. *Free culture: The nature and future of creativity*. New York: Penguin Press.

Lewinski, S.V., 1999. 'Proposed EC Directive on copyright and related rights in the information society as it progresses'. *International Review of Intellectual Property and Competition Law*, 30(7), pp. 767–82.

Netanel, N.W., 2008. *Copyright's paradox*. Oxford: Oxford University Press.

Nuttall, C., 1999a. 'Opposition grows to web caching ban'. *BBC*. Available at: http://news.bbc.co.uk/2/hi/science/nature/298498.stm [Accessed 13 July 2013].

Nuttall, C., 1999b. 'Tougher net piracy law backed'. *BBC*. Available at: http://news.bbc.co.uk/2/hi/science/nature/277126.stm [Accessed 13 July 2013].

Ohly, A., 2009. 'Economic rights'. In E. Derclaye, ed., *Research handbook on the future of EU copyright*. Cheltenham: Edward Elgar.

Osborn, A., 2000. 'Corrs join EU anti-piracy campaign'. *The Guardian*. Available at: www.guardian.co.uk/business/2000/jul/14/13?INTCMP=SRCH [Accessed 13 July 2013].

Patterson, L.R., 1968. *Copyright in historical perspective*. Nashville, TN: Vanderbilt University Press.

Perelman, M., 2004. *Steal this idea: Intellectual property rights and the corporate confiscation of creativity*. New York; Basingstoke, UK: Palgrave Macmillan.

Pidgeon, J., 2009. 'Music's intellectual-property eviction notice'. *The Guardian*. Available at: www.guardian.co.uk/music/2009/sep/24/music-copyright-ronald-prentice? INTCMP=SRCH [Accessed 14 July 2013].

Pinsent Masons, 2009. 'European Parliament backs 70-year copyright term for sound recordings'. *Out-Law*. Available at: www.out-law.com/page-9973 [Accessed 14 July 2013].

Pisuke, H., 2012. 'Duration of copyright and related rights'. In T.-H. Synodinou, ed., *Codification of European copyright law: Challenges and perspectives*. Alphen aan den Rijn: Kluwer Law International.

Powell, W.W. and Snellman, K., 2004. 'The knowledge economy'. *Annual Review of Sociology*, 30, pp. 199–220.

Samuelson, P., 1990. 'Digital media and the changing face of intellectual property law'. *Rutgers Computer & Technology Law Journal*, 16, p. 323.

Samuelson, P., 1996. 'The copyright grab'. *Wired*, 57.

Samuelson, P., 2002. 'Copyright and freedom of expression in historical perspective'. *Journal of Intellectual Property Law*, 10, pp. 319–44.

Schiller, H.I., 1981. *Who knows: Information in the age of the Fortune 500*. Norwood, NJ.: ABLEX.

Special Report, 1999. 'Business and the internet: The net imperative'. *The Economist*. Available at: www.economist.com/node/215657 [Accessed 12 July 2013].

Spinello, R.A. and Bottis, M., 2009. *A defense of intellectual property rights*. Cheltenham: Edward Elgar.

Spitzlinger, R., 2011. 'On the idea of owning ideas: Applying Locke's Labor Appropriation Theory to intellectual goods'. *Masaryk University Journal of Law and Technology*, 5, p. 273.

Stokes, S., 2009. *Digital copyright: Law and practice*. Oxford; Portland, OR: Hart.

Suthersanen, U., 2007. 'Copyright law: A stakeholders' palimpsest'. In F. Macmillan, ed., *New directions in copyright law, volume 5*. Cheltenham: Edward Elgar.

Towse, R., 2010. *A textbook of cultural economics*. Cambridge; New York: Cambridge University Press.

Toynbee, J., 2004. 'Musicians'. In S. Frith and L. Marshall, eds, *Music and copyright*. Edinburgh: Edinburgh University Press.

Tran, M., 2009. 'EU extends music recording rights to 70 years'. *The Guardian*. Available at: www.guardian.co.uk/world/2009/apr/24/eu-extends-copyright-70-years? INTCMP=SRCH [Accessed 14 July 2013].

Tritton, G. and Davis, R., 2008. *Intellectual property in Europe*. London: Sweet & Maxwell.

Tussey, D., 2011. *Complex copyright mapping the information ecosystem*. Burlington, VT: Ashgate.

Webster, F., 2006. *Theories of the information society*. London: Routledge.

Chapter 5

Networks of power II

The role of industry representatives in framing policies regarding the enforcement of copyright

> But now we are facing a very new and a very troubling assault on our fiscal security, on our very economic life and we are facing it from a thing called the video cassette recorder and its necessary companion called the blank tape.
>
> (Jack Valenti, 1978)

A frequently heard refrain in academic works discussing legal changes to copyright enforcement mechanisms in the EU is that of the 'impact of lobbying' upon the legislative process. However, many interested parties with very different agendas all undertake lobbying activities, be they civil society organizations, copyright holding industries and even other large commercial sectors, as this chapter shall demonstrate. A more interesting question is 'why are some lobbyists more successful than others in having their preferences taken into account?' The purpose of this chapter is to continue the analysis begun in Chapter 4 in order to demonstrate that the success of lobbying for copyright reform is more complex than big business getting the regime it wants, and is dependent on a combination of factors, such as perceptions of expertise and networked relations of power, low political salience and effective framing of issues in the media. This chapter will begin by exploring the dominant discourse in copyright enforcement legislation, particularly at the EU level, namely that of 'threat' – 'piracy' (among other forms of intellectual property infringement) poses numerous serious threats, not only to the economy through a loss of revenue due to infringement, but through associations with other more serious forms of crime. However, this is by no means an uncontested association, and the second section of this chapter will be dedicated to expanding upon the divisions in discourse, between those actors and academics who perceive copyright as posing a threat, and digital piracy having negative economic impacts, and those who feel that these associations have largely been constructed and the negative impact of digital piracy not yet proved. The third section will then consider the legislative process of the Information Society and Enforcement Directives, demonstrating the ability of entertainment industry representatives (and in particular, the International Federation of the Phonographic Industry, or IFPI) to effectively frame the discourse at the European level through the provision of information and expertise, strong connections to the Commission and European Parliament, and effective framing of the Enforcement Directive in the media as being necessary to combat serious crime. Taking place in low salience environments, the successful passing of the Information Society and Enforcement Directives are examples of industries taking advantage of quiet politics.

In the second part of this chapter, the development of a discourse of the responsibility for Internet Service Providers (ISPs) and other internet intermediaries will be discussed, beginning with brief consideration of the increased use of voluntary codes of conduct and agreements as a means of providing intermediaries with a more active role in managing copyright infringement, observing that much of the legal literature refers to these developments in light of principles of 'liability' as established in the E-Commerce Directive. The following chapter, however, will demonstrate that it is more effective to think of these developments in terms of 'regulation', and in particular networked governance and self-regulation, drawing upon the theories of regulatory capitalism. The final section of this chapter will then demonstrate how this discourse of intermediary responsibility has developed in a networked fashion, initially being adopted as a compromise initiated by the Council during deliberations over the Information Society Directive, but being taken and developed at both European and national levels, by both politicians and the entertainment industries. This section will also demonstrate the importance of expertise, networks and media framing in the legislative process, demonstrating that theoretically powerful lobbyists in the form of the telecoms industry were not able to influence legislation to the same extent as the entertainment industry, due to a combination of weaker associations with other actors, and an inability to effectively frame media coverage of the passing of the Directive. This will help to further develop the argument that knowledge and expertise in this respect can be more a effective explanation for law and policy in copyright law than referring solely to 'lobbying'.

The information society, enforcement and discourse: the rationale of threat

As Reinbothe has stated, 'the efforts and legislative measures at EU level to fight copyright piracy have not started with the Enforcement Directive, and they will not end with it' (Reinbothe 2010, sec. 1.A). Indeed, Directive 2001/29/EC on the protection of copyright in the Information Society sought to harmonize aspects of copyright law in order to ensure uniform protection in the Member States. The protection of copyright through TPMs, and indeed, the protection of TPMs, is one way of ensuring this protection. In the preamble to the Directive, recital 9 mentions that 'harmonisation of copyright and related rights must take as a basis a high level of protection, since such rights are crucial to intellectual creation', and recital 15 that there exists a need to 'fight piracy world-wide'. The 'piracy' of intellectual property generally, and 'copyright' specifically has been a consistent concern for right-holders for centuries, particularly with regard to the book trade in the early nineteenth century (see, generally Johns 2011; Seville 2010; Drahos and Braithwaite 2002, pp. 21–5). Seville states that the original use of piracy in this context was a neutral term, referring to 'infringement' without making a moral charge, although this had changed by the late 1830s (2010, p. 25). Interestingly, in the lobbying that followed the increased sale of British books in the US without the permission (or payment) of the author, lobbyists strongly argued that a 'right of property' should be protected (Seville 2010, p. 27). Johns argues that debates about intellectual property piracy have flared up repeatedly since the 1700s, and that 'the concept of piracy has always been shaped by perceptions of continuity and deviance' (2010, p. 48).

When discussions of piracy occur, the discourse is one of threat. Piracy presents risks, of various kinds, this discourse maintains. The quotation that begins this chapter comes from a statement made by Jack Valenti, who was then the head of the Motion Picture Association of America, to the US House of Representatives (1982). This discourse of the threat posed by piracy can be found at multiple levels of institutional actors, and at the level of academics and lobbyists. In this respect, the discourse of threat is networked, similar to the way in which the exercise of power is networked. Some examples of the pervasiveness of this discourse are as follows. Michele Barnier, the current European Commissioner for Internal Market and Services, has stated that 'Piracy undermines the very foundations of creative activity and a legal economy ... I intend to fight this scourge' (2011, p. 18). The previous Commissioner, Charlie McCreevy, spoke of his 'deep concern about the threat of counterfeiting and piracy – this menace that is growing more and more dangerous by the day' (2009). Lord Mandelson, discussing the Digital Economy Bill (that received royal assent in 2010) in the British House of Lords stated that 'this House is probably the one place in Britain where peer-to-peer file-sharing is associated more with passing notes in the Lords' tea room than with piracy, but, joking aside, this is a major problem for Britain's creative industries' (2009, col. 745). Academics have referred to piracy as having 'alarming dimensions' (Reinbothe 2010, sec. 1.A.), and that online infringement is 'the most serious threat to copyright ... [resulting] in huge losses of revenue and jobs in the copyright industry' (Iglezikas 2012, sec. 14.1), 'a daily phenomenon that needs to be tackled' (Kioupis 2010, sec. III). Representatives of business interests such as Philippe de Buck of BUSINESSEUROPE, a business consortium, have referred to 'counterfeiting and piracy [having] a profound impact on the world economy' (2011, p. 136), and IFPI has referred to piracy as 'significantly increasing business risk' (2004, p. 6).

As can be seen, references to 'threat' and 'risk' pervade discourse with regard to piracy, both as a general phenomenon, and with regard to online infringement specifically. Addressing the Centre for Intellectual Property Rights (CIR) in May 2002, the Senior Legal Advisor for European Affairs of IFPI, Olivia Regnier stated that the internet has 'turned out to be a great threat' to the music industry; 'the situation has done huge damage to the revenues of the industry and other rightholders' (Regnier 2003, p. 53). Laïdi hypothesizes that the European Union constitutes a 'risk averse power', defined as 'an international actor that defines and responds to the political stakes of a given identified risk in terms of a will to reduce its uncertainties and uncontrollable effects' (2010, p. 1). Laïdi goes on to state that a risk-averse power tends towards trying to protect 'global public goods' while mitigating the impact of 'global public bads', both externally in terms of reducing the risk of war, but also internally, for example by attempting to reduce or regulate the risk posed by genetically modified organisms (2010, p. 2). With the increased take-up of high-speed internet services, European citizens become part of that threat, through mass copying of digital works. A threat previously considered external, namely that of acts of infringement by and within third countries, develops an internal dimension (Farrand and Carrapico 2012, pp. 385–6; Reinbothe 2010, sec. C). If the European Union institutions are considered collectively as being a risk-averse actor, and given the statements by officials such as Commissioner Barnier quoted earlier, it may be inferred that the protection of intellectual property rights 'to a high standard' constitutes a public 'good', while the infringement of those rights constitutes a public 'bad'. Copyright, representing that good, must be protected while infringement, representing that bad, is a scourge to be fought (Barnier 2011, p. 18). However, despite the existence of an arguably dominant discourse of threat at the EU level, there is no consensus as to the extent or reality of that threat, as will be demonstrated in the next section.

Known knowns, known unknowns, unknown unknowns: the impact of digital piracy

Reyman has argued that the rhetoric and language of the piracy debate has 'been plagued by a series of polarized oppositions between villain pirates and victimized businesses, corporate greed and technological revolution, law and lawlessness, right and wrong' (2012, p. 26). These narratives, Reyman continues, represent different value systems at work, and create something of a binary debate, between 'open' and 'closed' visions of the internet, regulated and unregulated infringement, and so on (2012, pp. 26–7). The discourse of victimized business and the associated social costs has (perhaps unsurprisingly) formed the basis of a continuous narrative in the entertainment industry. One set of figures often cited by lobbyists in the US is that businesses lose $250 billion to piracy every year, as well as more than 750,000 jobs (see for example Patry 2009, p. 30). De Buck of BUSINESSEUROPE makes reference to the 'value of counterfeited and pirated products [being] as much as US $650 billion . . . and puts 2.5 million legitimate jobs at risk every year' (2011, p. 136). With regard to digital piracy, a narrative begins to be constructed by IFPI in 2000 in its music piracy report when it states that:

> Internet piracy spread rapidly in 1999 and early 2000, but it is too early to quantify the economic impact on the music market. Online piracy poses

exactly the same threat as its physical equivalent to the creativity of artists and the investment of record producers. Potentially its impact is far greater than physical piracy.

(2000, p. 5)

In 2001, statistics begin to be presented, with IFPI stating that in 'February 2001, some 2.8 billion songs were traded on Napster, according to internet research firm Webnoize' (2001, p. 8). In 2002, IFPI stated that while any official measurement of piracy was likely to be speculative, nevertheless 'in 2001, approximately 99 per cent of music files available online were unauthorised' (2002, p. 9). In 2004, with the first of IFPI's digital music reports, it was stated that unauthorized digital downloads were more likely to negatively impact music sales than promote them, with one survey finding that while 15 per cent of people who regularly downloaded unauthorized music bought more CDs, 27 per cent said that they bought less (2004, p. 11). The 2005 digital music report states that 'music industry sales declined by some 22 per cent over five years to 2003, a reduction of over US$6 billion, with some of the biggest drops in album and singles sales in countries with large or growing broadband penetration' (2005a, p. 18). This trend of a discourse of damage caused to the music industry by online piracy continues through subsequent reports (2006, p. 20; 2007, p. 18; 2008, p. 25; 2009, p. 5), with the use of statistics in support of this discourse. In 2011, the report states that while digital revenues are up 1,000 per cent, revenue is down 30 per cent, and that the 'overall impact of digital piracy has been to contribute substantially to the dramatic erosion in industry revenues in recent years' (2011, p. 14). As mentioned in Chapter 1 of this book, the use of statistics and empirical evidence is effective in the exercise of networked power, promoting the perception that the individual or institution presenting this information is an expert, legitimizing that particular form of discourse. Some academic studies have also supported IFPI's discourse concerning the decrease of revenue as a result of digital copyright infringement, finding varying degrees of loss of revenue apparently directly attributable to online copyright infringement, and others finding increases in revenue in the wake of the implementation of stricter enforcement mechanisms (Liebowitz 2005; Liebowitz 2006; Zentner 2006; Adermon and Liang 2010; Mortimer *et al.* 2010).

A counter-discourse runs that these arguments, particularly those of the music industry, must be viewed critically. With regard to the claim that piracy costs legitimate producers $250 billion annually, with a total of 750,000 lost jobs, Patry argues that the studies underpinning such claims are 'are obviously and fatally flawed' (2009, p. 30). Patry also states that depending on the needs of the particular actor, these figures either cover all intellectual property 'theft', that specifically attributable to piracy, or even that solely attributable to the counterfeiting of car parts (Patry 2009, p. 30). An investigation by Sanchez found that finding the original source of the $250 billion statistic is quite difficult to achieve, concluding that the earliest version of the claim he could find was found in an un-sourced figure in a *Forbes* magazine article from 1993, where it was stated that counterfeiting was a $200 billion enterprise worldwide and 'growing faster than many of the industries it's preying on' (2008). Similarly, the 750,000 lost jobs figure, according to Sanchez, was first printed in *The Christian Science Monitor* in 1986, when 'then-Commerce Secretary Malcom Baldridge . . . estimated the number of jobs lost to the counterfeiting of U.S. goods at "anywhere from 130,000 to 750,000"' (2008). Karaganis urges caution when considering the use of statistics by the entertainment industry, stating that in attempting to analyse the claims made by industry representative bodies, 'we see a serious and increasingly sophisticated industry research enterprise embedded in a lobbying effort with a historically very loose relationship to evidence' and dubious methodologies (2011, p. 4), a claim echoed by Boyle (2008, p. 220; 2010). Other academic studies by economists appear to suggest that the impact of digital piracy is minimal, 'statistically indistinguishable from zero' (Olberholzer-Gee and Strumpf 2007, p. 4), or could even have some potentially beneficial effects, such as music sales facilitated by the use of unauthorized downloads as a means of 'sampling' the product (Huygen *et al.* 2009, pp. 81–2; BBC News 2009; Norwegian Business School 2009) or promoting attendance of live performances (Cammaerts and Meng 2011, p. 6; Huygen *et al.* 2009, p. 82; *The Economist* 2010). Other factors, such as changing consumer-spending habits such as the increase in 'video-gaming' as a viable hobby have also been raised (Huygen *et al.* 2009, p. 82; Cammaerts and Meng 2011, pp. 4–7; Karaganis 2011, p. 40), as has the reduction in discretionary consumer spending as a result of the economic crisis (Farrand 2014; Nielsen 2012).

One particular discourse that became apparent during the mid-2000s was that of the link between piracy and other serious forms of crime. While IFPI had been discussing the mass-scale physical copyright infringement such as CD burning for sale in the black market in developing economies as an example of organized crime some years earlier (2000, p. 3), in 2005 IFPI released a report in which they stated that 'a series of raids was conducted in the UK, resulting in the arrest of nine individuals for organising the distribution of massive quantities of illegal material (music, films, software and paedophilia) on the Internet' (2005b, p. 6). Furthermore, IFPI argues, 'the most extreme form of organised crime affecting society today is that of terrorism . . . evidence and intelligence is available to prove that these groups are involved in the fabrication, distribution and sale of counterfeit music' (2005b, p. 3). Similarly, an OECD report into digital piracy makes the claim that 'there is an increasing concern that criminal networks (including organised crime and terrorist groups) are among the principal beneficiaries of . . . piracy activities, with the proceeds from their activities being used to finance a range of illicit activities' (2009, p. 15). This discourse serves to link the issue of digital piracy to serious forms of crime, seeking to establish as a dominant discourse that 'something must be done' about the former type of conduct, because of the networked effects of the latter type of conduct (Farrand and Carrapico 2012, p. 386). A well-known anti-piracy campaign ran by BREIN, a Dutch anti-piracy organization, states 'you wouldn't steal a car, you wouldn't steal a handbag, you wouldn't steal a television, you wouldn't steal a movie. Downloading pirated material is stealing. Stealing is against the law'. David notes that the use of such language is intended as a form of association building within anti-piracy discourse, helping to 'equate file-sharing with commercial piracy and counterfeiting' (2010, p. 98). Reyman states that this discourse 'suggests connections between criminals of much more dangerous crimes and participation on peer-to-peer file-sharing networks' (2012, p. 69). Nevertheless, David maintains that such a discourse should be viewed sceptically, as this association 'involves numerous deceptive claims and associations' (2010, p. 98), providing the example of a hearing of the United States' House Judiciary Committee's Subcommittee on Courts, the Internet and Intellectual Property attended by John Malcom. Malcom, representing the Department of Justice, was asked to give evidence linking internet-based piracy with organized crime or terrorism. In order to do so, according to David, Malcom 'sought to equate file-sharing networks with organised crime on the basis that they were international networks and they were enabling illegal activity' (2010, p. 99). Karaganis is equally sceptical, stating that his research team 'found no evidence of systematic links between media piracy and more serious forms of organised crime, much less terrorism, in any of our country studies' (2011, pp. 37–8).

There is, it seems, little common ground in the comparative discourses regarding piracy in the digital environment, and little consensus. To the entertainment industry, 'consumers want everything for free' (Reyman 2012, p. 5). To a range of other actors, strong enforcement is the result of a defensive industry unable or unwilling to create new business models in order to take advantage of technological change (Wikström 2009, p. 38; Boyle 2008, p. 56; Tapscott and Williams 2010, pp. 238–41; Hakfoort 2002; Kohli 2001, p. 20). What both discourses appear to have in common, however, is the difficulty in assessing the impact of digital piracy. Both those seemingly convinced that digital piracy is a significant threat to the music industry, and those who are cautious in making or accepting such claims, state that it is very difficult to assess and quantify the scale of piracy. For example, while stating that digital piracy is a serious threat and linking such activities to organized crime, the OECD still takes care to state that 'the overall degree to which products are being counterfeited and pirated is unknown, and there do not appear to be any method-ologies that could be employed to develop an acceptable overall estimate' (2009, p. 9). Similarly, a recently held symposium on the use of economic evidence in intellectual property policy made it clear that industry representatives, policy-makers and academics all found it incredibly difficult to collect and effectively assess data on both piracy generally, and digital piracy specifically, with the added difficulty that both 'sides' of the copyright debate seek out the (often-anecdotal) evidence that supports their discourse (Kretschmer and Towse 2013, p. 77). However, from this point, the views then diverge. Those in favour of increased copyright protection construct a discourse that underlines that we do not know the extent of the problem, yet we know it is one, and it must be tackled. Commissioner Barnier, for example, states that 'although accurate and reliable figures are difficult to obtain and are often contested, some people estimate the "black economy" on the Internet at 10 billion euros annually' (2011, p. 18). For this reason, he maintains, we require a strong enforcement system. In comparison, those that argue against a strong enforcement system, on the grounds it may unduly impact users, start from the basis that as the figures are debatable and contested, far-reaching legislative change should be avoided until stronger economic evidence is forthcoming (see for example Tapscott and Williams 2010, p. 241). However, policy actors at the EU level appear sure of the fact that digital piracy is a problem that must be tackled. In the next section, the networks of power underlying such a perception will be discussed.

Networks of power and quiet politics in the enforcement of copyright

European Commission discourse framing piracy as a serious threat can be traced back as far as the 1988 Green Paper mentioned in the previous chapter. According to this source, 'piracy has emerged as a serious problem for copyright industries and for creative artists' (1988, sec. 2.1.4). The source for the significant losses to the music industry quoted from sections 2.2.4–2.2.11 of the Green Paper is IFPI. This appears to suggest that the position of perceived expert has been held by this particular organization with regard to piracy for a significant period of time. In the 1991 Follow-Up, reference was made specifically to the creation of a proposal for a directive to harmonize 'certain neighbouring rights . . . intended . . . to fight piracy' (European Commission 1991, sec. 2.3.1). The 1995 Green Paper preceding the Information Society Directive referred to the 'danger of piracy . . . and the need for arrangements . . . for the progressive introduction of techniques to limit copying of this kind' (1995a, p. 28). The Commission's stance on piracy was largely influenced by a hearing in July 1994, in which various representatives of creation and innovation-led industries discussed the threats posed by piracy (a list of attendees can be found in European Commission 1995b, pp. iii–iv). Through perceived experts, knowledgeable in their own area of business activity (constituting an epistemic community), stating what they considered to be the most severe threat to their industries, these networked actors were able to begin influencing Commission policy on piracy. That the dominant discourse at the level of the Commission had become 'piracy is a threat' can be seen through the language of the Green Papers. However, this discourse becomes more prominent in a later Green Paper from 1998 on piracy and counterfeiting in the Single Market. Piracy, according to the Commission, 'has major economic and social consequences for national economies, [and is] a major threat to economies in general as it may destabilise the markets' (1998, pp. 10–11). This is despite the Commission admission that the exact scale of piracy and counterfeiting was difficult to quantify and the exact impact unclear (1998,

p. 10), supporting the earlier consideration of the Commission as a risk-averse actor that seeks to mitigate the impact of uncertain threats. It is in the 2000 Follow-up that the link is explicitly made to internet-based piracy. While reiterating that counterfeiting and piracy are serious issues, and stating that action must be taken, for the first time the Commission appears to consider the issue of piracy not only as serious in itself, but serious in its association to other activities. The Commission states that 'apart from the economic and social consequences, the phenomenon appears to be increasingly linked to organised crime and is developing in new ways with the Internet' (2000, para. 1). On this basis, the Commission states that 'combating this phenomenon is of vital importance to the European Union' (2000, para. 1), committing to an action plan that would include supplementing the provisions of the TRIPS Agreement (2000, para. 2), and to propose a Directive that would harmonize aspects of the enforcement regime relating to procedures (2000, para. 14).

The Proposal for Directive 2004/48/EC on the enforcement of intellectual property rights was published in 2003. According to this Proposal, piracy and counterfeiting pose a significant threat to both economic and social structures, and 'in the context of the Internet, the rapidity of illegal operations and the difficulty of tracking the operations further reduce the risks for the criminal . . . counterfeiting and piracy thus appear to be a factor in promoting crime, including terrorism' (European Commission 2003, p. 12). So serious is the threat, according to the discourse of the Commission, that piracy on a commercial scale is more attractive to criminal organizations than drug trafficking (2003, p. 12). This particular argument is also raised in the 2005 IFPI report on piracy and serious crime, where it is stated that crime groups have been attracted to music piracy due to a perception due to 'high profits and the low risk of detection' (2005b, p. 5). Indeed, the link between organized crime and music piracy appears to have originated with these industry representatives – according to the Proposal, this information came from consultation with 'interested parties', which exposed the 'links between counterfeiting and piracy and organised crime' (2003, p. 12). These 'interested parties', states a 1999 press release, included 'trade associations, intellectual property right-holders, companies, lawyers, academics, national administrations [and] other EU institutions' (European Commission 1999). No reference was made to user groups or citizens. While internet user activist organizations were involved in lobbying the European Parliament after the Proposal became public (Haunss and Kohlmorgen 2010, p. 249), according to Haunss and Kohlmorgen, semi-structured interviews conducted with twenty-five key actors led to the finding that IFPI was actively involved in the drafting of the Enforcement Directive, and 'exerted great influence from the start' (2010, p. 255). The success of IFPI in being able to take an active role in drafting the proposal, and ensuring its smooth transmission through the Parliament, was largely down to a combination of 'good contacts with the European Parliament [and] active cooperation with the European Commission' (Haunss and Kohlmorgen 2010, p. 257). This appears to demonstrate significant network power being exercised by IFPI over the legislative process, operating at both the levels of the Parliament and Commission to ensure that favourable legislation is passed. It also demonstrates the dual power/knowledge functions in operation – first the power/knowledge that comes from perceptions of expertise, such as IFPI's ability to present statistics, demonstrate knowledge of the market and assist the Commission in the drafting process, and also the power that is exercised through knowledge of the lobbying system in the EU; having contacts among MEPs and good working links with the Commission. It would also seem to support the view of legal academics who suspect that within the European Commission's discourse on piracy, 'the threatening statistics emanated from trade groups and lobbyists' (Tapper 2010, p. 256). Indeed, as Bernhagen and Braüninger state, 'business lobbyists have incentives to misrepresent the size and likelihood of a policy's negative inducement effects. The problem for policymakers is that they often lack the information necessary to assess the accuracy or veracity of business' predictions' (2005, p. 47). In a position where an industry representative can exercise power over the legislative process in the way IFPI was apparently able, they are able to use the information asymmetry existing in order to ensure a favourable outcome. The discourse that appeared to begin with statements made by IFPI remained in the finalized Directive published in April 2004, where in recital 9 it is stated 'infringements of intellectual property rights appear to be increasingly linked to organised crime. Increasing use of the Internet enables pirated products to be distributed instantly around the globe'.

So was this an issue of pure regulatory capture, where no matter the public visibility of the struggle, the result was never in doubt? This is somewhat unlikely, and it would appear that IFPI in this particular instance benefited from the Enforcement Directive being drafted in an environment of quiet politics. According to Haunss and Kohlmorgen, the contention concerning the Enforcement Directive was only publicly visible between September 2003 and March 2004 (2009, p. 112), with only forty-seven claims (statements made in favour of or against the Directive) in that time, indicating that this issue was likely of low political salience (respective of the average voter). In comparison, lobbying over proposals regarding software patents (that was ultimately shelved by the Commission) was visible for a much longer period of time, with initial reporting beginning in 2009, with more than 277 claims being made (Haunss and Kohlmorgen 2009, pp. 112–13). Furthermore, coverage of the Enforcement Directive in the media was predominantly favourable, with the first statements being made exclusively by the Commission, whereas coverage of the proposal for software patents was largely negative. This appears to be confirmed by investigation into reporting by the BBC News website, and archives for *The Guardian*, *Telegraph* and *Daily Mail* for this time period. The BBC News archive had four stories, two representing views in favour of the Directive, one view opposing, and one neutral. The *Guardian* only had two stories, one positive and one negative, whereas the *Daily Mail* and *Telegraph* had no stories on the Enforcement Directive. According to Haunss and Kohlmorgen, the successful group of actors in both these conflicts were those who had their claims most reported in the media (2009, pp. 112–13). This assessment fits effectively the framework provided by Iyengar (1991), in which it was determined that the success of an actor in achieving its objectives in policymaking is determined by the ability to frame the issue effectively in the media. Through a combination of low salience and favourable media coverage, entertainment industry representatives were able to secure a Directive that was favourable to their interests.

The enforcement of copyright and intermediaries: the rationale of regulated self-regulation

Copyright enforcement on the internet is increasingly characterized by a more active form of intermediary involvement, largely reliant upon voluntary codes of conduct and agreements with right-holders (see for example Hugenholtz 2010; Swartout 2011; Bonadio 2011). For example, a voluntary agreement between enforcement agencies and Dutch Internet Service Providers was published in 2008 (Hugenholtz 2010, sec. II). The Dutch Code states that where informed of unlawful content being available, including copyrighted material (Code of Conduct 2008, p. 7), intermediaries should review the content and if satisfied that it is unlawful, immediately remove it without the need for any judicial involvement (2008, p. 3). Another example is the voluntary code adopted by Internet Service Providers in France prior to the HADOPI anti-piracy laws (IFPI 2008, p. 3; Swartout 2011, pp. 389–90). A significant body of the legal literature discusses these developments in terms of liability and legal obligation (see, for example, Hays 2007; Wei 2006; Strachan 2004; Rudkin-Binks and Melbourne 2009; Iglezikas 2012). This is understandable, given that the role of intermediaries as originally envisaged was covered by the E-Commerce Directive 2000/31/EC, which provides for an exclusion of liability for internet intermediaries involved in transmission ('mere conduit' under Article 12), caching (Article 13) and hosting (Article 14) of illegal content, so long as that service provider does not initiate the transmission of that illegal content, or in the case of caching or hosting, 'acts expeditiously' to remove that content once informed of its existence (Articles 13(e) and 14(b) respectively). Combined with Article 15's statement that intermediaries have no general obligation to monitor their services, nor actively seek out facts or circumstances indicating illegal activity, the role of the ISP became seen as being a 'passive' one (Swartout 2011). The adoption of more active modes of managing infringement, particularly through voluntary agreements, have therefore been interpreted in light of the exclusion of liability terms of the E-Commerce Directive, with writers attempting to reconcile the legal position with the observed practices. Others have gone beyond discussions of liability to discuss the role of internet intermediaries in regulation (Hugenholtz 2010; Swartout 2011; Frabboni 2010). It is submitted that considering intermediaries in terms of regulation is more effective than considering them in terms of liability, particularly given the dominant discourse concerning regulation and self-regulation that can be seen in discussions of governance. After all, if we consider that power is exercised through networks, and that networked forms of governance are increasingly displacing hierarchical modes of governance based on state or sovereign power, then changes to the role of intermediaries from passive to active nodes within that regulatory framework are more easily explained and understood in terms of regulation.

Regulatory capitalism, the internet and regulated self-regulation: a frame for the responsibility of intermediaries

The way in which state functions, services and regulatory mechanisms operate is understandably a particularly large field of research, characterized by many different perspectives, both descriptive and normative. One strand of this research characterizes the changing role of the state, subsequent to the reforms made by the Reagan and Thatcher governments, as 'neoliberalism'. Neoliberalism, according to Harvey, is a political ideology that maintains 'that human well-being can best be advanced by the maximisation of entrepreneurial freedoms within an institutional framework characterised by private property rights . . . the role of the State is to create and preserve an institutional framework appropriate to such practices' (2007, p. 22). In terms of practical effect, neoliberalism envisages a return to, and an expansion of, 'classical liberalism, entailing limited government, unregulated free markets and the sanctity of private property' (Robertson 2008, p. 27). Neoliberalism, put simply, is about minimizing state involvement in markets, 'cutting red tape' through deregulatory measures and creating the optimal environment for trade and commerce, such as through the creation of 'free trade agreements'. Another aspect of this neoliberal shift is privatization in various sectors, such as energy, transportation and, of particular relevance to this book, telecoms. However, as Braithwaite states, in the 1990s people 'started recognizing that while the state was running fewer things, it was regulating more of them' (Braithwaite 2008, p. xi). Copyright law, as this book has demonstrated, is one of these areas, in which from the 1990s onwards the number of regulatory instruments has substantially increased. As Levi-Faur and Jordana put it, 'if we were to judge neoliberalism by the degree of "deregulation" it attained, it would be a failure. If we were to judge it by the degree of "regulation" it promoted, it would be, on its own terms, a fiasco' (2005, p. 7). Instead, a more nuanced conceptualization of contemporary regulatory structures is that of 'regulatory capitalism'. Regulatory capitalism, according to Levi-Faur, who began the development of the concept, is:

> A distinctive order that critically differs from laissez-faire capitalism. In regulatory capitalism, the state retains responsibility for steering, while business increasingly takes over the functions of service provision and

technological innovation . . . [it entails] a restructuring of the state (through delegation and the creation of regulatory agencies) and the restructuring of business . . . through the creation of internal controls and mechanisms of self-regulation.

(2005, p. 15)

For Braithwaite, the term 'regulatory capitalism' more effectively describes the realities of contemporary regulation than terms such as 'regulatory society' or 'regulatory state' (2008, p. ix). The concept of regulatory capitalism is one that is highly compatible with the networks of power analysis undertaken in this book, as its emphasis lies on the networked nature of regulation in the twenty-first century. Bevir and Rhodes, for example, consider that government has shifted from the government of a unitary state to governance in and by networks (2003, p. 1), in which governmental institutions are just individual nodes within a greater network of regulators (and indeed, the regulated). Lazer states that the role of regulators has shifted from one of 'primarily being somewhat isolated decision makers to rich informational nodes in an international network' (2005, p. 54). In this way, regulation has been decentralized. In this respect, a view of regulatory capitalism as networked regulation fits effectively with Foucault's notion of governmentality; Leviathan has been struck down, and the state is not the highly centralized sovereign exercising power hierarchically upon subjects. Instead, regulation is performed and power exercised by and through various nodes within a network. The power is multilateral, and while there may be asymmetries in the ability to exercise that power, each node is nevertheless capable of exercising it. The role of the state in this conceptualization is as a regulator of regulators, or rather, 'rule-making displace public ownership and centralised administration through privatisation and the growth of autonomous regulatory agencies' (Wright 2011, p. 31). Within this framework, governments or legislative institutions pass laws or regulations that dictate how a particular sector should be regulated (for example, copyright law). However, the government does not take an active role in this regulation, but instead facilitates an environment in which autonomous agencies carry out this regulation. These 'regulated self-regulators' (Braithwaite 2008, p. 43; Parker 2002) are then responsible for activities within that particular sector.

As issues become transnational, the frame of reference for assessing power relations changes, and the state 'changes its role, its structure, and its functions, gradually evolving toward a new form of state: the network state' (Castells 2011, p. 18). In a system of globalization, the state 'becomes just a node (however important) of a particular network' (Castells 2011, p. 19). Internet intermediaries (used to distinguish specifically from Internet Service Providers, or ISPs) also form nodes within this global network. As Mueller states, 'most of the real world governance of the Internet is decentralised and emergent: it comes from the interactions of tens of thousands of network operators and service providers' (2010, p. 9). For example, the Internet Corporation for Assigned Names and

Numbers (ICANN) is a non-profit private organisation (neither controlled nor accountable to a governmental body) responsible for the coordination of the Internet Protocol address spaces, and their assignment to regional internet registries. ICANN is also responsible for maintaining the Domain Name System, which communicates a website address (such as www.google.com) into an IP address that a computer system can use to communicate with the requested service. The internet represents what Mueller refers to as a system of distributed control, distributing 'participation in and authority over networking' (2010, p. 4). This has repercussions for the state (or indeed, European institution) that attempts to control it. This is due to the combination of the scope of communication, which is transnational in nature and crosses jurisdictional boundaries, and the sheer volume of communications data, overwhelming 'the traditional governmental process to respond' (Mueller 2010, p. 4). Levi-Faur explicitly refers to the internet functioning in a networked fashion within a regulatory capitalism frame, with various nodes being involved in regulating different types of activities without direct governmental oversight (2006), as does Lazer (2005). Bartle and Vass also argue for the internet constituting forms of 'regulated self-regulation' (a term coined by Price and Verhulst 2005), providing examples of actors such as the Internet Watch Foundation who are actively involved in the identification and removal of child abuse images without any specific government mandate or statutory basis for its activities (2007, p. 894). For Christou and Simpson, the highly decentralized, globalized and complex nature of the internet has meant that self-regulation has featured prominently in deliberations concerning internet governance (2006, p. 49).

With regard to copyright, an example might make this difficulty clearer. At the height of its popularity, Napster was alleged to have over 80 million registered users exchanging digital music files (Gowan 2002). Napster use was international, and not limited to any one state. Should a state wish to assist private parties in proceedings against individuals for copyright infringement, their ability would be limited by jurisdiction. If, for example the state in question were the US, the only cases that could be brought would be against users within the US. Furthermore, the state would be limited in ability to process the amount of data that would be required to do so. For this reason, some of the earlier 'cyber-libertarian' internet governance literature argues that the state does not and cannot have a place on the internet. Instead, the internet would be governed by its own rules and regulations, as a place separate and distinct from the nation state (see, for example, Johnson and Post 1996; Friedland 1996). However, this view was quickly dispelled by cases such as *LICRA v Yahoo!* (2000), in which France successfully managed to ensure that online auctions of Nazi memorabilia could not be accessed within French territory (Goldsmith and Wu 2006, pp. 2–6). Goldsmith and Wu consider this an example of the way in which the state is still able to exercise power in the online environment, showing in their view that the internet is not 'a technology that resists territorial law [but] one that facilitates its enforcement' (2006, p. 10). While this may be to an extent true, this does seem to dismiss somewhat the ability for the internet to be used as a means of resistance (as shall be discussed in more detail in Chapter 8), and does not consider that states are not the only regulators on the internet. After all, to block the access to particular auctions in France required the intervention of an internet intermediary with the ability to perform that activity. Power is exercised through a node, in this instance an internet intermediary, by another node, in this instance a state. Yet this book has demonstrated throughout the last two chapters that this relationship is not one where power is exercised unilaterally. Nodes such as intermediaries, or business groups, are also able to exercise power upon states, or supranational organizations. For this reason, the discourse of the internet as governed by networks is more convincing as a means of understanding the way in which the internet is currently regulated.

Self-regulation in this form has become influential as a discourse since the late 1990s, when national and supranational bodies began to adopt these networked approaches to regulation. Lutz *et al.* argue that voluntary accords and codes of best practice 'are becoming increasingly prominent in European capitalism' (2011, p. 315), stating that the code movement began in the UK in the early 1990s and spread to almost all the Member States of the EU by 2001 (2011, p. 316). Ronit similarly argues that the EU has become increasingly interested in these 'new' or 'alternate' forms of governance (2008), a view that appears to be supported by the release of a Commission White Paper on Governance in 2001. This White Paper stated that 'co-regulation' (synonymous with regulated self-regulation according to Bartle and Vass (2007, p. 893) and Christou and Simpson (2006, p. 48)) may be appropriate as a form of regulation in certain areas, combining 'legislative and regulatory action with actions taken by the actors most concerned, drawing on their practical expertise', should such action not be in conflict with fundamental rights (2001, p. 21). The European Union in this respect sees itself as a 'facilitator' of self-regulation, in which industries are tasked with regulating their own activities (based on perceptions of expertise) rather than seeking to enforce top-down regulation of those industries (Knill and Lehmkuhl 2002). As Black maintains, this is at least partly due to the increasingly complex nature of the activities being regulated, with the result that knowledge and expertise are diffused among different actors, public and private, within a regulatory network (Black 2001). The next section of this chapter will analyse the way in which this discourse of regulated self-regulation began to be applied to ISPs and other internet intermediaries, and the role of knowledge, expertise and framing in embedding that discourse within European policy institutions.

Networks of power, quiet politics and intermediary involvement in the regulation of copyright

The development of a discourse in which internet intermediaries form an active node within the networked regulation of copyright enforcement appears to have been a gradual one. The 1988 Green Paper on challenges to copyright posed by technology makes no reference to the internet, intermediaries or end-user infringement, largely because in 1988, the fact that the internet would become a mass-scale network of access for the average person was not yet known. Instead, the predominant focus on enforcement action appeared to be upon the right to inspect factories and places of business in order to identify infringing materials (1988, sec. 2.6.27–40) and seizure at customs points on entry to the EEC (1988, sec. 2.6.41–54). Similarly, no mention is made of the internet in the 1990 Follow-Up, and the only reference made in the 1995 Green Paper is to the fact that even if people have not yet used the internet, they have 'at least heard talk of it' (1995a, p. 54). No mention is made of the role of online intermediaries (including ISPs) and their role in copyright enforcement in the 1995 Green Paper, or in the Proposal for the Directive or 1998 Green Paper on combating piracy. The Information Society Directive, however, directly makes reference to the role of internet intermediaries in the prevention of piracy, stating in recital 59 that 'in many cases such intermediaries are best placed to bring such infringing activities to an end'. Yet, where did this addition come from?

Analysis of Council deliberations on the Information Society Directive is enlightening in this respect. It appears that the Council, according to a document from 4 June 1999, included intermediaries in the form of a new right for rightholders to request injunctions against 'service providers' in order to prevent ongoing infringements as a 'compromise' (Council of the European Union 1999a, p. 3). This compromise was sought due the European Parliament wanting a strict application of the temporary reproduction rule, allowing for it only in instances where reproduction was carried out during use permitted by a rightholder, and the Commission, who wanted to ensure that temporary reproductions with no independent economic significance would be exempt (1999a, pp. 2–3). This resulted in an amendment of Article 8(2) to allow for injunctions in instances where 'service providers' are used by third parties to create temporary reproductions on the internet, 'knowing or having reasonable grounds to know that their activities would entail the infringement of a copyright or related right'. However, the Italian delegation in particular was sceptical of this addition to the paragraph, instead urging the Council to use more precise language and create the right as a new Article 8(3) (1999c, pp. 2–3). As a result of concerns of the Austrian and French delegations that 'service provider' was too narrow a term (1999c, p. 2), deliberations resulted in the adoption of a text on 23 November 1999 that referred specifically to intermediaries in Article 8(3) and created a new recital 36(bis) that became Recital 59, which included the text 'intermediaries are best placed to bring an end to such infringing activities' (1999b, pp. 13–14). In January 2000, this wording was largely accepted by the Member States at the Council (2000a, p. 6), and remained in the consolidated version of the Directive submitted to the Commission and European Parliament on 28 March 2000 (Council of the European Union 2000b). Interestingly, in a 2007 Report, the Commission made explicitly clear that this injunctive relief against ISPs was separate and independent from the liability provisions of the E-Commerce

Directive (2007, p. 10), indicating that the perception of the role of ISPs with regard to copyright infringement was increasingly being influenced by the concepts of networked governance.

By the time of the drafting of the Proposal on an Enforcement Directive, the role of intermediaries in copyright infringement processes appeared to be well established, with the ability of judicial bodies to grant injunctions against intermediaries being stated in then Article 11 (European Commission 2003, p. 37). While several Member States' delegations in the Council expressed reservations at the inclusion of intermediaries, the Commission maintained that there were no contradictions or incompatibilities with the proposed legislation and the 'safe-harbor' provisions of the E-Commerce Directive (Council of the European Union 2003, p. 7). Nevertheless, injunctions against intermediaries remained despite subsequent modifications of the Proposal by the Council (Council of the European Union 2004, p. 7) and were contained in the finalized Directive, with the proviso that rules concerning injunctions against internet service providers were already sufficiently harmonized by Article 8(3) of the Information Society Directive (Directive 2004/48/EC recital 23). However, as Reinbothe argues, this nevertheless means that injunctions can still be made against internet service providers, and that the right to information contained in Article 8 of the Enforcement Directive still applies in the case of all intermediaries (2010, sec. 8). ISPs lobbied heavily against their inclusion in the Enforcement Directive in a very heated battle between lobbyists representing two major industries, namely the intellectual property industry and the telecoms industry. Nevertheless, as was stated in an earlier section, this 'battle', while heated, was not particularly visible. Through an effective framing process and positive media coverage, the entertainment industry, and in particular IFPI, was able to secure the passing of the Enforcement Directive. As Haunss and Kohlmorgen found, the three biggest lobbyists against the Directive were British Telecom, Telecom Italia and Nokia (2009, p. 116), working under the auspices of the umbrella organization the European Telecommunications Network Operators Association (ETNO). Despite active lobbying on behalf of European telecoms companies, ETNO did not appear at all in media coverage of the Enforcement Directive process. This meant that the main thrust of ETNO's lobbying campaign, namely that the Directive would 'impose high costs on internet providers [was prevented from] entering the public discourse about the directive' (2009, p. 120). In this low salience conflict (as discussed with regard to the Enforcement Directive more generally), the ability to effectively frame the issue in the media is essential, and the fact that ISPs were not able to have their claims represented in the media was highly detrimental to their campaign. In comparison, as has been discussed, the frame in which new enforcement mechanisms were necessary to combat criminal activity became the dominant one, ensuring that the discourse concerning the Directive was one 'about fighting product piracy and [it] was necessary to protect consumers from counterfeit goods' (Haunss and Kohlmorgen 2009, p. 119). Furthermore, the strength of network relations played an important part in the passing of the Directive – whereas IFPI formed a strong 'single-issue' coalition with other intellectual property-based industries under the banner of the 'Anti-Piracy Coalition', the network of anti-Directive groups was much more fragmented, with consumer organizations representing consumer interests, and telecoms industry representatives focusing on costs to ISPs. As a result of this divided platform, IFPI were better placed to control the framing of discourse concerning the passing of the Directive (Haunss and Kohlmorgen 2010, pp. 255–7). The network opposing the Directive was comparatively weak, as well as being 'too small and developed too late to exert significant influence on the decision-making process' (Haunss and Kohlmorgen 2010, p. 257).

In the light of their success with the Enforcement Directive and the dominant discourse of regulating copyright infringement as a means of countering criminal activity, IFPI appears to continue solidifying a discourse in which ISPs and other internet intermediaries should function as self-regulating regulators taking an active role in 'policing' infringing activity on the internet. IFPI's Online Music Report 2004 discusses the role of ISPs in taking down infringing material, stating that in the 'vast majority of cases, they have voluntarily blocked or taken down the sites or files identified as infringing [and that] no legal proceedings or other formal procedures are required' (2004, p. 14). This theme continues in the 2005 Report (2005a, p. 21), and in 2006 IFPI states that the 'music industry and its ISP partners have a shared interest and a shared responsibility in controlling copyright infringement on the internet' (2006, p. 17). In 2007, IFPI referred to this responsibility as 'an accepted principle' (2007, p. 3). This responsibility as perceived by IFPI was made clear when it drafted a code of conduct for ISPs with regard to tackling copyright infringement that was then presented to ISPs at the 2005 ETNO conference (European Digital Rights (EDRI) 2005). While ETNO appeared to have been resistant to such demands, this discourse of ISP responsibility became dominant among policymakers at both the national and European levels. According to one report, in 2008 Lord Triesman, then UK Minister for Intellectual Property, threatened ISPs with legislation should they not come to an agreement with the entertainment industry regarding means of tackling online infringement of copyright (Williams 2008). This statement followed the conclusion in the Gowers Review that agreements between the ISPs and copyright holders should be encouraged as a means of tackling online infringement, and that 'if there is a failure to agree, the Government should look towards establishing an appropriate statutory protocol' (Gowers 2006, sec. 5.99). The European Commission also appears to share the view that agreements between intermediaries and right-holders are to be encouraged, stating in a 2009 Communication that such arrangements could 'become a foundation for best practice in the fight against counterfeiting and piracy at global level' (2009, sec. 4.2). Should these voluntary agreements not take place, the Commission indicated that it was 'ready to consider alternative approaches, if needed in the future' (2009, sec. 4.2). In a subsequent Resolution, the Council stated that it encouraged 'relevant stakeholders to pursue on-going dialogues and to resolutely seek agreements on voluntary practical measures aimed at reducing counterfeiting and piracy in the internal market' (Council of the European Union 2010, para. 40).

It would therefore seem that the view of intermediaries as regulatory nodes, well placed to monitor and tackle infringement in co-operation with right-holders has become dominant in European institutional discourse. That this view appears to have become dominant can be evidenced by a Commission Communication from December 2010, where it is stated that 'given intermediaries' favourable position to contribute to the prevention and termination of online infringements, the Commission could explore how to involve them more closely' (2010, sec. 3.3). That there is a threat of subsequent legislation should voluntary arrangements not be achieved does not necessarily mean that actions taken by ISPs within this framework do not constitute self-regulated acts. According to Bartle and Vass, it is often implicit within the tacit monitoring that there is a threat of the introduction of state-led regulation if the industry does not make significant changes (2007, p. 895). ' "Voluntary" action of self-regulators, though important, is conditioned and constrained by action (often implicit) of the state' (Bartle and Vass 2007, p. 895). That the Commission maintains the view that intermediaries form an important node in the regulation of copyright infringement online can be seen in an April 2013 Working Document released subsequent to the review of the E-Commerce Directive, where it is stated that with regard to civil enforcement of intellectual property rights, 'voluntary collaborative approaches can strengthen the protection of both right holders and consumers' (European Commission 2013, p. 18). What is particularly interesting about the concept of the intermediary as regulator is the networked development of the concept – what initially began as the result of a textual compromise in the 2001 Directive was gradually built upon within a 'regulated self-regulation' framework into a discourse concerning the responsibility of intermediaries as part of a diffuse, decentralized system of copyright regulation. Nevertheless, while intermediary regulation of copyright infringement appears to be a principle accepted by European policy institutions, it is by no means a settled matter, as shall be discussed in further detail in Chapters 7 and 8.

Concluding remarks

As was discussed in the previous chapter of this book, the success of the entertainment industry in ensuring that legislation beneficial to their perceived interests is not solely attributable to European institutions wishing to keep 'big business' happy. In both the development of the Information Society Directive and the Enforcement Directive, IFPI was very actively involved in the early stages of both legislative processes, both providing expert data and setting the frame for acceptable discourse. While this was discussed with regard to the passing of the Information Society more generally in the previous chapter, this chapter has demonstrated how the provision of data on rates of infringement prior to the development of proposals in both instances was influential in determining the approach that the Commission and other European institutions took to the issue of copyright enforcement (irrespective of the contentiousness of the data provided by the entertainment industry). The reliance of the Commission on this perceived expertise can also in part be explained by the strong network relations existing between IFPI and European institutions, which in turn is also explained by knowledge produced and possessed by representatives such as IFPI. After all, as Foucault discussed, while power operates through networks and all nodes are theoretically able to exert influence, some are preferential nodes, more effectively able to exercise power than others. Becoming a preferential node is somewhat reliant on dominant discourses and operations of power/knowledge, as demonstrated by the success of IFPI in framing copyright debates. In comparison, representatives of telecoms agencies such as ETNO constituted less privileged actors, coming into the legislative process relatively late in the development of the Enforcement Directive, maintaining weaker network relationships, and attempting to act against a dominant discourse.

The importance of effective framing should not be underestimated, based on the discussion in this chapter. Through the research performed by Haunss and Kohlmorgen, it becomes readily apparent that proponents of the Enforcement Directive were much more visible in the media than those opposed to the Directive. Despite the fact that 'behind the scenes' an intense lobbying campaign was apparently being waged by ETNO, the views of ISPs were not represented in the media at all, with the effect that the discourse of the Enforcement Directive as a means of combating illegal activities dominated what little reporting there was. The paucity of news coverage concerning the Enforcement Directive also contributes to the notion that in low salience issues, those industries most able to position themselves as experts, develop good working relations with institutions such as the European Commission and ensure positive media coverage, are more likely to ensure that their preferences are secured, even where other lobbying bodies are also large corporate organizations. As shall be demonstrated in the next chapter, these networks of power are not only useful in cases where certain industries or actors wish to see legislative changes being made. An environment of quiet politics can be equally useful to industries wishing to ensure that certain legislation is not passed, or non-favourable clauses removed from intended legislation, which can have a negative impact on policy objectives of European institutions such as the Commission.

Bibliography

Adermon, A. and Liang, C.Y., 2010. 'Piracy, music and movies: A natural experiment'. Working Paper, Uppsala University. Uppsala: Sweden.

Barnier, M., 2011. 'To be or not to be: Copyright makes all the difference'. In F. Gevers and E. Cornu, eds, *The future prospects for intellectual property in the EU: 2012–2022*. Brussels: Bruylant.

Bartle, I. and Vass, P., 2007. 'Self-regulation within the regulatory state: Towards a new regulatory paradigm?' *Public Administration*, 85(4), pp. 885–905.

BBC News, 2009. 'File-sharers are big spenders too'. *BBC*. Available at: http://news. bbc.co.uk/2/hi/technology/8337887.stm [Accessed 17 July 2013].

Bernhagen, P. and Bräuninger, T., 2005. 'Structural power and public policy: A signaling model of business lobbying in democratic capitalism'. *Political Studies*, 53(1), pp. 43–64.

Bevir, M. and Rhodes, R.A., 2003. *Interpreting British governance*. London: Routledge.

Black, J., 2001. 'Decentring regulation: Understanding the role of regulation and self regulation in a "post-regulatory" world'. *Current Legal Problems*, 54(1), pp. 103–46.

Bonadio, E., 2011. 'File sharing, copyright and freedom of speech'. *European Intellectual Property Review*, 33(10), pp. 619–31.

Boyle, J., 2008. *The public domain: Enclosing the commons of the mind*. New Haven, CT: Yale University Press.

Boyle, J., 2010. 'Fantasy and reality in intellectual property policy'. *The Public Domain*. Available at: www.thepublicdomain.org/2010/12/01/fantasy-reality-in-intellectual-property-policy/ [Accessed 17 July 2013].

Braithwaite, J., 2008. *Regulatory capitalism: How it works, ideas for making it work better*. Cheltenham: Edward Elgar.

Buck, P. de, 2011. 'Expectations of European companies as regards intellectual property in Europe and globally'. In F. Gevers and E. Cornu, eds, *The future prospects for intellectual property in the EU: 2012–2022*. Brussels: Bruylant.

Cammaerts, B. and Meng, B., 2011. *Creative destruction and copyright protection: Regulatory reponses to file-sharing*. London: London School of Economics and Political Science, Department of Media and Communications.

Castells, M., 2011. *Communication power*. Oxford: Oxford University Press.

Christou, G. and Simpson, S., 2006. 'The internet and public-private governance in the European Union'. *Journal of Public Policy*, 26(1), pp. 43–61.

Code of Conduct, 2008. *Notice-and-takedown code of conduct*. The Netherlands. Available at: www.isoc.nl/info/nieuws/NTD_CodeOfConduct.pdf [Accessed 15 July 2013].

Council of the European Union, 1999a. *Amended proposal for a Directive of the European Parliament and of the Council on the harmonisation of certain aspects of copyright and related rights in the Information Society*. Brussels: Council of the European Union.

Council of the European Union, 1999b. *Amended proposal for a Directive of the European Parliament and of the Council on the harmonisation of certain aspects of copyright and related rights in the Information Society: Revised version*. Brussels: Council of the European Union.

Council of the European Union, 1999c. *Proposal for a European Parliament and Council Directive on the harmonisation of certain aspects of copyright and related rights in the Information Society: Consolidated text of Article 5*. Brussels: Council of the European Union.

Council of the European Union, 2000a. *Amended proposal for a Directive of the European Parliament and of the Council on the harmonisation of certain aspects of copyright and related rights in the Information Society*. Brussels: Council of the European Union.

Council of the European Union, 2000b. *Amended proposal for a Directive of the European Parliament and of the Council on the harmonisation of certain aspects of copyright and related rights in the Information Society: Consolidated text*. Brussels: Council of the European Union.

Council of the European Union, 2003. *Proposal for a Directive of the European Parliament and of the Council on measures and procedures to ensure the enforcement of intellectual property rights.* Brussels: Council of the European Union.

Council of the European Union, 2004. *Proposal for a Directive of the European Parliament and of the Council on the measures and procedures to ensure the enforcement of intellectual property rights: Outcome of the European Parliament's first reading (Strasbourg, 8–11 March 2004).* Brussels: Council of the European Union.

Council of the European Union, 2010. *Commission Communication: Enhancing the enforcement of intellectual property rights in the internal market: Adoption of a Council Resolution.* Brussels: Council of the European Union.

David, M., 2010. *Peer to peer and the music industry the criminalization of sharing.* Los Angeles, CA: Sage.

Drahos, P. and Braithwaite, J., 2002. *Information feudalism: Who owns the knowledge economy?* London: Earthscan.

European Commission, 1988. *Green Paper on copyright and the challenge of technology: Copyright issues requiring immediate action.* Brussels: European Commission.

European Commission, 1991. *Follow-up to the Green Paper: Working programme of the Commission in the field of copyright and neighbouring rights.* Brussels: European Commission.

European Commission, 1995a. *Green Paper: Copyright and related rights in the Information Society.* Brussels: European Commission.

European Commission, 1995b. *Replies from interested parties on copyright and neighbouring rights in the Information Society.* Luxembourg: European Commission.

European Commission, 1998. *Green Paper: Combating counterfeiting and piracy in the Single Market.* Brussels: European Commission.

European Commission, 1999. 'Counterfeiting and piracy: Munich hearing endorses need for EU action'. *Europa.* Available at: http://ec.europa.eu/internal_market/smn/smn17/s17mn37.htm [Accessed 17 July 2013].

European Commission, 2000. *Communication from the Commission to the Council, the European Parliament and the Economic and Social Committee: Follow-up to the Green Paper on combating counterfeiting and piracy in the single market.* Brussels: European Commission.

European Commission, 2001. *European Governance: A White Paper.* Brussels: European Commission.

European Commission, 2003. *Proposal for a Directive of the European Parliament and of the Council on measures and procedures to ensure the enforcement of intellectual property rights.* Brussels: European Commission.

European Commission, 2007. *Report to the Council, the European Parliament and the Economic and Social Committee on the application of Directive 2001/29/EC on the harmonisation of certain aspects of copyright and related rights in the information society.* Brussels: European Commission.

European Commission, 2009. *Communication from the Commission to the Council, the European Parliament and the European Economic and Social Committee: Enhancing the enforcement of intellectual property rights in the internal market.* Brussels: European Commission.

European Commission, 2010. *Application of Directive 2004/48/EC of the European Parliament and the Council of 29 April 2004 on the enforcement of intellectual property rights.* Brussels: European Commission.

European Commission, 2013. *Commission Staff Working Document: E-Commerce Action plan 2012–2015, State of play 2013*. Brussels: European Commission.

European Digital Rights (EDRI), 2005. 'ISP self-regulation proposal entertainment industry'. *EDRI*. Available at: www.edri.org/edrigram/number3.7/takedown [Accessed 22 July 2013].

Farrand, B., 2014. 'The digital agenda for Europe, the economy and its impact upon the development of EU copyright policy' (forthcoming).

Farrand, B. and Carrapico, H., 2012. 'Copyright law as a matter of (inter)national security? The attempt to securitise commercial infringement and its spillover onto individual liability'. *Crime, Law and Social Change*, 57(4), pp. 373–401.

Frabboni, M.M., 2010. 'File-sharing and the role of intermediaries in the marketplace: National, European and international developments'. In I.A. Stamatoudi, ed., *Copyright enforcement and the Internet*. Alphen aan den Rijn, The Netherlands; Frederick, MD: Kluwer Law International.

Friedland, L.A., 1996. 'Electronic democracy and the new citizenship'. *Media, Culture and Society*, 18, pp. 185–212.

Goldsmith, J.L. and Wu, T., 2006. *Who controls the Internet? Illusions of a borderless world*. Oxford: Oxford University Press.

Gowan, M., 2002. 'Requiem for Napster'. *TechHive*. Available at: www.techhive.com/article/100004/article.html [Accessed 18 July 2013].

Gowers, A., 2006. *The Gowers review of intellectual property*. HM Treasury.

Hakfoort, J., 2002. 'Copyright in the digital age: The economic rationale re-examined'. In R. Towse, ed., *Copyright in the cultural industries*. Cheltenham: Edward Elgar.

Harvey, D., 2007. 'Neoliberalism as creative destruction'. *The ANNALS of the American Academy of Political and Social Science*, 610(1), pp. 21–44.

Haunss, S. and Kohlmorgen, L., 2009. 'Lobbying or politics? Political claims making in IP conflicts'. In S. Haunss and K.C. Shadlen, eds, *Politics of intellectual property: Contestation over the ownership, use, and control of knowledge and information*. Cheltenham: Edward Elgar.

Haunss, S. and Kohlmorgen, L., 2010. 'Conflicts about intellectual property claims: The role and function of collective action networks'. *Journal of European Public Policy*, 17(2), pp. 242–62.

Hays, T., 2007. 'Secondary liability for infringements of copyright-protected works: Part 2'. *European Intellectual Property Review*, 29(1)(15–21).

Hugenholtz, P.B., 2010. 'Codes of conduct and copyright enforcement in cyberspace'. In I.A. Stamatoudi, ed., *Copyright enforcement and the Internet*. Alphen aan den Rijn, The Netherlands; Frederick, MD: Kluwer Law International.

Huygen, A., Helberger, N., Poort, J., Rutten, P., Eijk, and N. van, 2009. *Ups and downs; economic and cultural effects of file sharing on music, film and games*. Rochester, NY: Social Science Research Network. Available at: http://papers.ssrn.com/abstract=1350451 [Accessed 17 July 2013].

IFPI (International Federation of the Phonographic Industry), 2000. *Music piracy report 2000*.

IFPI, 2001. *Music piracy report 2001*.

IFPI, 2002. *Music piracy report 2002*.

IFPI, 2004. *IFPI online music report 2004*.

IFPI, 2005a. *IFPI digital music report 2005*.

IFPI, 2005b. *Music piracy: Serious, violent and organised crime*.

IFPI, 2006. *IFPI digital music report 2006.*

IFPI, 2007. *IFPI digital music report 2007.*

IFPI, 2008. *IFPI digital music report 2008.*

IFPI, 2009. *IFPI digital music report 2009.*

IFPI, 2011. *IFPI digital music report 2011.*

Iglezikas, I., 2012. 'The legal struggle in the EU against online piracy'. In T.-H. Synodinou, ed., *Codification of European copyright law: Challenges and perspectives.* Alphen aan den Rijn: Kluwer Law International.

Iyengar, S., 1991. *Is anyone responsible?: How television frames political issues.* Chicago, IL: University of Chicago Press.

Johns, A., 2010. 'Language, practice and history'. In L. Bently, J. Davis, and J.C. Ginsburg, eds, *Copyright and piracy: An interdisciplinary critique.* Cambridge; New York: Cambridge University Press.

Johns, A., 2011. *Piracy: The intellectual property wars from Gutenberg to Gates.* Chicago, IL: University of Chicago Press.

Johnson, D. and Post, D.G., 1996. 'Law and borders: The rise of law in cyberspace'. *Stanford Law Review, 48*, p. 1367.

Karaganis, J., 2011. *Media piracy in emerging economies.* United States of America: Social Sciences Research Council.

Kioupis, D., 2010. 'Criminal liability on the internet'. In I.A. Stamatoudi, ed., *Copyright enforcement and the Internet.* Alphen aan den Rijn, The Netherlands; Frederick, MD: Kluwer Law International.

Knill, C. and Lehmkuhl, D., 2002. 'The national impact of European Union regulatory policy: Three Europeanization mechanisms'. *European Journal of Political Research, 41*(2), pp. 255–80.

Kohli, V., 2001. 'Mutilating music: A critical look at the copyright and business issues in online music distribution'. *Entertainment Law Review, 121*(1), pp. 15–24.

Kretschmer, M. and Towse, R., 2013. *What constitutes evidence for copyright policy.* Poole, UK: Bournemouth University.

Laïdi, Z., 2010. 'Europe as a risk averse power: A hypothesis'. *Garnet Policy Brief 11*, pp. 1–18

Lazer, D., 2005. 'Regulatory capitalism as a networked order: The international system as an informational network'. *The ANNALS of the American Academy of Political and Social Science, 598*(1), pp. 52–66.

Levi-Faur, D., 2005. 'The rise of regulatory capitalism: The global diffusion of a new order'. *The ANNALS of the American Academy of Political and Social Science, 598*(1), pp. 12–32.

Levi-Faur, D., 2006. 'Regulatory capitalism: The dynamics of change beyond telecoms and electricity'. *Governance, 19*(3), pp. 497–525.

Levi-Faur, D. and Jordana, J., 2005. 'Globalizing regulatory capitalism'. *The ANNALS of the American Academy of Political and Social Science, 598*(1), pp. 6–9.

Liebowitz, S.J., 2005. 'Economists' topsy-turvy view of piracy'. *Review of Economic Research on Copyright Issues, 2*(1), pp. 5–17.

Liebowitz, S.J., 2006. 'File-sharing: Creative destruction or just plain destruction?' *Journal of Law and Economics*, April, pp. 1–28.

Lütz, S., Eberle, D. and Lauter, D., 2011. 'Varieties of private self-regulation in European capitalism: Corporate governance codes in the UK and Germany'. *Socio-Economic Review, 9*(2), pp. 315–38.

McCreevy, C., 2009. *Closing remarks: High level conference on counterfeiting and piracy.* Brussels: European Commission.

Mandelson, P., 2009. *Digital economy bill second reading [HL]*. Westminster: Hansard. Available at: www.publications.parliament.uk/pa/ld200910/ldhansrd/text/91202–0002.htm [Accessed 15 July 2013].

Mortimer, J.H., Sorensen, A. and Nosko, C., 2010. 'Supply responses to digital distribution: Recorded music and live performances'. Working Paper, Harvard University.

Mueller, M., 2010. *Networks and states: The global politics of Internet governance*. Cambridge, MA: MIT Press.

Nielsen, 2012. *Consumer confidence, concerns and spending intentions around the world*, nielsen. Available at: http://tw.nielsen.com/documents/NielsenGlobalConsumerConfidenceReportQ32012.pdf [Accessed 15 July 2013].

Norwegian Business School, 2009. 'Downloading music and CD purchases'. *Norwegian Business School*. Available at: www.bi.no/en/About-BI/News/News-archive-2009/Downloading-music-and-CD-purchases/ [Accessed 17 July 2013].

Olberholzer-Gee, F. and Strumpf, K., 2007. 'The effect of file sharing on album sales: An empirical analysis'. *Journal of Political Economy*, 115, p. 1.

Organization for Economic Cooperation and Development, 2009. *Piracy of digital content*.

Parker, C., 2002. *The open corporation: Effective self-regulation and democracy*. New York: Cambridge University Press.

Patry, W.F., 2009. *Moral panics and the copyright wars*. New York: Oxford University Press.

Price, M.E. and Verhulst, S.G., 2005. *Self-regulation and the internet*. The Hague; Frederick, MD: Kluwer Law International; Aspen.

Regnier, O., 2003. 'The point of view of the music industry'. In F. Gotzen, Katholieke Universiteit te Leuven and Centrum voor Intellectuele Rechten, eds, *The future of intellectual property in the global market of the information society: Who is going to shape the IPR system in the new millennium?* Bruxelles: Bruylant.

Reinbothe, J., 2010. 'The EU Enforcement Directive 2004/48/EC as a tool for copyright enforcement'. In I.A. Stamatoudi, ed., *Copyright enforcement and the internet*. Alphen aan den Rijn, The Netherlands; Frederick, MD: Kluwer Law International.

Reyman, J., 2012. *The rhetoric of intellectual property: Copyright law and the regulation of digital culture*. New York: Routledge.

Robertson, M., 2008. 'Property and privatisation in RoboCop'. *International Journal of Law in Context*, 4(3), pp. 217–35.

Ronit, K., 2008. 'Self-regulation and public regulation: Financial services and the out-of-court complaints bodies'. In J.-C. Graz and A. Nölke, eds, *Transnational private governance and its limits*. London; New York: Routledge.

Rudkin-Binks, J. and Melbourne, S., 2009. 'The new "three strikes" regime for copyright enforcement in New Zealand: Requiring ISPs to step up to the fight'. *Entertainment Law Review*, 20(4), pp. 146–9.

Sanchez, J., 2008. '750,000 lost jobs? The dodgy digits behind the war on piracy.' *Ars Technica*. Available at: http://arstechnica.com/tech-policy/2008/10/dodgy-digits-behind-the-war-on-piracy/ [Accessed 17 July 2013].

Seville, C., 2010. 'Nineteenth-century Anglo-US copyright relations: The language of piracy versus the moral high ground'. In L. Bently, J. Davis, and J.C. Ginsburg, eds, *Copyright and piracy: An interdisciplinary critique*. Cambridge; New York: Cambridge University Press.

Strachan, J., 2004. 'The internet of tomorrow: The new-old communications tool of control'. *European Intellectual Property Review*, 26(3), pp. 123–36.

Swartout, C.M., 2011. 'Toward a regulatory model of internet intermediary liability: File-sharing and copyright enforcement'. *Northwestern Journal of International Law and Business, 31*, p. 499.

Tapper, C., 2010. 'Criminality and copyright'. In D. Vaver and L. Bently, eds, *Intellectual property in the new millennium: Essays in honour of William R. Cornish*. Cambridge: Cambridge University Press.

Tapscott, D. and Williams, A.D., 2010. *MacroWikinomics: Rebooting business and the world*. London: Atlantic.

The Economist, 2010. 'What's working in music: Having a ball'. *The Economist*. Available at: www.economist.com/node/17199460 [Accessed 17 July 2013].

Valenti, J., 1978. *Hearings before the subcommittee on Courts, Civil Liberties and the Administration of Justice of the Committee on the Judiciary: Home recording of copyrighted works*. Washington: US Government Printing Office.

Valenti, J., 1982. *Home recording of copyrighted works*. Washington, DC: US Government Printing Office.

Wei, W., 2006. 'The liability of internet service providers for copyright infringement and defamation actions in the United Kingdom and China: A comparative study'. *European Intellectual Property Review, 28*(10), pp. 528–34.

Wikström, P., 2009. *The music industry: Music in the cloud*. Cambridge: Polity.

Williams, C., 2008. 'Government piles filesharing pressure on UK ISPs'. *The Register*. Available at: www.theregister.co.uk/2008/01/08/triesman_isps_legislation_timetable [Accessed 22 July 2013].

Wright, J.S., 2011. 'Regulatory capitalism and the UK Labour Government's reregulation of commissioning in the English National Health Service'. *Law and Policy, 33*(1), pp. 27–59.

Zentner, A., 2006. 'Measuring the effect of file sharing on music purchases'. *Journal of Law and Economics, 49*, pp. 63–90.

Chapter 6

Networks of power III

The role of industry representatives in framing policies regarding cross-border licensing

> Competition has been shown to be useful up to a certain point and no further, but cooperation, which is the thing we must strive for today, begins where competition leaves off.
>
> (Franklin D. Roosevelt, 3 March 1912)

The issue of the slow growth in multi-territory cross-border licensing in the EU is a highly complex issue and, as demonstrated in Chapters 2 and 3, one that both legislative and judicial bodies have not been effectively able to address. Nevertheless, new proposals for a Directive on cross-border licensing have been introduced that seek to ensure that multi-territory licensing is facilitated by means of ensuring free and effective competition in the market for licensing services. Indeed, the lack of multi-territory licenses for European digital music provision has been effectively framed as being a competition issue, rather than a harmonization one. This chapter will seek to demonstrate how this has occurred, and the direct and indirect roles that the music industry has had in this framing through the provision of expert knowledge.

The structure of this chapter is as follows. Given the high complexity of collective management, the chapter will begin with an overview of the traditional role of collecting societies as territorially bound 'monopolies' that exist for the protection of right-holders. The chapter will continue by examining these justifications in greater detail, demonstrating the traditional acceptance of these monopolies on the grounds of the protections they afforded, the economies of scale and reduction of transaction costs afforded by collecting societies having territorial exclusivity, and the role of competition law as a regulator rather than a breaker of these monopolies.

What is a collecting society and how does it function?

A collecting society is an organization responsible for the management of the economic rights of the right-holders it represents. Towse defines them as 'membership collectives that administer specific rights accorded to authors and publishers under copyright law, by licensing users and distributing the revenues to their members' (2004, p. 64). An important characteristic of collecting societies is their position as the administrator of the rights of all members within a particular geographical location. For example, PRS for Music administers musical copyrights in the UK. SACEM administers those same rights in France. GEMA manages rights in Germany. Collecting societies are organized country-by-country and profession-by-profession (IRIS 2009, p. 2) meaning that each collecting society manages the rights of a particular type of right-holder. For example, whereas PRS for Music represents composers and performers in the UK, the Artists Collecting Society, or ACS, administers artists' (such as painters and sculptors) resale rights. Different collecting societies within a given territory tend not to compete but specialize in various sets of rights and/or types of right-holders (Handke and Towse 2007, pp. 940–1). It is possible for collecting societies to manage both types of right (such as SACEM does), or for the rights to be managed separately by different collecting societies (as was the case in the UK with the MCPS managing mechanical rights and the PRS managing public performance rights, until the two bodies merged to form the PRS for Music organization).

With regard to the management of music, collecting societies manage two particular rights – the mechanical reproduction right, and the public performance right. The mechanical reproduction right is that over the reproduction of the musical work on the mechanical form on which it is stored. It covers, for example, the reproduction of an album by making pressings of CDs, which are then sold in music stores, and ultimately constitutes 'the right of the author to authorise the sound recording of its work' (Sterling 1998, p. 778). The public performance right concerns the interest of an artist to be reimbursed for the public performance of their work. According to Dehin, this distinction arose prior to the online exploitation of music, at a time when reproduction and performance were two distinct activities (2010, p. 221). Brinker and Holzmuller state that the territoriality of licensing is to be expected, given that copyright is a nationally exercised right, stating that as long as 'the principle of territoriality remains undisputed in the European Union, copyright and related rights originate and exist independently in each Member State' (2010, p. 553). Licenses, therefore, are also territorially limited. As such, the position of a collecting society within a Member State is that of a national monopoly. This chapter will also discuss the perceived role of major music publishers as members of these collecting societies, and the potentially negative impact on smaller right-holders and individual authors, composers and performers, before giving consideration to the changing role of collecting societies online. The chapter will conclude by considering the predominant discourse of competition in which the legislative initiatives concerning collecting societies have taken place, and the construction of the problem of multi-territory licensing as one of competition. In these final two sections, the role of the music industry in framing collecting societies' anti-competitive practices as being at the heart of limited provision of multi-territory licenses rather than a lack of harmonization of certain aspects of copyright law will be analysed, demonstrating how an environment of high technical complexity and low political salience allow industry experts to both frame and work within dominant discourses.

The traditional perception of the role of collecting societies

The position of collecting societies as national monopolies has generally been tolerated, as traditionally they have been perceived as an efficient way of overcoming the problem of high transaction costs for administering copyright (Handke and Towse 2007, p. 938). According to Handke and Towse, due to the complexity of music markets, and identifying right-holders on the one hand and users of content on the other, the transaction costs that accrue just for the purposes of finding potential trading partners and to negotiate the terms of trade can be very high (2007, p. 938). WIPO states that an average of 60,000 musical works are broadcast on television each year, necessitating the identification, contacting and negotiation with artists in order to be able to license that content (WIPO 2013). By having an organization that collectively assigns and licenses these rights, this discourse maintains, the potential search costs of copyright users decreases substantially. Collecting societies achieve this reduction in costs by granting blanket licenses to copyright users that allow them, for a pre-determined fee, to use any and all of the works managed by a particular collecting society. This view was held by the US Supreme Court in *BMI v CBS* (1979), where the Court determined that the issuing of blanket licenses is by far the most effective system for both right-holders and right users due to the simplification of the purchasing and granting of licenses, and the reduced complexity in monitoring the public performance of works (1979, para. 20 of the judgment). In essence, the question is a simple 'does the user have a license?', rather than 'does the user have a license for this particular work?'. The argument, ultimately, is one of 'convenience and practicality' (Wallis *et al.* 1999, p. 11). Similarly, this discourse runs, collecting societies benefit from economies of scale, insofar as where licenses are identical (as each user is granted a blanket license) and the means of gaining licenses for particular works requires making one general inquiry about an entire repertoire, rather than being based on selection of a certain number of songs, 'the average cost of monitoring and enforcing the copyright of thousands, even millions of works . . . falls rapidly with the number of works represented' (Handke and Towse 2007, p. 939; see also Katz 2005, p. 554). In other words, by granting blanket licenses, and controlling the complete repertoire available in a particular territory, it actually becomes easier and more cost-effective to monitor the usage of this music. For these reasons, Posner argues that the position of collecting societies is one of the 'natural' monopolist, in which a monopoly is actually more efficient and effective than a competitive market (Posner 2001, pp. 30–1).

The view of the CJEU, it would appear, is that collecting societies constitute necessary actors in copyright management, and will not normally be considered as being in breach of competition law as a general principle. As Brinker and Holzmuller state, when the question is asked whether the restriction of the licensing and granting of licenses to a particular Member State is anti-competitive, 'the clear answer is no' (2010, p. 553). According to the *BRT v SABAM* (1974) case, this is because collecting societies are viewed as protecting the interests of its right-holding members, and operates on a scale necessary to perform this activity (paras 9–10 of the decision). This reasoning was expanded upon by Advocate General Mayras, who stated that as an individual author or publisher is not in a position to effectively monitor and administer their own rights effectively, therefore it is necessary to assign those rights to a body able to manage them on their behalf (*BRT v SABAM*, Advocate General's Opinion at p. 324). The question has been raised whether the formation of collecting societies may constitute an anti-competitive agreement between the members of a collecting society. The rationale for such consideration is based in the fact that because licensing operates in the form of blanket licensing, this helps to eliminate competition between artists who no longer have any need to compete; 'by pooling costs, the authors of the most popular works end up indirectly subsidising other members' (Handke and Towse 2007, p. 944). From the Commission decision in *Re GEMA Statutes*, it would appear that these agreements are deemed to have no object or effect beyond the normal activities and purposes of a copyright collecting society (1982, para. 54 of the decision). As Brinker and Holzmuller state, a collecting society is akin to a union for authors, and the elimination of price competition between members of a collecting society has been recognized as a 'necessary counterbalance to the superior market power of industrial right users' (Brinker and Holzmuller 2010, p. 554). A 2004 European Parliament Resolution on the issue of collective management and cross-border licensing made it clear that in the Parliament's opinion, the position of de facto national monopoly that collecting societies in the EU enjoy does not in principle pose a problem for competition, and that collecting societies carry out tasks in the public interest and in the interests of right-holders and users (European Parliament 2004, sec. 14). Furthermore, the European Parliament stated that it sees collecting societies as constituting an 'indispensable link between creators and users of copyrighted works' (European Parliament 2004, sec. 25). However, the Parliament also stated that it is important for competition law authorities to subject collecting societies to scrutiny in individual cases of suspected abuse, 'so as to be able successfully to ensure rights management also in the future' (2004, sec. 14).

Competition authorities can intervene where it is determined that a collecting society's terms of membership are deemed to be unduly onerous, as in *BRT v SABAM*, where it was determined the assignment of rights to the collecting society should be limited to what is appropriate and absolutely necessary to meet the goals of collective administration (1974, para. 11). For this reason, the assignment of not only existing but also future rights for an extended period after the ending of the business relationship between collecting society and member would constitute an abuse of a dominant position (1974, para. 12). This decision was in essence the confirmation of a 1971 decision of the Commission in *Re GEMA (No. 1)* in which the Commission determined that an obligation to assign an unduly broad category of rights, in this case all existing and future rights over a worldwide repertoire, would constitute the abuse of a dominant position (Guibault and Gompel 2006, p. 121). Furthermore, and of relevance to cross-border rights, *Re GEMA (No 1)* established that collecting societies may not refuse nationals of other Member States as members of that collecting society, nor may they discriminate between nationals and non-nationals (see Bently and Sherman 2009, p. 298). This was confirmed in *GVL v Commission* (1983, paras 55–6). The case law regarding the relationship between collecting societies and its members under Article 102 TFEU focuses mainly on principles of equal treatment and universal access for right-holders. The Court's attempt to ensure, as it is generally accepted that collecting societies are a necessary market force, that their power is balanced against the protection of its author members. The mere existence of a collecting society, however, is not deemed to be anti-competitive.

There is of course a countervailing discourse that argues that collecting societies are either inefficient or unnecessary. Katz (2005) and Wallis *et al.* (1999) have argued that blanket licensing is inefficient as a licensee will not require the entire repertoire licensed by the collecting society. One example provided is that in licensing music for use in television broadcasts or movies, for example, rights users will only desire access to a relatively limited class of works, such as top-selling artists such as Lady Gaga, or classic artists such as Elvis or the Rolling Stones (Wallis *et al.* 1999, p. 18). In support of this is the finding that of the 15,500 PRS members mentioned in a 1996 investigation into collective management by the Monopolies and Mergers Commission, 7,900 had no music performed in the UK giving rise to royalty distribution (Monopolies and Mergers Commission 1996, p. 65). The CJEU has appeared to view the possibility of separating part of the repertoire as being theoretically possible, but determined that it was for national authorities to assess whether this would be possible without substantially increasing costs (*Tournier* 1989, para. 34 of the judgment). Katz also argues that there is no reason why multiple collecting societies could not operate within a territory (2005, p. 558). However, Drexl disputes such a claim, stating that a higher number of providers in itself is no guarantee of competition, and may potentially increase search costs (2007, p. 12). In markets such as the US, where multiple collecting societies operate, the repertoire tends to be divided between them, with licensees invariably requiring licenses from both (Drexl 2007, p. 13). Another criticism of collecting societies is that they constitute a reproduction of the intermediary role already played by music publishers who hold the copyright of individual authors (Kretschmer 2002). As was discussed in Chapter 4, copyrights held by composers and performers are often assigned to publishers as a matter of course (Greenfield and Osborn 2004). For this reason, WIPO has stated that 'collective management without the incorporation of publishers quickly stagnates and loses its meaning' (1998, pp. 374–5). Kretschmer argues that this raises more questions about the role of authors than it does about publishers (2002, p. 128).

Kretschmer's concern is that this system does not treat individual authors, composers or performers particularly well, citing inequality of bargaining power in the transfer of rights to large intermediary organizations such as publishers (2002, p. 128). These publishers are also represented by collecting societies and, according to one study, of the money received from the sale of a CD in the UK, the retailer receives 30 per cent of the sale price, 17 per cent goes towards tax (this figure would now be 20 per cent), 15 per cent to other costs and the remaining amount is divided between artist and record label. This is by no means an equal split – of the leftover 39 per cent, only 18 per cent goes to the artist, meaning that the record label takes 82 per cent of the remainder, or 32 per cent of the overall retail price (Kretschmer *et al.* 1999, p. 165). In a study performed by the Monopolies and Mergers Commission into collecting society practices in 1996, it was found that the vast majority of artists did not make enough money through royalty payments to live on, with 95 per cent making less than £10,000 (1996, p. 63). There were similar findings in Germany, where in 1996/1997, '5 per cent of members received 60 per cent of the distributed money. Also, 80 per cent of the fees being processed by the major collecting societies come from or flow to only five (now four) media companies' (Jenny 2007, p. 362).

Record labels are large organizations, and are often part of a larger conglomerate undertaking. For example, Universal Music Group has its own publishing arm, Universal Music Publishing Group, constituting a form of vertical integration. It is an asset of the international media conglomerate Vivendi, which also owns the television network group Canal+Group, and Activision games. According to Kretschmer, these vertically integrated music companies have an interest in making collecting societies compete to represent their repertoires (2002, p. 133). With regard to mechanical rights, in 1995 an agreement was concluded between the five major record labels existing in 1995 and thirteen mechanical rights societies. The Cannes Agreement (named after the city in which the negotiations were concluded) sought to create a 'one-stop shop' for mechanical rights licensing in Europe. Under this agreement, a record label can choose one collecting society to collect all royalties for mechanical reproduction in Europe (known as a Central Licensing Agreement, or CLA), irrespective of where that reproduction was made, reducing transaction costs. While this may seem beneficial, Montgomery argues that this leads to a weakening of the principle of reciprocity as collecting societies not party to this agreement see their revenues decrease (Montgomery 1994). Furthermore, as Kretschmer *et al.* demonstrated, the Cannes Agreement resulted in collecting societies decreasing their commission fees from 8 per cent to 6 per cent (1999, p. 171), with the result that collecting societies made up the difference in lost fees by means of 'a sharp increase in commission on royalties collected from smaller record labels' (Kretschmer 2002, p. 133; see also Wallis *et al.* 1999, p. 117). Wallis argues that collecting societies acted as a result of the perceived threat that vertically integrated media companies would bypass them entirely, and that collecting societies are in an increasingly weak position in comparison to the major publishers they ostensibly represent (1999, pp. 117–18).

The internet has changed everything (except collecting society practices): reciprocity off and online

In comparison to the handling of mechanical rights for major publishers, which since the mid-1990s have been handled through CLAs, the cross-border management of performing rights has been handled through the principle of reciprocity. The principle of reciprocity in agreements between collecting societies has been referred to as 'the cornerstone of international collaboration' (Wallis *et al.* 1999, p. 14). A reciprocity agreement is the result of each collecting society operating in a limited geographical territory, such as a Member State. A reciprocal agreement allows for the collection of fees outside of a collecting society's boundaries by ensuring that another collecting society will collect those royalties on the first collecting society's behalf, wherever there is a performance by one of its artists in another collecting society's territory (Wallis *et al.* 1999, p. 14). This allows each society to have access to the world repertoire, rather than just the repertoire of the artists of that Member State. This type of agreement can be in the form of a 'Type A' agreement, or a 'Type B' agreement. A 'Type A' agreement includes the exchange of both rights and royalties collected, whereas a 'Type B' agreement provides for an exchange of repertoire but no transferal of royalties (Tuma 2006, p. 222). Batchelor has argued that any restriction of competition that results from collective action pursuing collecting societies' legitimate aims is the essence of the functioning of the society and therefore not contrary to Article 101 TFEU (2007, p. 218). In the cases of *Tournier* and *Luzazeau*, the CJEU determined that although it may well be the case that reciprocal agreements between collecting societies could result in the partitioning of the single market, the purpose of such agreements is to ensure that all musical works are subject to the same conditions within a Member State. This allows collecting societies to rely on a collecting society in another Member State to afford equal protection to the works of its own members (*Tournier* 1989, para. 19). However, where exclusivity clauses are written into the reciprocal agreement that forbid direct access to their repertoires by users of music in a different Member State, this clause can be considered as being in breach of Article 101. Users of copyrighted materials should have the right to be able to seek licenses in another Member State – any agreement that prevents a collecting society from granting such a license will be deemed to be anti-competitive (*Tournier* 1989, para. 20). In other words, competition for users of rights is encouraged.

A primary difficulty experienced by content providers online is that in order to legally offer works online, it is necessary to both gain a license for the reproduction right and the performance right, held usually by the artist or creator themselves. In the case of collecting societies such as PRS for Music, which is an amalgamation of the reproduction and performance rights societies, only one license in needed. However, in Member States where the mechanical right and performance right are not held by the same entity, a license is needed from two separate societies, meaning that there is significant fragmentation of the rights that content providers need to seek in order to offer a work online, even in one sole Member State. The territorial nature of copyright licensing means that if a content provider wanted to create a pan-European music service, clearance and a license to exploit such works must be obtained in all twenty-seven Member States, necessitating negotiations with at least twenty-seven different collecting societies (Dehin 2010, p. 227). The Commission determined that the best way to ensure that licensing was made simpler was 'not necessarily by building on existing models that originate in the analogue environment' (European Commission 2005a, p. 7). It may be for this reason that initial attempts by collecting societies to simplify licensing were viewed dimly by the Commission.

In order to facilitate multi-territory licensing, collecting societies initially attempted to rely upon reciprocity agreements. The first, the Barcelona Agreement, was intended to allow users to gain a multi-territory performance rights license to be exploited throughout the European Union. The second, the Santiago Agreement, concerned the reproduction rights. However, both agreements contained 'user allocation' clauses, only permitting collecting societies to provide these licenses to users within their territory. The Commission considered these clauses to be anti-competitive restrictions on the provision of cross-border services that had the impact of distorting the internal market and demanded that they were removed from the agreements (European Commission 2005a, p. 9). As a result of this demand, the Barcelona Agreement was not renewed in 2005, whereas the Santiago Agreement was never concluded. According to GESAC, a representative organization for a number of European collecting societies, this was because ending territoriality was not deemed to be beneficial to the authors and composers it represented, as 'forum shopping' by large commercial users would result in a 'race to the bottom', with each collecting society attempting to undercut the others in order to conclude agreements (European Commission 2005a, p. 9). A final decision was made in *CISAC*, which concerned a standard form Model Agreement for bilateral relations between collecting societies. The members of CISAC, an umbrella organization, comprise 232 societies from 121 countries, 24 of which operate in the European Economic Area. When refused a multi-territory license for online music exploitation by GEMA, RTL Group issued a complaint to the Commission, which then decided to investigate. The CISAC Model Agreement, drafted in 1936, contained three clauses that prevented collecting societies party to the Agreement from issuing multi-territory licenses outside of their own territory. The first was a membership clause, and the second and third were a pair of territorial clauses. In 2006, the Commission issued a Statement of Objections, stating that the application of these clauses in contracts for online exploitation were anti-competitive (European Commission 2006). When CISAC made a series of commitments to mitigate any anti-competitive effects, the Commission began an investigation into whether CISAC's commitments would be enough. Ultimately, the Commission determined that they would not, stating that unlike physical markets, there was no need for territorial restrictions on the granting of licenses on the internet in order to meet collecting societies' legitimate aims (European Commission 2008, para. 190). The Commission also determined that the individual acts of collecting societies in choosing to issue licenses in their own territory only was indicative of a concerted practice. However, the EU's General Court was highly critical of this conclusion by the Commission, concluding in the *CISAC v Commission* case that the Commission had not proved the existence of any concerted practice (2013, para. 132 of the judgment). Furthermore, as was discussed in Chapter 3, the General Court appeared sceptical about the Commission's general approach to collecting societies, stating that the 'arrival of new information technologies allowing the exploitation of works online does not mean that those structures are suddenly obsolete' (2013, para. 130 of the judgment).

Nevertheless, through the Commission Decision in *CISAC* and the 2005 Recommendation discussed in Chapter 2, the Commission has sought to replace reciprocity with active competition. The Commission considered the Recommendation the 'most effective model to remedy all identified concerns: it created a competitive environment among collecting societies and allowed right-holders to appoint the most effective ones, i.e., those with low administrative rates and effectives/transparent royalties distribution systems' (Dehin 2010, p. 227). Furthermore, it was hoped that with the *CISAC Decision*, national monopolies would be broken up, and collecting societies would actively compete for both users and right-holders throughout Europe (Brinker and Holzmuller 2010, p. 556). However, Brinker and Holzmuller state that the result was not what the Commission appeared to intend – rather than collecting societies offering their entire repertoire under a multi-territory license, a patchwork of different agreements and provisions displaced national 'one-stop' services for rights, increasing complexity (2010, pp. 556–7). In particular, the major publishers (who had already demonstrated significant power in mechanical rights licensing) removed the most valuable part of their repertoire, known as the 'Anglo-American' repertoire, from traditional collecting society control and have instead entered into agreements with specific collecting societies for multi-territory online licensing. EMI was the first, forming the CELAS joint venture with the UK's PRS for Music and Germany's GEMA collecting societies in 2006 (see Frabboni 2008, p. 101; Brinker and Holzmuller 2010, p. 555). Warner Music Group quickly followed, creating the Pan-European Digital Licensing (hereby PEDL) collective management group with PRS for Music, BUMA-STEMRA (the Netherlands), SACEM (France), SGAE (Spain) and STIM (Sweden) in June 2006, with SABAM (Belgium) joining in 2009

(Warner Music Group 2009). This joint venture 'offers pan-European digital licences in Warner/Chappell's Anglo-American repertoire' (Warner Music Group 2009). Universal entered into agreements with SACEM, SIAE (Italy), SGAE (Spain), and SPA (Portugal) for ARMONIA (European Commission 2012a, p. 105). Finally, SONY made an agreement with GEMA in February 2009 for the creation of Pan-European Central Online Licensing GmbH (PAECOL), a 100 per cent subsidiary of GEMA that manages the Anglo-American repertoire of SONY – based on 'the online recommendation of the European Commission from October 18, 2005' (PRS for Music 2010).

The result of this is that the market for multi-territory licensing has become more, rather than less fragmented, with users wishing to start an online music service needing to gain four licenses for the Anglo-American repertoire, in addition to negotiating licenses with collecting societies for more local or niche music not represented by the major publishers (Brinker and Holzmuller 2010, pp. 556–7; Graber 2012, pp. 42–3; Dehin 2010). Indeed, the impact of the *CISAC Decision* and the Recommendation appears to have been the opposite of what was intended. Graber considers that the position of smaller collecting societies and less popular music that is not represented by major publishers has become more difficult, and has had a negative impact on cultural diversity (2012, pp. 39–40). Mazziotti states that one study has found that the result of the changes online have threatened the economic viability of smaller collecting societies, and the fragmentation of repertoires into the popular Anglo-American repertoire and local/niche interest repertoires provides an incentive for commercial users to choose to license only the commercially appealing music (2010, pp. 792–3). This strikes at the heart of the solidarity between artists, composers and performers that collective management was based on, which was intended to ensure that they could not be taken advantage of by large commercial users. Drexl *et al.* state that it is the larger right-holders, i.e., the major record publishers, that have benefitted from the changes in the online licensing system, not individual artists (2013, pp. 14–15; see also Gyertyanfy 2010). Recognizing that the Recommendation had not had the desired effect of creating a regime of multi-territory licensing for entire repertoires rather than individual publisher repertoires, the Commission launched further actions in this field, as described in Chapter 2, including the Creative Content Online initiative and the proposal for a Directive on cross-border music licensing. However, despite the apparent difficulties caused by basing multi-territory licensing on competition rather than reciprocity and co-operation, the Commission nevertheless proposes a Directive based strongly on competition principles.

Is competition always the best policy? Discourses concerning multi-territory licensing and the construction of collecting societies as a competition problem

Akman and Kassim state that in the field of competition policy, the EC and EU Treaties have 'granted the Community extraordinary powers, but in a context where the regulation of anti-competitive practices was a novelty. These circumstances urgently required the Commission to provide a strong and persuasive justification for Community action' (2010, p. 112). In this respect, the Commission and DG Competition have needed to ensure that their activities are perceived as legitimate, necessitating 'myth-making' regarding the institutions of competition policy. 'Myth-making' is a process by which 'social organizations ... develop myths in order both to legitimize their functions externally and to provide purpose, direction and identity for those who work in them' (Akman and Kassim 2010, p. 113). In a Foucauldian approach, 'myth-making' would be referred to (as discussed in Chapter 1) as the production of knowledge. Through this process, the Commission embeds a discourse in which competition is both foundational and essential to the functioning of the EU and linked to single market aims and consumer protection, both of which can only be protected through Commission intervention (Akman and Kassim 2010, pp. 115–18). This discourse has become institutionalized, accepted and reiterated by future generations of Competition Commissioners, such as Neelie Kroes, who in 2009 stated that 'competition policy is essential to ensure that there is a level playing field and that all national markets are open for all competitors' (2009). This conceptualization has become dominant, becoming part of established political discourse (Akman and Kassim 2010, p. 122).

That a discourse of the Commission as protector of competition is largely dominant at the European level is relevant to the consideration of multi-territory licensing as being best ensured through a competition approach. As the Commission made clear in its 2008 Report on Competition Policy, its perception concerning CISAC was that the 'exclusivity clause and the concerted practice impeded the emergence of competition between societies for licensing of rights and the emergence of multi-territorial licenses' (European Commission 2009b, sec. 77). The Commission appears to have determined that reciprocity constitutes a significant barrier to multi-territory licensing, stating in its Notice published after the Santiago Agreement investigation that 'each national collecting society is given absolute exclusivity for its territory as regards the possibility of granting multi-territorial/multi-repertoire licenses for online music rights' (European Commission 2005c, para. 6). By allowing for right-holders to choose which collecting society to assign their rights to for online pan-European exploitation, transaction costs could be further decreased and remove the price distortion caused by national monopolies (Thakker 2009, p. 126). Maziotti argues that the Commission view is that 'collective management of online rights should be based on a free and EU-wide market where collective rights management organizations compete with one another on the grounds of their services and of the appeal of their repertoires' (2010, p. 770), and that with changes brought by the internet, national exclusivity for monitoring and royalty collection are no longer necessary (Mazziotti 2010, p. 770). This is a view shared by some academics in the field of competition law (see generally Vinje and Niiranen 2007; Katz 2006). Indeed, in the US, both Universal and Sony have removed their repertoires from the control of US-based collecting societies for exploitation in the online market, managing these rights directly (Pakinkis 2013). In the face of the difficulties that have been caused by its forays into the online music-licensing arena, the Commission has appeared to determine that increased regulatory involvement in order to ensure competition thrives is the best approach to the slow growth of multi-territory licensing initiatives. In this way, the collecting society is discursively constructed as a threat to competition – they at best constitute a grudgingly accepted necessity in offline markets, but in online markets they pose significant competition concerns, distort markets and increase transaction costs. In the Proposal for the Directive, other potential methods of ensuring multi-territory licensing were dismissed in favour of the 'European Passport' model, in which the licensing of rights would take place through multi-territorial licensing infrastructures. Under this model, the Directive would 'lay down common rules for all collective licensors throughout the EU and would create competitive pressure on societies to develop more efficient licensing practices' (European Commission 2012b, p. 6). Competition was therefore determined as being the best means of ensuring multi-territory licensing. The possibility of multi-territory licensing through a 'country of origin' principle, or through a centralized portal, in which collecting societies would pool the repertoire for multi-territory licensing online, were both dismissed as not sufficiently inducing competition (2012b, pp. 6–7).

The Commission discourse concerning the difficulty in achieving a streamlined multi-territory licensing as being a competition issue has been challenged by various actors unconvinced by the Commission's reasoning. Drexl *et al.* argue that collecting societies constitute a form of natural monopoly, and an effective market solution (2013, p. 5). 'Law should not try to impose competition on natural monopolies; otherwise it would endanger the efficiencies arising from the monopoly' (Drexl *et al.* 2013, p. 5). According to Lapuerta and Moselle, inducing competition in these areas can lead to grossly inefficient duplication of services (1999, p. 455). For this reason, Drexl *et al.* advocate using competition law as a means of countering abuse by these monopolies, rather than as a means of reforming the collecting society sector, as to do so may result in increasing the power of a few large collecting societies (2013, p. 5). As was discussed earlier in this chapter, this appears to have been the result, with larger collecting societies such as PRS for Music, GEMA and SACEM gaining exclusive rights over the Anglo-American repertoire, which has been withdrawn from the smaller societies. In the European Parliament Report on the Recommendation, this concern was expressed when it was stated that the result would likely be that major publishers would withdraw the 'so-called "international" repertoire they control from the network of national collective rights management societies (CRMs) and place it in the hands of one or a very few large CRMs with an exclusive mandate' (2007, p. 11). Albeit trying to increase competition in the market, the European Parliament believed that 'such action is potentially anti-competitive, as it is likely to lead to a *de facto* oligopoly' (2007, p. 11).

Not only has this benefited certain major collecting societies, but it has also increased the strength of the major record labels, according to Batchelor (2007), Mazziotti (2010) and Nerisson (2012). According to Mazziotti, rather than mitigate the potential for abuse by collecting societies, this has instead transferred that potential to major record publishers. Mazziotti suggests that this was intentional on the part of the Commission, stating that the Commission's advocating of 'monorepertoire collective management was intended to be mostly beneficial for the four international media conglomerates which own 70 per cent of the world music repertoire' (2010, p. 788). Drexl *et al.* argue that the repertoire of each record label is complementary rather than substitutable, meaning that in the current agreements between major labels and individual collecting societies, new monopolies are created over the repertoire over a particular label (2013, p. 6). The result is that the 'location' of the monopoly changes, from the territory to the product. Mazziotti argues that the Commission's objective is in fact the restructuring of the online music licensing market and giving the ability to negotiate licenses directly to major right-holders, rather than collecting societies (2010, p. 779). Evidence for this can be found in the Commission decision in the Universal/BMG merger Decision, where it is stated that:

> after the withdrawal from the traditional collecting society system, all vertically integrated music companies will in the future be able to negotiate the access to the combined package of recording rights and publishing rights including fully and partly owned publishing rights.
>
> (European Commission 2007, sec. 282)

With the move to vertical integration, large media companies control both the recording and publishing of music. Batchelor argues that in this system, the 'power of collecting societies may no longer be a concern, but to the contrary, that power may shift to the major music publishers' (2007, p. 221). Again, the Universal/BMG Decision seems to indicate this as being a preference on the part of the Commission, where it was stated that the Commission foresaw collecting societies adopting 'a role as agents and service providers for the publishers and [they] will no longer act in the traditional sphere of the usual membership agreement and collecting societies' statutes' (European Commission 2007, sec. 223). Mazziotti and Nerisson suggest that this system allows for potential abuse by major record labels (2010, p. 791; 2012, p. 141 respectively), leading to questions as to why the Commission has chosen a competition-based approach to multi-territory licensing that results in not mitigating, but transferring the potential for monopoly abuse.

Finally, it has been argued that the competition-based approach of the Commission has not succeeded in simplifying licensing, and has instead led to increased fragmentation of repertoires (Mazziotti 2010, p. 794; Graber 2012, p. 42; GESAC 2010, p. 10; Drexl *et al.* 2013, p. 27), making the system for multi-territory licensing more complex, rather than less. Rather than focusing on the issue of multi-territory licensing being a 'pure' competition problem, there have been suggestions that deeper integration or harmonization are necessary in order to create a digital single market. Brinker and Holzmuller argue that a harmonization of collective management laws is necessary in order to effectively ensure multi-territory licensing, given substantial differences between national systems governing collecting societies (2010, pp. 558–9). As Tuma states, there are different models of collective management in Europe that reflect cultural, social and historical differences (see Tuma 2006, pp. 221–2). For example, in the UK, collecting societies are private, not-for-profit organizations that are governed by principles of contract law, with no governmental oversight. In comparison, Tuma states that there is a Central European model, best exemplified by Germany and Austria, where collective management is a public regulatory function with strong governmental oversight, and where deductions are made for cultural purposes on the basis of societal benefit (2006, p. 221). The French model is somewhere in between the two systems, operating with limited government oversight and being regulated by the Intellectual Property Code, whereas in Italy, the collecting society SIAE is part of the government itself (Tuma 2006, p. 222). Whereas Brinker and Holzmuller argue that these rules should be harmonized, Tuma is sceptical of the ability of European institutions to do so, given the complex cultural and political sensitivities involved (2006, p. 225; see also Hilty 2012, sec. 18.3.3). Many smaller collecting societies also hold this position, arguing that reciprocity remains the best way of ensuring a 'one-stop' multi-territory licensing system that ensures equal treatment of all right-holders rather than just the major publishers (Frabboni 2008, pp. 104–5). Mazziotti argues in favour of harmonization based on a 'country of origin' principle and reciprocity, as this would both facilitate multi-territory licensing, while ensuring protection of smaller right-holders (2010, p. 804).

The division of rights into mechanical/reproduction and performance/communication rights has also been raised as a problem in multi-territory licensing, which could be remedied through the integration of those rights. Drexl *et al.* state that the division between these two rights causes significant uncertainty, referring to an ongoing German case concerning the legality of the separating of the two rights in the German context (2013, p. 10). This division, they continue, constitutes a substantive issue that must be tackled by the EU if successful multi-territory licensing is to be achieved (2013, p. 11). While the Wittem Group Copyright Code (The Wittem Group 2011) goes some way to addressing the concerns of lack of harmonization of certain aspects of copyright law by providing a substantive framework for a unitary copyright, the code maintains the distinction between reproduction and performance rights, meaning that while the Code seeks to incorporate elements of both the utilitarian (generally Anglo-American) and natural rights (generally Continental) traditions, its ability to redress this difficulty in cross-border licensing is limited. The Commission appears to be of the opinion that more substantive harmonization of copyright, or the role of collecting societies, is unneeded, with recital 1 stating that directives that have been adopted in the area of copyright 'already provide a high level of protection for right-holders and thereby for a framework where the exploitation of content protected by these rights can take place', seemingly without the need for additional harmonization of these principles. This view appears to be reinforced by a statement by Commissioner Barnier in 2012 that he envisages the market for creative work as 'a Single Market – but not a uniform one' (2011, p. 18). Instead, the Commission appears to favour a harmonization based on overarching principles of good governance and transparency, as provided for in the first part of the proposed Directive. Similar to the principles of regulated self-regulation discussed in Chapter 5, the Commission states in the Proposal that collecting societies need to ensure 'transparency, governance and the handling of rights revenue collected on behalf of rightholders. Notably, concerns have been expressed with regard to the accountability of certain societies to their members in general' (2012b, p. 2). Therefore, the Commission determined that the best approach was to 'codify the existing principles and provide a more elaborate framework of rules on governance and transparency' (2012b, p. 6). Nevertheless, this governance and transparency framework is equally based on ensuring certain principles of competition, with Article 5(2) of the proposed Directive reiterating the freedom to choose both which collecting society will manage rights and the scope of the rights to be transferred. Drexl *et al.* consider that while desires for increased transparency are commendable, the proposals as written risked further fragmentation of repertoires, as well as potentially reducing protection for smaller right-holders in comparison to larger right-holders and commercial users (2013, pp. 22–3). It would appear, then, that the Commission remained strongly of the view that the difficulty in establishing multi-territory licensing was a competition problem, with collecting societies as its source.

Networks of power, quiet politics and initiatives in the field of cross-border licensing

As was demonstrated in Chapter 3 of this book, and may be apparent from the preceding sections of this chapter, the issue of cross-border licensing is complex and appears difficult to address. Indeed, Commission interventions in this field appear to have increased rather than decreased the perceived difficulties, if the goal was to ensure streamlined multi-territory licensing. This section will seek to evaluate the development of the above-noted policies, addressing first the issue of competition and second the issue of further harmonization of law, seeking to identify power relationships within these policy decisions.

As the preceding section demonstrated, the Commission has developed cross-border licensing policies based strongly on a 'traditional' competition approach. While this is explainable in part by the dominant discourse of competition policy and the Commission as a protector of effective competition, certain publishers and major collecting societies have also been very favourably predisposed towards the market for multi-territory licensing functioning along traditional competition principles. In choosing 'Option 3' in its 2005 Impact Assessment, the Commission intended to introduce competition at the level of right-holders and collective rights manager (European Commission 2005b, p. 26), allowing right-holders to freely choose who would administer their rights in the online environment (2005b, p. 27). The Impact Assessment shows that the consulted parties most in favour of this approach were music publishers, namely BMG, EMI, Sony, Universal and Warner-Chappell (as they were at that time) (2005b, p. 35). The submissions of these stakeholders are not available publicly, and it is therefore difficult to determine whether there was direct correlation between the statements of these right-holders and the wording of the Impact Assessment and Recommendation. It is interesting to note, however, that in the 2005 Commission Study, it is stated that as well as ensuring the general benefits of competition, adopting Option 3 would be 'particularly interesting' for authors whose work is exploited on a large scale across the EU, as only needing to license their works once for the entirety of the EU would result in lower collecting society deductions, increasing author revenue (European Commission 2005a, p. 35).

As a result of the 2008 Consultation that followed the 2007 Creative Content Online Communication, EMI published a response in which it was stated that the Recommendation had been effective in ensuring that the licensing of its repertoire was now the 'result of free market forces' (EMI Publishing 2008, p. 3), and indicated that a reduced role for collecting societies was much more efficient (2008, p. 3). Furthermore, in response to the 2010 Consultation, EMI specifically stated that 'importance of choice and competition as the drivers of improvements in licensing for users and representation for rights holders' is essential, and that competition was the best way to ensure innovation and efficiency in licensing (EMI Publishing 2010, p. 1). Similarly, Universal Music Publishing Group stated in its response to the 2010 Consultation that 'competition in the market needs to exist in terms of competition between the collecting societies for repertoire' (UMPG 2010, p. 9). This discourse remains prevalent in the 2012 Impact Assessment, where in Annex B the Commission refers to the response of major music publishers in bilateral discussions. According to this annex, major music publishers advocated for strong pro-competitive policies in music licensing (European Commission 2012a, p. 60). Earlier in the Impact Assessment, the Commission states that in taking the 'European Passport' approach to licensing, competition would be ensured between collecting societies for the rights to repertoires to exploit on a pan-European basis (European Commission 2012a, p. 48). This was reiterated in the Explanatory Memorandum accompanying the Proposal for the Directive, in which it was stated that adopting the European Passport approach would ensure 'competitive pressure on societies to develop more efficient licensing practices' (European Commission 2012b, p. 6). Indeed, the representations of major publishers and IFPI consistently framed the lack of multi-territory licensing as being a competition problem, and more precisely, the result of collecting societies' practices. EMI stated 'that the general lack of competitive tension in the traditional European CMO [Collective Management Organizations] environment has ultimately been to the detriment of both rightsholders and CMOs' (EMI Publishing 2010, p. 8), whereas UMPG referred to being 'forced to mandate rights to a national monopoly society' (UMPG 2010, p. 4). IFPI in turn mentioned 'authors' societies' rigid and uniform pricing practices and their reluctance to negotiate' (2010, p. 9). Such statements fit effectively within a more general discourse of ensuring competition, perhaps leading to these statements having more influence over the Commission than counter-statements by collecting societies that favoured reciprocity, which the Commission already appeared to perceive as being anti-competitive.

In comparison, responses from other bodies to the 2008 and 2010 consultations and in the bilateral discussions covered by Annex B of the Impact Assessment showed differing views on the best approach to these issues. While the larger collecting societies were broadly in favour of the new pan-European licensing arrangements and supported a competitive approach to licensing of certain repertoires, other smaller societies were against such an approach (European Commission 2012a, p. 59; see also PRS for Music 2010, p. 1). Representative bodies such as IFPI suggested a return to reciprocity as means of ensuring effective licensing (2012a, p. 61) but at the same time expressed that right-holders should be free to remove their repertoire in order for it to be individually managed on a pan-European basis (IFPI 2010, p. 5), whereas commercial users such as music service providers discussed the need for flexibility and adaptability, desiring a competitive environment and avoidance of 'one-size-fits-all' approaches to licensing (European Commission 2012a, p. 62). As with previous initiatives, the 2012 Impact Assessment makes it clear that there is little consensus between the various stakeholders regarding the preferred means of giving effect to multi-territory licensing. The fact that the Commission chose to adopt a competition-based approach is likely to be the result of a combination of factors, including that the promotion of competition is a dominant discourse within European law and policy more generally, and that several large collecting societies and publishers favoured such an approach, thereby adding legitimacy to the decision taken. In this respect, power would appear to operate both ways in this relationship – major music publishers seeming to benefit from the environment of open competition supported the Commission in adopting such an approach, and by reference to this support, the Commission could adopt a policy towards collecting societies that fit within the discourse of the Commission being the protector of competition. The Commission statements discussed earlier in the context of the Universal/BMG Decision appear to further support such a conclusion.

In areas where there was general agreement, however, it appears that industry players were more effectively able to frame the Commission response. In particular this is the case when it concerns further harmonization of copyright laws or an end to territoriality. As was mentioned in Chapter 2, in a 2009 Reflection Document the Commission discussed the possibility of alleviating the difficulties of multi-territory or pan-European licensing through the implementation of more far-reaching reforms to copyright, such as a unitary code (European Commission 2009a, p. 18). Responses to this proposal by stakeholders in the 2010 Consultation were overwhelmingly negative. EMI stated that the 'current legal regime does not in itself limit the ability to licence online services' (EMI Publishing 2010, p. 7) and that harmonizing rights through unifying copyright law or creating a voluntary unitary title would not only be 'fraught with difficulties but would also add to rather than reduce complexity' (2010, p. 7). Similarly, Universal stated that 'no changes in the copyright regime are needed' (UMPG 2010, p. 3). IFPI was also negatively predisposed to the proposal (IFPI 2010, p. 7), as was GESAC (GESAC 2010, p. 20). These submissions appeared to be supported by the study commissioned by the Commission, which reported in 2010 that 'territoriality and exclusivity do not per se prevent the licensing of audiovisual works' (KEA European Affairs and MINES ParisTech Cema 2010, p. 192), and that 'regulatory focus should shift from the ambition to review copyright standards' to the issue of licensing specifically (2010, p. 195). That there was no industry support for this approach appears to have influenced the tone of the 2012 Impact Assessment, which did not address potential harmonization as a means of addressing the problems in multi-territory licensing. Furthermore, the Explanatory Memorandum to the Proposal specifically states that the EU had 'already enacted legislation which harmonises the principal rights of rightholders that are managed by collecting societies' (European Commission 2012b, p. 7; see also Drexl et al. 2013, p. 10). In this respect, it would appear that pre-legislative involvement from industry stakeholders in the consultation process managed to ensure that harmonization of rights or a unitary copyright title were removed from the agenda.

The view of stakeholders concerning adopting a principle for music licensing akin to the 'country of origin' principle in the Satellite and Cable Directive 1993 was also negative (EMI Publishing 2010, p. 8; UMPG 2010, p. 8; IFPI 2010, p. 6; GESAC 2010, p. 14; PRS for Music 2010, p. 6), and the commissioned study from 2010 also states that 'it is difficult to understand in which way the extension of the country of origin principle to "broadcast-like services" would make the current licensing process easier or more efficient' (KEA European Affairs and MINES ParisTech Cema 2010, p. 148). This appears to have registered with the Commission, as in the 2012 Impact Assessment, it is stated that a 'country of origin' approach would not lead to making the licensing process simpler and 'would also not lead to aggregation of repertoire' (2012a, p. 48). This option was therefore dismissed in favour of the 'European Passport', in which aggregation would be possible, an approach favoured by IFPI (IFPI 2010, p. 6), EMI (EMI Publishing 2010, p. 5) and Universal (UMPG 2010, p. 10).

The low salience environment in which these discussions took place may explain these developments. Gormley states that antitrust (or competition, to use EU terminology) is an issue that is notable for its high complexity and low salience (1986, p. 600), a point reiterated by Baker almost twenty years later (Baker 2005).

This particularly applies to natural monopolies, argues Gormley, which are much more complex and difficult to regulate (1986, p. 601). If competition policy is a low salience issue, then it may well be safe to conclude that the regulation of collecting societies is also an issue of (extremely) high complexity and low salience. In the period between the release of the 2009 reflection document and the release of the Directive proposal, BBC News has one story from July 2012, which presents a largely neutral view, contrasting artist dissatisfaction with the proposal to the positive perception of PRS for Music (BBC News 2012). The *Telegraph* also has one story, which is slightly more positive in tone, warning about the risk of media concentration, but also quoting Commissioner Barnier as stating the changes are necessary (Warman 2012). In comparison, the *Guardian* and *Daily Mail* newspapers both had no stories on either the consultation or the proposed Directive. This would suggest that, in the UK at least, the role and reform of collecting societies is not an issue of high political salience, meaning that businesses are able to dictate the terms of legislative development. This would help to explain why, despite academic arguments that there is a need to address territoriality in copyright, and perhaps consider the deeper harmonization of copyright law, these policy options were not represented in the Impact Assessment or proposed Directive.

However, in this instance, there are strong business interests competing in order to influence the direction of Commission policy. Culpepper refers to these conflicts in formal rule-making settings in low salience environments (such as the Commission determining the content of a Directive) as being characterized by 'bureaucratic network negotiation' (2011, p. 181). In these instances, Culpepper argues that expertise is key, as 'bureaucracies prioritize the input of social actors by the expertise they bring to the table' (2011, p. 182). As the 2010 study by KEA and MINES was specifically commissioned by the Commission to assess these issues, it is likely that their expertise was relied on substantially, as would be the responses of regular providers of expert information such as IFPI (Gormley 1986, pp. 604–5). Culpepper states that where particular actors are known to possess expertise and have developed long-term relationships with policymakers, they are more likely to be relied upon in disputes between groups of industry representatives (2011, p. 182). As was demonstrated in Chapters 4 and 5, the working relationship between the Commission and IFPI is both decades old and particularly strong. The 2012 Impact Assessment is also heavily reliant on IFPI-provided data (see, for example European Commission 2012a, pp. 72, 76, 78, 80 and 86), indicating that they are a network actor with significant ability to influence policy decisions through expertise possessed/knowledge produced. Where information produced by competing sets of experts (record labels on the one hand and collecting societies on the other, both considered expert in their respective area of activity), then that expertise that fits within the dominant form of discourse, namely competition, is more likely to have influence. Finally, Gormley states that where an issue is determined in a low salience environment through negotiations between large industry representatives, the regulatory typology is that of 'boardroom politics', marked by a 'mixture of concessions for both groups' (1986, p. 607). In this respect, the compromise may have been the determination that pursuing a competition-based approach would be the Commission's priority, supported by the views of some major business actors, with the concession being that many of the more objectionable proposals, such as reforming copyright law, ending territoriality and adopting a country of origin principle, were discounted either before or during the impact assessment stage. Gormley maintains that in these situations 'the dominant participants will be members of the business community' (1986, p. 608). Where that business community proposes solutions based on competition principles already comprising a dominant discourse within the European Commission, then it is submitted that the ability to frame policy becomes stronger.

Concluding remarks

As this chapter has demonstrated, the effective means of regulating multi-territory, cross-border licensing in the EU is a highly complex issue with different actors proposing substantially different solutions to the problem. Whereas many smaller collecting societies and some academics argue in favour of systems of reciprocity and co-operation as a means of ensuring solidarity between large and small right-holders, a discourse of competition has instead become dominant, in which reciprocity constitutes a barrier to cross-border trade, with collecting societies being the source of this difficulty. The role of the Commission is as protector of competition in the internal market, and one of the founding principles of the Commission cannot be underestimated in this, although this perceived role is not the sole explanation for the current approach to collecting societies.

Given the significant difficulties the Commission has experienced in facilitating multi-territory licensing in the digital market, a number of proposals have been raised, which have included the harmonization of copyright law generally through a unitary code, through to specific rights harmonization as a means of simplifying online licensing. However, as has been demonstrated, the majority of stakeholders in the discussion process prior to the creation of the Proposal were unified in rejecting such proposals, with the result that these proposals did not survive to be considered in the 2012 Impact Assessment or finalized Proposal. Where consulted 'experts' were divided, however, those that offered solutions that fit within the discourse of ensuring competition, thus having added legitimacy and acceptability, were arguably more successful in influencing the Commission's response. Given the high complexity of collective management, combined with its very low salience, discussions concerning multi-territory licensing took place in an environment of quiet politics, which tends to benefit large business interests. Where harmonization was therefore seen as posing potential threats to those interests, consulted right-holders were in a position to prevent those harmonization provisions from being incorporated.

What these three chapters have demonstrated is that both successful and failed initiatives to harmonize copyright law have been directly and indirectly influenced by large right-holders and representative groups, both through the expert evidence and business knowledge they construct or otherwise possess, and through the dominant discourses in which these negotiations take place. If 'business gets what business wants', then it is the result of being able to both frame the acceptable limits of discourse and provide knowledge in the form of solutions within this discourse. In this respect, it is not only expert knowledge concerning the business activities these organizations represent that is important, but also the expert knowledge concerning the processes of European institutions. In 'quiet politics' environments, in which issues are complex and not of particular interest to a large body of the general public, and either positively framed in the media or not framed at all, business interests are able to exercise significant power over other institutional actors. However, this is not to say that business will 'win' every 'conflict' in legislative development. As the next two chapters will demonstrate, resistance both within and without existing frames of discourse is possible, particularly when an issue moves from being one of low political salience to one of high political salience. In the next chapter, this concept will be expanded upon, and its relevance to the final chapter explained.

Bibliography

Akman, P. and Kassim, H., 2010. 'Myths and myth-making in the European Union: The institutionalization and interpretation of EU competition policy'. *Journal of Common Market Studies*, 48(1), pp. 111–32.

Baker, J.B., 2005. 'Competition policy as a political bargain'. *Antitrust Law Journal*, 73, p. 483.

Barnier, M., 2011. 'To be or not to be: Copyright makes all the difference'. In F. Gevers and E. Cornu, eds, *The future prospects for intellectual property in the EU: 2012–2022*. Brussels: Bruylant.

Batchelor, B., 2007. 'Antitrust challenges to cross-border content licensing: The European Commission investigations of collecting societies and iTunes'. *Computer and Telecommunications Law Review*, 13(8), pp. 217–22.

BBC News, 2012. 'Artists angered by copyright plan'. *BBC*. Available at: www.bbc.co.uk/news/entertainment-arts-18801119 [Accessed 31 July 2013].

Bently, L. and Sherman, B., 2009. *Intellectual property law*. Oxford: Oxford University Press.

Brinker, I. and Holzmuller, T., 2010. 'Competition law and copyright: Observations from the world of collecting societies'. *European Intellectual Property Review*, 32(11), pp. 553–9.

Broadcast Music, Inc. v Columbia Broadcasting System, Inc, 441 US 1 (1979).

Case 127/73 *BRT V SABAM* [1974] ECR 313.

Case 7/82 *GVL v Commission* [1983] ECR 483.

Cases 110–242/85 *Lucazeau v SACEM* [1989] ECR 281.

Case 395/87 *Ministere Public v Tournier* [1989] ECR 2521.

Case T-442/08 *CISAC v. European Commission* (12 April 2013).

Commission Decision 82/204/EEC *Re GEMA Statutes* OJ L 94/12 08/04/82.

Commission Recommendation of 18 May 2005 on collective cross-border management of copyright and related rights for legitimate online music services (2005/737/EC).

Culpepper, P.D., 2011. *Quiet politics and business power: Corporate control in Europe and Japan.* Cambridge: Cambridge University Press.

Dehin, V., 2010. 'The future of online music services in the European Union: A review of the EU Commission's recent initiatives in cross-border copyright management'. *European Intellectual Property Review, 32*(5), p. 220.

Drexl, J., 2007. 'Collecting societies and competition law'. Working Paper, pp. 1–31.

Drexl, J., Nerisson, S., Trumpke, F. and Hilty, R.M., 2013. 'Comments of the Max Planck Institute for Intellectual Property and Competition Law on the Proposal for a Directive of the European Parliament and of the Council on collective management of copyright and related rights and multi-territory licensing of rights in musical works for online uses in the internal market'. Max Planck Institute for Intellectual Property and Competition Law Research Paper, No. 13-04, pp. 1–37.

EMI Publishing, 2008. *Communication on creative content online: Response by EMI Music Publishing.* Hamburg: EMI Music Publishing.

EMI Publishing, 2010. *Response of EMI Music Publishing to the Reflection Document of DG INFSO and DG MARKT.* Hamburg: EMI Music Publishing.

European Commission, 2005a. *Commission Staff Working Document: Study on a Community Initiative on the Cross-Border Collective Management of Copyright.* Brussels: European Commission.

European Commission, 2005b. *Impact Assessment reforming cross-border collective management of copyright and related rights for legitimate online music services.* Brussels: European Commission.

European Commission, 2005c. *Notice published pursuant to Article 27(4) of Council Regulation (EC) No 1/2003 in Cases COMP/C2/39152 – BUMA and COMP/C2/39151 SABAM (Santiago Agreement – COMP/C2/38126).* Brussels: European Commission.

European Commission, 2006. *Commission sends Statement of Objections to the International Confederation of Societies of Authors and Composers (CISAC) and its EEA Members.* Brussels: European Commission.

European Commission, 2007. *Universal/BMG Music Publishing – Regulation (EC) No 139/2004 Merger Procedure.* Brussels: European Commission.

European Commission, 2008. *Commission Decision of 16/07/2008 relating to a proceeding under Article 81 of the EC Treaty and Article 53 of the EEA Agreement – (Case COMP/C2/38.698 – CISAC).* Brussels: European Commission.

European Commission, 2009a. *Creative content in a European digital single market: Challenges for the future: A Reflection Document of DG INFSO and DG MARKT.* Brussels: European Commission.

European Commission, 2009b. *Report from the Commission: Report on Competition Policy 2008.* Brussels: European Commission.

European Commission, 2012a. *Impact Assessment accompanying the Proposal for a Directive of the European Parliament and of the Council on collective management of copyright and related rights and multi-territorial licensing of rights in musical works for online uses in the internal market.* Brussels: European Commission.

European Commission, 2012b. *Proposal for a Directive of the European Parliament and of the Council on collective management of copyright and related rights and multi-territorial licensing of rights in musical works for online uses in the internal market.* Brussels: European Commission.

European Parliament, 2004. *European Parliament resolution on a Community framework for collective management societies in the field of copyright and neighbouring rights*. Brussels: European Parliament.

European Parliament, 2007. *Report on the Commission Recommendation of 18 October 2005 on collective cross-border management of copyright and related rights for legitimate online music services (2005/737/EC)*. Brussels: European Parliament.

Frabboni, M.M., 2008. 'From copyright collectives to exclusive "clubs": The changing faces of music rights administration in Europe'. *Entertainment Law Review*, *19*(5), p. 100.

GESAC, 2010. *GESAC submission to the consultation on the reflection document on creative content in a European digital single market*. Brussels: GESAC.

Gormley, W.T., 1986. 'Regulatory issue networks in a federal system'. *Polity*, *18*(4), pp. 595–620.

Graber, C.B., 2012. 'Collective rights management, competition policy and cultural diversity: EU lawmaking at a crossroads'. *The WIPO Journal*, *4*(1), pp. 35–43.

Greenfield, S. and Osborn, G., 2004. 'Copyright law and power in the music industry'. In S. Frith and L. Marshall, eds, *Music and copyright*. Edinburgh: Edinburgh University Press.

Guibault, L. and Gompel, S. van, 2006. 'Collective management in the European Union'. In D.J. Gervais, ed., *Collective management of copyright and related rights*. Alphen aan den Rijn: Kluwer Law International.

Gyertyanfy, P., 2010. 'Collective management of music rights in Europe after the CISAC decision'. *International Review of Intellectual Property and Competition Law*, *41*(1), p. 59.

Handke, C. and Towse, R., 2007. 'Economics of collecting societies'. *International Review of Intellectual Property and Competition Law*, *38*(8), p. 937.

Hilty, R.M., 2012. 'Reflections on a European copyright codification'. In T.-H. Synodinou, ed., *Codification of European copyright law: challenges and perspectives*. Alphen aan den Rijn: Kluwer Law International.

IFPI (International Federation of the Phonographic Industry), 2010. *IFPI's response to: Creative content in a European digital single market: Challenges for the future: A reflection document of DG INFSO and DG Markt*. Brussels: IFPI.

IRIS, 2009. *Creativity comes at a price: The role of collecting societies*. Brussels: European Audiovisual Observatory.

Jenny, F., 2007. 'EC competition law enforcement and collecting societies for music rights: What are we aiming for?' In C.-D. Ehlermann and I. Atanasiu, eds, *European competition law annual 2005: The interaction between competition law and intellectual property law*. Oxford: Hart.

Katz, A., 2005. 'The potential demise of another natural monopoly: Rethinking the collective administration of performing rights'. *Journal of Competition Law and Economics*, *1*(3), pp. 541–93.

Katz, A., 2006. 'The potential demise of another natural monopoly: New technologies and the administration of performing rights'. *Journal of Competition Law and Economics*, *2*(2), p. 245.

KEA European Affairs and MINES ParisTech Cema, 2010. *Multi-territory licensing of audiovisual works in the European Union: Final report prepared for the European Commission, DG Information Society and Media*. Brussels: European Commission.

Kretschmer, M., 2002. 'Copyright societies do not administer individual property rights: The incoherence of institutional traditions in Germany and the UK'. In R. Towse, ed., *Copyright in the cultural industries*. Cheltenham: Edward Elgar.

Kretschmer, M., Klimis, G.M. and Wallis, R., 1999. 'The changing location of intellectual property rights in music: A study of music publishers, collecting societies and media conglomerates'. *Prometheus*, *17*(2), pp. 163–86.

Kroes, N., 2009. *How competition policy benefits SMEs*. Brussels: European Economic and Social Committee.

Lapuerta, C. and Moselle, B., 1999. 'Network industries, third party access and competition law in the European Union'. *Northwestern Journal of International Law and Business*, *19*(3), p. 454.

Mazziotti, G., 2010. 'New licensing models for online music services in the European Union: From collective to customized management'. *Columbia Journal of Law & the Arts*, 34, p. 757.

Monopolies and Mergers Commission, 1996. *Performing rights. A report on the supply in the UK of the services of administering performing rights and film synchronisation rights*. Westminster: Department of Trade and Industry.

Montgomery, R., 1994. 'Central licensing rights in Europe: The journey towards the single copyright'. *European Intellectual Property Review*, *16*(5), p. 199.

Nerisson, S., 2012. 'Ownership of copyright and investment in teams and networks: Need for new rules?' In J. Rosen, ed., *Individualism and collectiveness in intellectual property law*. Cheltenham: Edward Elgar.

Pakinkis, T., 2013. 'Universal Music Publishing to withdraw digital rights control from ASCAP, BMI'. *MusicWeek*. Available at: www.musicweek.com/news/read/universal-music-publishing-to-leave-ascap-bmi/053431 [Accessed 2 August 2013].

Posner, R.A., 2001. *Antitrust law*. Chicago, IL: University of Chicago Press.

PRS for Music, 2010. *Response to the Commission's Reflections Paper 'Creative Content in a European Digital Single Market'*. London: PRS for Music.

Re GEMA (No 1) [1971] CMLR D-35.

Re GEMA's Statutes (No 2) [1972] CMLR D-115.

Sterling, J.A.L., 1998. *World copyright law*. London: Sweet & Maxwell.

Thakker, K., 2009. 'Conflicts between EU collecting societies and EC competition law'. *Columbia Journal of European Law*, 16, p. 121.

The Wittem Group, 2011. 'European copyright code'. *European Intellectual Property Review*, *33*(2), p. 76.

Towse, R., 2004. 'Copyright and economics'. In S. Frith and L. Marshall, eds, *Music and copyright*. Edinburgh: Edinburgh University Press.

Tuma, P., 2006. 'Pitfalls and challenges of the EC Directive on the collective management of copyright and related rights'. *European Intellectual Property Review*, *28*(4), pp. 220–9.

UMPG (Universal Music Publishing Group), 2010. *Response by Universal Music Publishing to Creative Content Reflection Document*. London: UMPG.

Vinje, T. and Niiranen, O., 2007. 'The application of competition law to collecting societies in a borderless environment'. In C.-D. Ehlermann and I. Atanasiu, eds, *European competition law annual 2005: The interaction between competition law and intellectual property law*. Oxford: Hart.

Wallis, R., Baden-Fuller, C., Kretschmer, M., Klimis, G.M., 1999. 'Contested collective administration of intellectual property rights in music: The challenge to the principles of reciprocity and solidarity'. *European Journal of Communication*, *14*(1), pp. 5–35.

Warman, M., 2012. 'EU plans pan-European music stores'. *Telegraph.co.uk*. Available at: www.telegraph.co.uk/technology/news/9394998/EU-plans-pan-European-music-stores.html [Accessed 31 July 2013].

Warner Music Group, 2009. 'SABAM joins Warner/Chappell's pan-European digital licensing initiative'. *Warner Music Group*. Available at: www.wmg.com/newsdetails/id/8a0af81223ca5ea0012477f6614d50dd [Accessed 2 August 2013].

WIPO (World Intellectual Property Organization), 1998. *Intellectual property reading Material*, 2nd edn. Geneva: World Intellectual Property Organization.

WIPO, 2013. 'Collective management of copyright and related right'. *World Intellectual Property Organization*. Available at: www.wipo.int/about-ip/en/about_collective_mngt.html [Accessed 30 July 2013].

Chapter 7

Power and resistance I

Where there is power, there is resistance

> If an individual can remain free, however little his freedom may be, power can subject him to government. There is no power without potential refusal or revolt.
>
> (Foucault 2002, p. 324)

While the previous three chapters have sought to demonstrate the ways in which power exercised through networked relationships has impacted and framed the development of copyright law and policy, the purpose of this chapter is to begin to apply the theory of resistance to this analysis. As Foucault says, where there is power, there is resistance. This chapter will begin by outlining some of the key concepts in Foucault's conceptualization of resistance as a phenomenon, beginning by reiterating Foucault's desire that power not be perceived as something naturally negative or oppressive, but merely the exercise of influence over other actors that can be used to either oppress or to produce. Whereas power is everywhere and permeates social relationships, so too does resistance, or contestation, the refusal to submit to influence or the unpredicted response to an exercise of power. Resistance, as this chapter will demonstrate, is the necessary corollary of power, as resistance is in itself an exercise of power. As with power, resistance is equally exercised through networks, and acts to change or transform the established networks of power.

This chapter will continue by applying these theories to possible sites of resistance to changes in copyright law, focusing first on the courts, and second on academic writing. In order to assess the Court of Justice of the European Union (CJEU) as a site of resistance, the second section of this chapter will apply the resistance theory to the cases of *Promusicae* (2008), *Scarlet* (2011) and *Netlog* (2012), demonstrating that resistance is possible through the courts, yet that any resistance within these institutions is ultimately a limited and 'internalized' form of resistance. As the CJEU in these cases is asked to interpret provisions of legislation, resistance is permitted only insofar as that resistance fits within the legitimate interpretation of laws by the CJEU. While the CJEU can be a site of possible individual acts of micro-resistance, it may be difficult to affect radical change in copyright law through this institution.

In the third section of this chapter, the role of academic writing as a point of resistance will be considered. As previous chapters have demonstrated, academics are prolific in their writings criticizing policymaking in the field of copyright law. As each of the studied Directives and the proposed Directive have been drafted and then implemented by the European institutions, these developments have been subject to criticism by academics. While these writings constitute a valid nodal point of resistance to networks of power in copyright law, their ability to affect the passing of these laws and transform the networks of power are limited by the relative lack of reach of these writings, catering as they do for a relatively small audience. Furthermore, due to the low political salience of copyright reform, the ability of academics to establish a dominant discourse or frame developments appears to be relatively unsuccessful in comparison to better-placed nodes such as industry representatives. If this is the case, then what does this mean for resistance in copyright's networks of power?

Power and resistance

Foucault has been criticized for his conceptualization of power, on the basis that if power is all-pervasive, then nothing can change. Some see the strength of his work as also being its weakness, stating that Foucault 'presents such a bleak view of disciplinary society that he ultimately paralyzes, rather than promotes resistance' (Pickett 1996, p. 445). Fraser argues that without providing a normative assessment of the 'wrongness' of power, Foucault leaves us with no reason to challenge it – 'Why is struggle preferable to submission? Why ought domination to be resisted?' (1981, p. 283). Indeed, for Foucault, power is everywhere, a constant within societal relations. 'Power relations are rooted deep in the social nexus, not a supplementary structure over and above "society"' (Foucault 2002, p. 343). For Habermas in particular, who conceptualizes power as a 'negative', or a distortion of communicative relations (Habermas 1987, chap. 10; see also Pickett 1996, p. 445; and Lukes 2005, chap. 2 for a general critique of Foucualt's conceptualization of power and resistance), Foucault's conceptualization of power as being intrinsic to society rather than an extrinsic force applied over society was the subject of substantial debate between the two scholars. Similarly, Harstock considers that by placing the individual as the subject of power relations upon which power is exercised, Foucault places individuals in the position of victims of power, rather than actors capable of resistance (1990, pp. 171–2). If this is the case, then Foucault presents a significantly dystopic view of social relations, in which individuals seem almost 'predestined' to be subject to dominance and/or oppression.

However, it is important to remember that, as discussed in Chapter 1, Foucault sought to move away from definitions and understandings in which power is a negative, used solely as a means of repression, censorship or domination. As stated in Chapter 1, 'power is productive', and we 'must cease once and for all to describe the effects of power in negative terms' (Foucault 1991a, p. 194). As Gaventa states, Foucault 'recognises that power is not just a negative, coercive or repressive thing that forces us to do things against our wishes, but can also be a necessary, productive and positive force in society' (2003, p. 2). If power is perceived as being a purely negative phenomenon, then the ubiquity of power leaves actors trapped within an oppressive system of relations that they have no influence over. This reasoning, however, relies on the assumption that power is a negative force that must be overthrown, or abolished (Kelly 2012, p. 112). As Kelly states, to abolish power 'would mean nothing less than the destruction of all actions upon actions. It cannot be done by appealing to a higher action upon actions that will keep power in check, since that would of course itself still be power' (2012, p. 112). However, the corollary of this is that if power is everywhere, so is resistance. If power is ubiquitous, so too is resistance. The way this is explained by Foucault is that:

> Where there is power, there is resistance, and yet, or rather consequently, this resistance is never in a position of exteriority in relations to power. Should we say that we are necessarily 'inside' power, that we cannot 'escape' it . . . This is to misunderstand the strictly relational character of power relations.
> (1978, p. 95)

Kelly summarizes this by stating that since 'power is everywhere in society, it means that resistance is everywhere too' (2012, p. 107). Power and resistance are co-extensive. If power is the exercise of power in order to influence the conduct of others, then resistance is the exercise of power against that influence. To use a basic example, should someone be listening to music, and another person request they turn the volume down, this is an attempted exercise of power, an attempt to influence someone's conduct. Should that first person turn the volume up, rather than down, then that is an act of resistance, in that the attempt to influence conduct has resulted in the opposite intended conduct. However, both acts are exercises of power and occur within the relationship in operation at that time. If the second person then threatens to call the police, resulting in the first person turning down the music, then again we have examples of power and resistance. This is what Foucault meant when he said that resistance is never in a position of exteriority to power. As Kelly states, 'when we resist, it is never a matter of us doing exactly what we would have had done had no one acted upon our actions: the specific character of resistance is itself influenced by the power it opposes' (2012, p. 108).

Resistance can take place at the micro-level and the macro-level. At the micro-level, which is the main focus of this chapter, resistance is on a personal scale, such as in the act of refusal. For example, an individual may disagree with increasing sanctions for copyright infringement on the internet. They may believe that there is a right to free access of information and so willingly ignore and refuse that governmentality, or regulatory logic that dictates that individuals do not break laws and infringe copyright. In so doing, that individual downloads music as a means of protesting, or resisting, that system. However, this resistance is at a micro-level, which Kelly refers to as 'micro-resistance' (2012, p. 109). These resistances, while taking place at a personal level and being an exercise of power in themselves, nevertheless represent 'no overall conflict with the network of power relations' (Kelly 2012, p. 110). Another example is that of resistance by prisoners in a jail. While their resistance to authority may constitute an exercise of power, these micro-resistances do not change the nature of the criminal justice system. They are already factored into the management of the prison system (the macro-level institution) and the governmentality of the prison (the corresponding institutional logic by which conduct is regulated), with resistance forming the basis for further disciplinary action (see Kelly 2012, p. 110). This 'co-option' will be discussed in greater detail in relation to copyright law and policy in the subsequent sections of this chapter. A greater resistance, one that has the ability to substantially transform the existing networks of power, is referred to as being macro-resistance. Foucault, however, never gave explicit criteria for establishing where the lines between micro- and macro-resistance should be drawn, nor did he explicitly refer to resistance in these precise terms, instead discussing resistance in terms of 'multiplicity' and 'individuality' (Kelly 2012, pp. 110–11), those acts of resistance that come from multiple nodes in order to challenge a dominant discourse, and those individual acts of resistance important at the individual level but that pose little threat to the existing networks of power.

As with power, resistance is also exercised through networks. Foucault refers to resistance traversing social stratifications, forming 'a thick fabric which traverses apparatuses and institutions, without precisely localising itself in them' in the same way as power (Foucault 1978, p. 96). Resistance is mobile and transitory, operating within and upon particular nodes within a network, 'mobilizing groups or individuals in a definite way, inflaming certain points of the body, certain moments in life, certain types of behaviour' (Foucault 1978, p. 95; see also Reyman 2012, pp. 30–1). In this respect, there is no utopian ideal of an escape from forms of power suggested in this resistance, but causing 'ruptures', changing or transforming existing networks of power. One example would be the French Revolution, in which huge societal upheaval ended the monarchy (at least for a time), and drastically reduced the influence of the Church as a node in the networks of power active in France. The Revolution was the result of a combination of factors, including the development of nodal relationships between different groups and organizations seeking to resist what was increasingly being seen as a form of unjust and illegitimate power. The networks of power within France were changed, removing the King and the logic of sovereign rule. However, resistance is a constant, as is power. France then went through 'The Reign of Terror' as the result of conflict and contention between political bodies with different visions of what a French Republic should be, and later through another transformation of the networks of power as a sovereign entity once again arose in the form of Napoleon Bonaparte. For this reason, it is impossible to disassociate resistance from power, and indeed the idea of 'freedom from' power.

Power is a societal constant, albeit being exercised in different ways and to different degrees by actors within societies networks. Therefore, 'resistance' should not be perceived as an act of liberation in the sense of the abolition of power, but the abolition or dramatic restructuring of specific power relations (see Kelly 2012, pp. 112–14). With regard to copyright law and policy then, the purpose of resistance would not be to eliminate all power from the system of governance, to overthrow all relations relating to the creation of works, and leave an anarchic vacuum. Such action would not be possible, as power would always operate to some extent within such a system. For example, to eliminate copyright protection in its entirety may potentially result in a 'true' neoliberal approach to intellectual property, in which powerful market actors do as they will with no rule or regulation to prevent potentially abusive conduct. Alternatively, it may result in the creation of 'copyright co-operatives' that have a more communitarian bent. The purpose of this book, however, is not to explore what would happen in the absence of a legal framework for copyright, except to say that a system in which law was removed would not result in the removal of power, but would result in power being expressed and exercised in different ways. In the next sections, examples of the exercise of resistance as a form of power in copyright law and policy will be provided, considering resistance as exercised through the judicial system, and then through academic writing, seeking to identify potential points and, indeed, the likely effectiveness of such resistance.

Resistance and the Court of Justice of the European Union: an internalized resistance in the discourse of copyright enforcement

As was discussed in Chapter 5, a growing discourse in the field of copyright enforcement is that of the 'responsibility' of intermediary service providers on the internet. Their systems are used to infringe upon copyright and, therefore, there is a duty to bring an end to these infringements. Statements made by entertainment industry representatives go as far as to suggest that there should be active monitoring of services by service providers in order to prevent those infringements. However, there has been some resistance to this discourse, which has taken place at the level of the CJEU in the form of conflicts concerning the interpretation of sections of legislation. These conflicts constitute a form of 'internalized' resistance, operating within the existing dominant discourses, as will be demonstrated in this section.

The first case is *Promusicae* (2008). This case concerned the right to information provided for under Article 8 of the Enforcement Directive, and the duty of ISP Telefónica de España to release information to right-holders concerning the identity of an alleged infringer using that service. Telefónica resisted this request for information, claiming that the right to information was only prescribed in cases concerning criminal proceedings rather than civil proceedings, and that there was no obligation to provide that information (see paras 29–34 of the decision). In its deliberations, the CJEU noted that the right to information had to be interpreted in light of other European legislation concerning the protection of personal information under Directives 95/46/EEC and 2002/58/EC (para. 44). Under Article 15(1) of Directive 2002/58/EC, Member States must ensure the confidentiality of communications by means of a public communications network and publicly available electronic communications services, and of the related traffic data, and must inter alia prohibit, in principle, the storage of that data by persons other than users, without the consent of the users concerned. Nevertheless, Member States are free to legislate for the release of that confidential information in circumstances pertaining to national and public security and/or the detection, investigation, prevention and prohibition of crime or unauthorized use of electronic communications systems (para. 49). The CJEU concluded that with regard to civil proceedings there is nothing in Directive 2002/58/EC that precludes 'the possibility for the Member States of laying down an obligation to disclose personal data in the context of civil proceedings' (para. 54), but also that the Directive 'cannot be interpreted as compelling the Member States, in the situations it sets out, to lay down such an obligation' (para. 55).

In this respect, the *Promusicae* decision has been referred to as being somewhat non-committal, or in the words of Stamatoudi, comparable 'to the ambiguous oracle of Pythia: it says everything and nothing at the same time' (2010, p. 231), leaving the matter of whether the information should be disclosed to the Member State. This has nevertheless been referred to as being a 'blow' to copyright holders (Davies and Helmer 2008, p. 308) and complicating the position of right-holders wishing to seek redress for copyright infringement (Massey 2008, p. 161). The CJEU's actions may be phrased in terms of resistance. In this particular case, we have right-holders wishing to ensure the protection of copyright, and thus relying upon enforcement principles provided for in the Enforcement Directive. They therefore request information, under the national implementation of Article 8 of the Directive, from Telefónica. Telefónica refuses, in itself an act of resistance. Promusicae attempted to exercise power over Telefónica, influencing the company's actions, whereas Telefónica refused to act in accordance with those wishes. As Foucault states, 'to say no is the minimum form of resistance' (Foucault 2000, p. 168). As a result, the matter is referred to the national court, which then referred the matter 'up' to the CJEU. This helps to demonstrate that resistance, even in its simple form (the act of saying no) is also dependent on the exercise of power through networks. The CJEU, through determining that this was a matter for the Member States to decide, and giving a decision in which the provision of information was neither precluded nor prohibited, in essence also was engaged in a form of resistance. When asked to decide, to determine whether information should or should not be passed on, it resisted that call, instead referring the matter back to national authorities. In this respect, the act is one of micro-resistance. There was no challenging of the discourse of the need to protect copyright, and indeed the CJEU reiterated the belief in the existence of 'the fundamental right to property, which includes intellectual property rights such as copyright' (para. 62). The resistance in this instance is 'internalized', insofar as it operates within the existing frame of discourse (copyright must be protected). The dominant discourse is accepted, rather than challenged, and resistance occurs by way of reference to another competing interest and discourse, namely that of data protection and privacy (para. 63). The CJEU states in para. 68 of the decision that the Directives must be interpreted in a way that allows for 'a fair balance to be struck between the various fundamental rights protected by the Community legal order'. Therefore, there are two competing interests that must be addressed, but the legitimacy of those interests is not challenged and the matter is referred back to the national court. This micro-resistance, then, provides a minor setback for right-holders as the CJEU did not oblige Telefónica to provide information, but at the same time it did not critique the general discourse of copyright protection. Indeed, should a national law be introduced in order to oblige ISPs to provide information, then on this reading of the case, the CJEU would not prevent such a law from being enforced.

More recently, the CJEU has decided upon the issue of intermediary service provider filtering in the cases of *Scarlet* (2011) and *Netlog* (2012). These cases have somewhat similar facts. In both cases, SABAM, the collecting society responsible for representing authors and composers of musical works in Belgium, brought actions against service providers arguing that they were best placed to end copyright infringement by their users. In *Scarlet*, SABAM brought the action against Scarlet, an ISP (2011, paras 16–18), and in *Netlog*, against Netlog, a social network platform popular in Belgium (2012, paras 16–18). In the first case, Scarlet was subject to legal proceedings in the national court, where it was decided that Scarlet was obliged to render the transmission of copyrighted musical works through peer-to-peer transmission 'impossible'. Scarlet argued that this was both infeasible and contrary to Article 15 of the E-Commerce Directive, which states that Member States must not impose upon intermediaries a general obligation to monitor information transmitted or stored (2011, paras 20–1). Similarly, Netlog was ordered to take action to prevent the transmission or making available of music through its platform, which Netlog argued was both impossible to achieve and contrary to the to Article 15 of the E-Commerce Directive (2012, paras 21–3). In *Scarlet*, the CJEU affirmed the right of right-holders to seek injunctions against intermediaries under Article 8(3) of the Information Society Directive and Article 11 of the Enforcement Directive, and stated that national courts must be able to order that 'intermediaries to take measures aimed not only at bringing to an end infringements already committed against intellectual-property rights using their information-society services, but also at preventing further infringements' (2011, paras 30–1). However, the CJEU determined that Article 15 'prohibits national authorities from adopting measures which would require an ISP to carry out general monitoring of the information that it transmits on its network', and furthermore that the costs involved in such activity would be considered unfair and disproportionate under Article 3 of the Enforcement

Directive due to the need to install a complicated and expensive filtering system (2011, paras 36 and 48). In *Netlog*, similar conclusions were reached, relying predominantly on the decision in *Scarlet* (2012, paras 28–34). Active monitoring or filtering would constitute a breach of Article 15 of the Information Society Directive, and Article 3 of the Enforcement Directive, therefore 'precluding an injunction made against a hosting service provider which requires it to install the contested filtering system' (2012, para. 52).

These cases, then, appear to challenge the discourse concerning the responsibility of intermediaries for infringement undertaken using the intermediaries' services. According to Gardiner and Abbotts, these decisions reassure ISPs and create complications for right-holders (2012, p. 77). Under this ruling, ISPs can take the view that they have no duty to act until requested to by the courts, and that there is no responsibility on their part for infringements on their services (Meale 2012, p. 647). EDRI declared the *SABAM* decision in particular to be 'hugely important for the openness of the Internet, and therefore for the fundamental rights value and the economic value of the Internet' (EDRI 2011). EDRI also argued that in this decision, the CJEU protected ISPs, recognizing that they perform the role of infrastructure providers and conduits for data transfer, not a private copyright enforcement mechanism (2011). Again, we can see forms of resistance operating through networks in these decisions. In both instances, attempts were made to influence the conduct of intermediaries, through requiring or urging them to introduce filtering systems. In both instances, those intermediaries objected, refusing to do so. Their cases were referred to the CJEU, which in these cases also resisted demands for active monitoring of intermediary services. In both cases, therefore, we see micro-resistance. We have intermediaries resisting through saying 'no', and the CJEU resisting calls for active monitoring. Nevertheless, this resistance still constitutes micro-resistance, as the dominant discourses are not challenged. Whereas the active monitoring of services is precluded, the discourse of the need for copyright enforcement is reiterated in both cases, with the CJEU stating in *Scarlet* that there was a need to ensure 'a fair balance be struck between, on the one hand, the protection of the intellectual-property right enjoyed by copyright holders, and, on the other hand, that of the freedom to conduct business enjoyed by operators such as ISPs' (*Scarlet* 2011, para. 49; see also *Netlog* 2012, para. 51). Both categories of right are regarded as important, but the discourse of the Court is one of the need to balance these competing interests.

It is equally important to consider the nature of the CJEU's 'resistance' in these matters. While working at the level of micro-resistance, the CJEU ultimately decides in cases on the basis of legal provisions, and its interpretations of those provisions. In *Scarlet* and *Netlog*, the decisions of the CJEU rested upon the interpretation of (in particular) Article 15 of the E-Commerce Directive. The CJEU is a limited, and indeed self-limiting actor, working within the acceptable discourses and accepted frames of legal review (see generally St Clair Bradley 2011; Sweet 2011). The purpose of the Court in these cases was to review the application of the relevant Directives in national law and determine whether that implementation was compliant with the Directives as drafted. While there is an element of resistance in the CJEU's decisions, this resistance is limited to micro-resistance, in which interpretations of the law are challenged, rather than the law itself. The source of the CJEU's legitimacy, in other words, is also its limiting factor. Should Article 15 not be part of the E-Commerce Directive, remaining silent on an obligation to monitor, then it may be possible that the CJEU would leave the decision of whether to oblige intermediaries to monitor their services to the Member States. The Court, by working within the framework of the Directives, provides legitimacy for those Directives, validating the dominant discourses in doing so (Kelly 2012, p. 110). This is not to say, however, that the CJEU can never substantially alter discourses that result in institutional changes – Sweet provides examples such as the CJEU determining that EU competition rules should apply to the telecommunications and air transport sectors (2011, p. 147). This decision challenged, and in essence changed, the dominant discourse in competition law at that time, in which policymakers generally considered these sectors as being outside the remit of competition policy. Instead, what is being stated is that in these particular instances, the dominant discourses have not been challenged. The discourse that the protection of copyright is 'fundamental' is not challenged, either by *Promsuicae* or the *Scarlet-Netlog* decisions, and neither is the growing discourse of intermediary responsibility. Nevertheless, as Culpepper argues, courts are institutions that, while not swayed by political salience in the same way as other actors such as governments or legislatures, 'usually resolve political struggles on questions of expertise and interpretation' (2011, p. 192). While they are less likely to be influenced by public opinion on an issue, or alternatively by the usual forms of influence exerted on institutional actors such as parliaments, the CJEU is more limited in its ability to act as a node of resistance due to the fact that its role is to interpret the law based on the questions referred, and to work within the framework of the Directive(s) that form the basis of that request for interpretation.

For example, while *Scarlet* and *Netlog* state that intermediaries are not obliged to have general systems of monitoring in order to protect copyright as a result of Article 15 of the E-Commerce Directive, this does not preclude obligations to apply targeted monitoring, as was discussed in *eBay* (2011). In this case, it was determined that a general obligation to monitor was prohibited under Article 15 (2011, para. 139) and would also breach Article 3 of the Enforcement Directive (2011, para. 140), 'injunctions which are both effective and propor-tionate may be issued against providers such as operators of online marketplaces' in order to prevent repeat infringement by known individuals (para. 141). In this instance, eBay installed specific filters to detect listings that potentially infringed upon intellectual property rights and developed a notice and take-down programme intended to provide right-holders with assistance in removing infringing listings from the marketplace (para. 46), a system that was not considered as being contrary to Article 15. By accepting such a system the CJEU legitimizes, rather than challenges, the discourse concerning the responsibility of intermediaries. Indeed, national court decisions in the UK appear to support such a view. In *Dramatico Entertainment Ltd* (2012), Arnold J. considered whether the decisions in *Scarlet* and *Netlog* prevented the granting of injunctions that oblige ISPs to apply filters that block websites deemed to infringe copyright, determining that specific acts of filtering are not contrary to those decisions (2012, para. 8) and that applying an IP address-based filter is appropriate and proportionate in order to block an infringing website such as the 'Pirate Bay' (see also Meale 2012, pp. 647–8). This was reaffirmed in *EMI Ltd* (2013). Again, this demonstrates that the resistance shown in the preceding CJEU cases constitutes a form of micro-resistance, but one that works within the bounds of the laws that the Court interprets. As such, this resistance does not challenge the dominant discourses in operation in copyright law, meaning that the acts of resistance, while successful at the micro-level, are integrated into the general scheme of discourse. In this discourse, copyright must be protected and inter-mediaries do have responsibilities to ensure the protection of copyright, but this responsibility is not all encompassing, being specifically limited by Directive. This internalized resistance, then, is factored into the existing network of power, limiting its ability to substantially alter those power relationships.

Resistance and academics: internalized resistance in the form of critique

Academics too can play a role in the resistance of dominant discourses in copyright law and policy. Equally, of course, they may also support and reaffirm those discourses. The prime contribution of academics to resistance is in the form of critique. Critique in its political context is about trying to transform relations of power, by uncovering their operation (Kelly 2012, p. 128). Dean argues that in analytics of government, critique is about asking questions 'about government, authority and power . . . [it is] a form of criticism that seeks to make explicit the thought that, while often taking a material form, is largely tacit in the way in which we govern and are governed' (2010, p. 48). The purpose of doing so, Dean continues, is so that it is possible to open up a space in which it becomes possible to think of ways of doing things differently, to highlight where resistance can be possible, and even to 'demonstrate the degree to which that transforma-tion may prove difficult' (2010, p. 48). Lemke states that this represents the transformation of a 'what' question, namely 'what is critique?', into a 'how' question, 'how is critique performed?' (2011, p. 58). In other words, through critique, it becomes possible to explain policy development in copyright law and, in so doing, provide a basis for those who wish to attempt to transform practices or the networks of power that guide conduct.

Critique can take place in a localized context, in which the challenge concerns particular policy developments. Examples include the critique concerning the passing of the Information Society Directive, on the grounds of it being perceived as highly imbalanced (for example, Hugenholtz 2000; Mazziotti 2008), and the criticisms of the use of economic evidence in the formulation of the Term Extension Directive (for example Helberger *et al.* 2008; Hilty *et al.* 2009). It may concern the role of lobbyists in the creation of the Enforcement Directive (Kierkegaard 2005), or Commission attitudes towards collective rights management as demonstrated in the proposed Directive on Cross-Border Licensing (Drexl *et al.* 2013). As has been discussed throughout the preceding chapters, many of these critiques focus on the role of 'lobbying' in the process, with a common theme being 'this result, which is perceived as wrong, or excessive, or misguided, would likely not have occurred if not for lobbying by those with vested interests.' Foucault describes this form of critique as being 'juridico-discursive' (Foucault 1978, p. 82), a technique based on judging, negating or rejecting (see also Lemke 2011, p. 58). Some examples include Hugenholtz stating that the Information Directive 'has little or nothing to offer in terms of legal certainty or harmonisation' (2000, p. 502), the Max Plank Institute's *Opinion on the Term Extension Directive*, in which it was stated that 'no persuasive economic or social reason can be found in favour of a term extension' (Klass *et al.* 2008, p. 596), and 'the regrettable passing of this Directive in the face of a substantial body of evidence arguing against it' (Farrand 2012, p. 204). Such arguments have as their basis the correction of errors, focusing on epistemological problems, and what is perceived as the distortion of knowledge (Lemke 2011, p. 59). In other words, these critiques take as their basis the perception that something went wrong, or was incorrect – for example, 'the term extension for sound recordings was based on flawed data, and will not achieve the aims that it sets out to achieve.' These acts form a body of resistance, internal to the discourses of copyright – 'we believe that artists should be fairly recompensed for their creative endeavors, but we do not believe this is the way to do it'.

However, this form of internalized resistance bears the risk of being 'co-opted', according to Kelly. Kelly gives the example of the punk subculture as a movement that was co-opted. 'Punk' as a social movement strongly associated with music as a form of resistance emerged in the mid-1970s, albeit as a dispersed movement with significantly different and distinct ideologies. For example, some punks were anarchists with a strong leftist lean, whereas others ascribed to neo-Nazi and 'white power' politics. Others, such as 'straight edge' punks, advocate abstinence from drugs, alcohol and cigarettes, with some also advocating veganism. Punk was the subject of moral panics in the mid to late 1970s, raising concerns regarding decadent lifestyles, rebellious counter-culture and violent crime, largely personified in the UK by the Sex Pistols. 'Early punk was a proclamation and embrace of discord ... Early punk sought to tear apart consumer goods, royalty, and sociability; it sought to destroy the idols of the bourgeoisie' (Clark 2003, p. 225). However, in time, punk began to occupy what Kelly refers to as 'a relatively stable niche in which there is no overall conflict with the network of power relations' (2012, p. 110). Youths taking on the appearance of punks, involving getting piercings and tattoos and listening to punk music, may constitute micro-resistance in the form of 'rite of passage' identity construction and may irritate parents, but it does not significantly threaten to transform the network of power relations. The 'shock rock' of artists like Marilyn Manson, associated with moral panics concerning youth disassociation, nihilism and violence in the early 2000s has also largely been incorporated in this sense (for more on this topic, see Wright 2000). Academics too face this risk of being co-opted, insofar as the writing of academic articles criticizing copyright policies becomes part of an accepted exercise of micro-resistance. These articles, critiquing developments in copyright law that are believed to have been made in error, become a 'mere' articulation of dissent on the part of academics writing for an academic audience, anticipated by institutional and non-institutional actors. They become part of the overall strategy of power – legal changes are made, 'lobbyist' involvement is suspected as being the driver of changes and articles are written criticizing these changes. 'For resistance to be effective, we must resist where it is not expected, in ways that are not foretold', reasons Voruz (2010, p. 3).

Alternatively, academics may become involved in advising in legislative policy, through the provision of expert submissions and reports, such as the IViR report on term extension (Institute for Information Law 2006), submitted to the European Commission as part of its review into the potential impact of the extension of the duration of protection for sound recordings. Unlike academic articles written for a limited audience, these expert submissions are direct attempts to influence policy. They make policy recommendations, such as 'extending the term of protection of performing artists should be considered only in connection with the harmonisation of statutory measures that protect the artists against overbroad transfers of rights' (Institute for Information Law 2006, p. v), or in the case of a Centre for Intellectual Property and Information Law (CIPIL) submission to the Gowers Review, 'we consider the case for an extension of the copyright term in sound recordings to be weak' (Centre for Intellectual Property and Information Law 2006, p. 49). These submissions work within the framework of copyright law and policy, seeking to influence decision making with regard to an aspect of copyright (in the examples provided, the term of protection for sound recordings, although the IViR Report was further reaching), again constituting forms of micro-resistance. They do not seek to change the copyright system in its entirety and do not propose significant challenges to the existing networks of power. They do not, for example, question the relevance or appropriateness of copyright. For this reason, they also constitute a form of internalized resistance, proposing reform, rather than revolution.

However, as has been demonstrated in previous chapters, the ability of this expertise to significantly alter dominant discourses and transform networks of power has been limited. While Gowers referred to the CIPIL study in determining that an extension to the term of protection for sound recordings was inadvisable, at the European level, the Commission referred to the CIPIL and IViR studies sparingly, and relied predominantly on studies provided by the entertainment industry. Arguably, large representative organizations such as IFPI have longer, stronger connections to the Commission than academics and a greater ability to exert influence over policy development, particularly in areas of low political salience. Where the dominant discourses of copyright policy concern high levels of protection, then alternate discourses that seek to challenge the established 'truth' are less able to instigate transformation in these networks. The existing relationships, involving particularly strong nodes (again, such as IFPI) are aligned against these alternate discourses, making internalized contestations more difficult. When the term of protection for sound recordings has been 'problematized', and is considered an issue that needs to be addressed, then those actors stating 'there is no problem' or 'the best course of action is to not act', although acting in resistance, are limited in their capacity to exert influence. There is also the possibility of suggesting pro-active reform, by proposing policies. One example is the IViR report into flexible interpretations in the exceptions and limitations in copyright (Hugenholtz and Senftleben 2011). This report seeks to determine whether incorporating US-style fair use into European law would be helpful in addressing imbalances in copyright law and concludes that, rather than incorporating fair use, a flexible interpretation of the exceptions and limita-tions already provided for under the Information Society Directive would be a preferable solution (see in particular 2011, p. 2). This type of proposal can be considered as 'reform', rather than 'revolution'. While revolution will be discussed in more detail in the next chapter, for now it is important to state that revolution does not (or, at least, does not necessarily) entail the violent overthrow of entire political systems, but can include engendering radical new ways of thinking or doing. On the topic of reform, Foucault states that this constitutes 'the wish to change the institution without touching the ideological system' (1977, p. 228). This does not mean that Foucault was against reform as a general approach to contesting established networks of power, as Kelly states (2012, p. 137). Instead, according to Voruz, while reform is important, 'reformism should not be substituted for "the radicality of a global approach"' (2010, p. 10). In this respect, Foucault was particularly critical of the penal reform movement, which he believed to be locked in stasis, continually articulating 'demands for reform of the prison system, while ultimately validating the prison system per se by doing so' (Kelly 2012, p. 110). Voruz paints an equally bleak picture, stating that 'the reformist project . . . inspires these critical, yet *relatively* ineffectual accounts of criminal justice . . .' (2010, p. 9). For reform to have more chance of success, it needs to be linked to a grander project, or critique of the established networks of power. It is yet to be determined how successful the call for greater flexibilities in applying the exceptions and limitations provided for under Article 5 of the Information Society Directive will be. While in the 2009 Reflection Paper, the Commission discussed the possibility of reform to the system of exceptions and limitations 'in the medium term', it nevertheless noted the significant divisions on the topic, with entertainment industry representatives strongly arguing against the 're-opening' of the debate over the Information Society Directive (2009, p. 15). This option is being considered as part of a review of the Directive, but at the time of writing this review is not yet complete. However, as with the penal reform movement, the desire to reform this aspect of the Directive potentially legitimizes that same Directive. By adopting a 'gradualist' approach to reform in this area, and suggesting modifications rather than repeal of the Directive, there is the possibility that this move is perceived by actors such as the Commission as an admission that the purpose and effect of the Directive has been accepted, subject to certain modifications. It is in this way that resistance in the form of calls for reform, while useful, can also be co-opted into the existing networks of power.

This is not to suggest that more radical calls will be successful. Revolution does not occur just because it is called for. In terms of larger critiques of copyright, the work of Boldrin and Levine (2008) stands out as an example of a call for radically changing the way that intellectual property is viewed. Summarizing their view in the title of the book, 'Against Intellectual Monopoly', Boldrin and Levine argue that rather than being conceptualized in terms of property and the protection of authors, we should instead conceptualize intellectual property rights as a form of monopoly. This monopoly distorts markets, supports protectionism and should be substituted for a system of free competition, which is a stronger guarantor of innovation and creation. While the authors suggest deregulation as one possible way of changing the copyright and patent systems, they go as far as to say that they favour abolition of the systems in their entirety (see generally the arguments raised in Boldrin and Levine 2008, chap. 10). There are also the writings of the late Patterson, who argued that rather than conceptualizing copyright as a form of 'intellectual property', it was better to think of copyright in terms of regulation. Patterson reasoned that the language used to describe copyright has an impact on the way the right develops, stating that 'copyright as property and copyright as a regulation are two distinct yet interrelated concepts' (Patterson 1986, p. 183). If conceptualized as property, then complete and exclusive control over a work fits within that discourse – however, if conceptualized as regulation, then copyright becomes limited by the explicit goals of that regulatory environment. Irrespective of whether the reader agrees with the views expressed by Boldrin and Levine, or by Patterson, it is these larger, more systematic critiques of copyright that have the potential to form the basis of a larger macro-resistance that is able to substantially alter dominant discourses and transform networks of power. For Foucault, 'conceptual activity is about trying to invent new ways of thinking – precisely as opposed to *discovering* deep truths' (Kelly 2012, p. 130). In other words, ideas, or new ways of thinking, can form the basis of resistance and, through this critique, open up new possibilities for resistance, either by the thinker himself, or (and potentially more likely) by activists who take up those ideas and seek to apply or use them in their own exercise of resistance. However, it is not just because an academic, or thinker, or philosopher decides that revolution is desirable that it automatically becomes so, nor does it mean that the 'banner of revolution' will be picked up and waved by others. For example, while Patterson's work on copyright as regulation was written in the early 1980s, arguably the property rhetoric of copyright is stronger than before. Similarly, Boldrin and Levine's discussions of abolition may have resonated within academic circles, but have not noticeably spread to legislative institutions or to the general public. As has been demonstrated in previous chapters, high complexity–low salience issues tend not to resonate with the 'average voter'. Gormley in particular gives patent regulation as an example of one of the issues with the highest complexity and lowest political salience (1986, p. 600), and while the issue may have become more salient in recent years, it is still a technically complex issue. As has also been demonstrated, copyright regulation has historically been an issue of low political salience, with media coverage concerning the Information Society and Enforcement Directives being scarce, and that on collective rights management being almost non-existent. Where existing network of power relationships are particularly strong, with influential nodes such as entertainment industry representatives being better placed to influence policy decisions, then even calls for revolution may be comparatively unsuccessful. If comparatively isolated nodes make those revolutionary calls, their ability to exert influence is ultimately limited, hindering any attempt to affect change in discourses concerning issues that the public may not consider to be important. As Foucault argues, if 'revolution' comes, it is for the public rather than intellectuals to pursue it. 'They are the ones who've got to choose collectively and individually' (Foucault 1991b, p. 172).

Concluding remarks

It could be concluded that the above discussion has painted a somewhat bleak picture of the possibilities for effective resistance in the field of copyright law. Whereas it would appear that resistance of a kind is possible through the court system of the EU, this resistance is limited by the limitations placed upon an institution such as a court. Resistance is effective insofar as it relates to the interpretation of law, but those interpretations exist within the dominant discourses and framework in which the laws were created. As such, any resistance in the courts is likely to take on the characteristics of micro-resistance. Micro-resistance can be important, and at an individual level is perceived as vital to those exercising that power to resist, but micro-resistance does not effectively transform existing relationships of power. Instead, it works within them, potentially legitimizing the system that resistance is exercised against.

Similar conclusions may be drawn concerning the writings of academics on the subject of copyright law. As with many forms of micro-resistance, the written critiques of developments in copyright law run the risk of being 'co-opted' into the existing networks of power, becoming an accepted and relatively harmless form of resistance. A law is passed, academics complain, but the law remains in place. The institutions and actors that are influential in passing that law recognize that academic resistance in this form is possible, and even likely, but are able to plan around it. Where academics provide direct guidance in the form of 'expert knowledge' produced in order to attempt to influence the direction of legislation, that ability has also been shown to be limited in the context of the Directives discussed in the previous three chapters of this book. Even larger, more radical critiques of copyright as a system of regulation have been limited in their ability to affect substantial change in the existing networks of power. Resistance is further complicated by the fact that it seeks to challenge established, dominant discourses, or, to use Gramscian terminology it seeks to challenge the hegemonic concepts, those that appear to be 'common sense'. They attempt to speak truth to power, and in so doing challenge the established networks in order to form new ones. However, even if an idea develops a considerable following in academic circles, this does not necessarily translate into general support or transformation of the networks of power.

So does this mean that resistance is doomed to failure and co-option? Foucault would argue that this is not the case, and that revolution is possible. Through linking the theories of quiet politics with Foucault's networks of power, it would appear that one of the key criteria for affecting networks of power is that of political salience. The more important an issue appears to be to citizens, and the more that issue is discussed in the media, the more likely it is that there can be a change in those networks of power. While transformation of the networks of power operating in copyright law and policy development is *difficult*, this does not mean that it is *impossible*. As will be demonstrated in the last chapter of this book, where an issue becomes politically salient thereby allowing for stronger interconnection between nodes in the network, it is possible to have a significant impact on the passing of legislation perceived by European voters as undesirable. In this last chapter, the possibility for resistance to be effectively exercised will be demonstrated by considering the controversy concerning the Anti-Counterfeiting Trade Agreement and its rejection by the European Parliament.

Bibliography

Boldrin, M. and Levine, D.K., 2008. *Against intellectual monopoly.* New York: Cambridge University Press.

Case C-275/06 *Productores de Música de España (Promusicae) v Telefónica de España SAU* [2008] ECR I-271.

Case C-324/09 *L'Oréal SA and Others v eBay International AG and Others* [2011] ECR I-6011.

Case C-70/10 *Scarlet Extended v SABAM* [2011] *ECR* I-0000.

Case C-360/10 *SABAM v Netlog* (16 February 2012).

Case HC11C04518 *Dramatico Entertainment Ltd & Ors v British Sky Broadcasting Ltd & Ors* [2012] EWHC 268 (Ch).

Cases HC12F4957–9 *EMI Records Ltd & Ors v British Sky Broadcasting Ltd & Ors* [2013] EWHC 379 (Ch).

Centre for Intellectual Property and Information Law, 2006. *Review of the economic evidence relating to an extension of the term of copyright in sound recordings.* Cambridge: University of Cambridge.

Clark, D., 2003. 'The death and life of punk, the last subculture'. In D. Muggleton and R. Weinzierl, eds, *The post-subcultures reader.* New York: Berg.

Culpepper, P.D., 2011. *Quiet politics and business power: Corporate control in Europe and Japan.* Cambridge: Cambridge University Press.

Davies, I. and Helmer, S., 2008. 'Productores de Musica de Espana ('Promusicae') v Telefonica de Espana SAU ('Telefonica') (C-275/06)'. *European Intellectual Property Review,* 30(8), p. 307.

Dean, M., 2010. *Governmentality: Power and rule in modern society,* 2nd edn. London: Sage.

Drexl, J., Nerisson, S., Trumpke, F. and Hilty, R., 2013. 'Comments of the Max Planck Institute for Intellectual Property and Competition Law on the proposal for a Directive of the European Parliament and of the Council on collective management of copyright and related rights and multi-territory licensing of rights in musical works for online uses in the internal market'. Max Planck Institute for Intellectual Property and Competition Law Research Paper, No. 13–14, pp. 1–37.

EDRI (European Digital Rights), 2011. 'Scarlet v SABAM: a win for fundamental rights and internet freedoms'. *EDRI.* Available at: www.edri.org/edrigram/number9.23/scarlet-sabam-win-fundamental-rights [Accessed 7 August 2013].

European Commission, 2009. *Creative content in a European digital single market: Challenges for the future: A reflection document of DG INFSO and DG MARKT.* Brussels: European Commission.

Farrand, B., 2012. 'Too much is never enough? The 2011 copyright in sound recordings extension directive'. *European Intellectual Property Review,* 34(5), pp. 297–304.

Foucault, M., 1977. *Language, counter-memory, practice: Selected essays and interviews.* D.F. Bouchard, ed. Ithaca, NY: Cornell University Press.

Foucault, M., 1978. *The history of sexuality: The will to knowledge.* London: Penguin.

Foucault, M., 1991a. *Discipline and punish: The birth of the prison.* London: Penguin.

Foucault, M., 1991b. *Remarks on Marx: Conversations with Duccio Trombadori.* New York: Semiotext(e) Foreign Agents.

Foucault, M., 2000. *Ethics: The essential works of Michel Foucault, 1954–1984: Subjectivity and truth.* P. Rabinow, ed. London: Penguin.

Foucault, M., 2002. *Power: The essential works of Michel Foucault 1954–1984.* J. Faubion, ed. London: Penguin.

Fraser, N., 1981. 'Foucault on modern power: Empirical insights and normative confusions'. *Praxis International,* 3, pp. 272–87.

Gardiner, P. and Abbotts, G., 2012. 'Scarlet extended reprieve from content filtering'. *Entertainment Law Review,* 23(3), pp. 75–7.

Gaventa, J., 2003. *Power after Lukes: A review of the literature.* Brighton: Institute of Development Studies.

Gormley, W.T., 1986. 'Regulatory issue networks in a federal system'. *Polity,* 18(4), pp. 595–620.

Habermas, J., 1987. *The philosophical discourse of modernity.* Cambridge, MA: MIT Press.

Harstock, N., 1990. 'Foucault on power: A theory for women?' In L. Nicholson, ed., *Feminism/postmodernism.* New York: Routledge.

Helberger, N., Dufft, N., Gompel, S. van and Hugenholtz, P.B., 2008. 'Never forever: Why extending the term of protection for sound recordings is a bad idea'. *European Intellectual Property Review,* 5, pp. 174–81.

Hilty, R.M., Kur, A., Klass, N., Geiger, C., Peukert, A., Drexl, J. and Katzenberger, P., 2009. 'Comment by the Max-Planck Institute on the Commission's proposal for a Directive to amend Directive 2006/116 concerning the term of protection for copyright and related rights'. *European Intellectual Property Review,* 31(2), pp. 59–72.

Hugenholtz, P.B., 2000. 'Why the copyright directive is unimportant, and possibly invalid'. *European Intellectual Property Review*, 11, pp. 501–2.

Hugenholtz, P.B. and Senftleben, M.R.F., 2011. *Fair use in Europe: In search of flexibilities.* Amsterdam: Institute for Information Law; VU Centre for Law and Governance.

Institute for Information Law, 2006. *The recasting of copyright and related rights for the knowledge economy.* University of Amsterdam.

Kelly, M.G.E., 2012. *The political philosophy of Michel Foucault.* London: Routledge.

Kierkegaard, S., 2005. 'Taking a sledge-hammer to crack the nut: The EU Enforcement Directive'. *Computer Law and Security Report*, 21(5), p. 488.

Klass, N., Drexl, J., Hilty, R.M., Kur, A. and Peukert, A., 2008. 'Statement of the Max Planck Institute for Intellectual Property, Competition and Tax Law concerning the Commission's plans to prolong the protection period for performing artists and sound recordings'. *International Review of Intellectual Property and Competition Law*, 39(5), pp. 586–96.

Lemke, T., 2011. *Foucault, governmentality, and critique.* Colorado, CO: Paradigm.

Lukes, S., 2005. *Power: A radical view*, 2nd edn. New York: Palgrave Macmillan.

Massey, R., 2008. 'Independent service providers or industry's secret police? The role of the ISPs in relation to users infringing copyright'. *Entertainment Law Review*, 19(7), p. 160.

Mazziotti, G., 2008. *EU digital copyright law and the end-user.* Berlin: Springer.

Meale, D., 2012. 'Avast, ye file sharers! The Pirate Bay is sunk'. *Journal of Intellectual Property Law and Practice*, 7(9), pp. 646–8.

Patterson, L.R., 1986. 'A regulatory theory of copyright: Avoiding a first amendment conflict'. *Emory Law Journal*, 35, p. 163.

Pickett, B.L., 1996. 'Foucault and the politics of resistance'. *Polity*, 28(4), pp. 445–66.

Reyman, J., 2012. *The rhetoric of intellectual property: Copyright law and the regulation of digital culture.* New York: Routledge.

St Clair Bradley, K., 2011. 'Powers and procedures in the EU constitution: Legal bases and the court'. In P. Craig and G. De Burca, eds. *The evolution of EU law.* Oxford: Oxford University Press.

Stamatoudi, I.A., 2010. 'Data protection, secrecy of communications and copyright: Conflicts and convergences – The example of Promusicae v Telefonica'. In I.A. Stamatoudi, ed., *Copyright enforcement and the internet.* Alphen aan den Rijn, The Netherlands; Frederick, MD: Kluwer Law International.

Sweet, A.S., 2011. 'The European Court of Justice'. In P. Craig and G. De Burca, eds, *The evolution of EU law.* Oxford: Oxford University Press.

Voruz, V., 2010. 'Politics in Foucault's later work: A philosophy of truth; or reformism in question'. *Theoretical Criminology*, 15(1), pp. 1–19.

Wright, R., 2000. ' "I'd sell you suicide": Pop music and moral panic in the age of Marilyn Manson'. *Popular Music*, 19(3), pp. 365–85.

Chapter 8

Power and resistance II
(In)civil society, changing networks and the unquiet politics

> Revolutionary action, on the contrary, is defined as the simultaneous agitation of consciousness and institutions; this implies that we attack the relationships of power through the notions and institutions that function as their instruments, armature, and armor.
>
> (Foucault 1977, p. 228)

In the previous chapter, the Foucauldian approach to resistance in networks of power was discussed, demonstrating that resistance is possible both at the individual micro level and at a more radical macro level, in which networks of power and dominant discourses can be transformed, substantially altering power relations. However, one of the limitations of resistance at the micro level is that this resistance can have the effect of legitimating existing networks of power, becoming 'co-opted' in the sense that resistance is incorporated and the influence of resisting actors reduced. In order for resistance to be able to substantially alter existing networks of power, it must be at a macro level, transforming dominant discourses and conceptualizations. In this final chapter, the theories and principles expanded upon in the previous chapters of this book will be applied to a specific legislative initiative that failed as the result of contestation by citizens and activist organizations despite the support for that initiative by entertainment industry representatives. This initiative, the Anti-Counterfeiting Trade Agreement (ACTA) was an international agreement intended to harmonize certain standards of protection and enforcement mechanisms for the protection of intellectual property. Whereas previous initiatives to harmonize enforcement mechanisms in the EU such as the Enforcement Directive had been successfully passed despite the criticism of academics and activists, the European Parliament rejected ACTA by a significant majority. The contentiousness of the Agreement, or rather the framing of the Agreement as controversial, resulted in significant reluctance on the part of the European Parliament to be seen as supporting ACTA.

This concluding chapter will begin by providing an overview of the sections of ACTA relevant to the consideration of the response to the Agreement, highlighting the perceived secretive and anti-democratic nature of negotiations, and identifying concerns on the part of academics regarding the substantive provisions of the Agreement. It will also consider the position of the Commission and industry representatives on ACTA, demonstrating the strong support for its quick ratification and entry into force. The next section will expand upon the resistance to ACTA, providing a consideration of the role of the internet in coordination and facilitating activism both online and offline. This section will provide an overview of the development of an 'Anti-ACTA' resistance movement, appearing to originate in Poland and other former Soviet states, in which social media such as Facebook was used to both provide information and coordinate protests against the Polish signing of the Agreement. The networked nature of the resistance to ACTA will be demonstrated, highlighting the role of internet-based activist organizations such as La Quadrature du Net in coordinating transnational resistance to ACTA, considering the way in which loosely connected nodes in an issue network are able to exert significant influence in a policy area traditionally dominated by strongly connected policy network nodes, actors that have strong ties to policymaking institutions such as the European Commission and Parliament. Through the coordination of both offline protest action and combined online and offline direct lobbying of the European Parliament, this issue network was able to influence the European Parliament's decision to reject ACTA.

The final section of analysis will expand upon the reasons for the success of this activist network, by considering the way in which the transformation of dominant discourses allowed for the rejection of ACTA. By campaigning on the grounds of democratic accountability and civil liberties, rather than a general protest against intellectual property, and using protest as a means of capturing media attention, activists were able to transform the ratification of ACTA from a low political salience issue of copyright regulation into a high political salience issue of democratic accountability. By creating an environment of 'noisy politics' or 'unquiet politics', traditionally influential actors were not able to exert their usual influence over the legislative process, allowing for individual citizens to have a substantial impact over the European Parliament. However, as will be discussed, although resistance to ACTA was successful, this has not necessarily changed the existing networks of power and dominant discourses over intellectual property law and policy, which may continue to be an issue of low political salience and subject to the effects of quiet politics.

The Anti-Counterfeiting Trade Agreement (ACTA)

The ACTA negotiations began in 2006 as a bilateral discussion between the US and Japan concerning the combating of piracy and counterfeiting by means of a plurilateral treaty (Swiss Federation of Intellectual Property 2009, p. 1). These initially informal discussions were followed by formalized negotiations that commenced in June 2008 between the US, Canada, Australia, the EU, Japan, Mexico, Morocco, New Zealand, the Republic of Korea, Singapore, Switzerland

and the US (Swiss Federation of Intellectual Property 2009, p. 1; see also Farrand and Carrapico 2012, p. 392). Initially, very little was known about the content of this Agreement, due to the highly secretive nature of the discussions (Farrand and Carrapico 2012, p. 393). However, after leaks of deliberative versions of the text by organizations such as Digitale Linke in March 2010, La Quadrature du Net (LQDN) in July 2010 and Knowledge Ecology International in August 2010, as well as the release of a draft text by the European Union in April 2010, it became apparent that ACTA was intended to cover infringements of copyright through use of the internet, in addition to offline counterfeiting. According to the deliberative text released by the European Union in April 2010, Article 2.14 provided for the imposition of criminal sanctions 'at least in cases of willful trademark counterfeiting or copyright or related rights piracy on a commercial scale', which was intended to include wilful copyright and related rights infringements 'that have no direct or indirect motivation of financial gain'. Article 2.18(1) specifically stated that these sanctions should be applied to cases of wilful infringement that take place by means of the internet/in the digital environment. In a subsection 3 *quater*, one possible option recommended by at least one party to the negotiations stated that: 'Each Party shall promote the development of mutually supportive relationships between online service providers and right holders to deal effectively with . . . copyright or related rights infringement which takes place by means of the Internet' (see European Commission 2010, p. 22). The wording of these sections on infringement lead to the conclusion that the intention behind the section on criminal sanctions was to ensure that all acts of infringement, either on or offline, could constitute criminal acts, in essence transforming copyright infringement online from a civil law 'wrong' to a criminal law 'offence' (Farrand and Carrapico 2012, p. 394).

The language of these sections was mollified somewhat in the finalized Agreement, with Article 23(1) stating that criminal sanctions should be applied in cases of copyright or related-rights 'piracy' on a commercial scale, intended to include 'at least those carried out as commercial activities for direct or indirect economic or commercial advantage'. Nevertheless, these sanctions should nevertheless be applied in cases of infringement of copyright online under Article 27(1), with each Party to the Agreement endeavoring 'to promote cooperative efforts with the business community to effectively address . . . copyright or related rights infringement . . . while preserving fundamental principles such as freedom of expression, fair process, and privacy.' Despite the change in language between versions, ACTA caused considerable concern to a range of actors including academics and civil society organizations. Blakeney and Blakeney in 2010 referred to ACTA being 'dogged by controversy over the lack of transparency' (2010, p. 91), with no public releases of any negotiation document up until the first leak by Wikileaks in 2008, and many subsequent releases of information being in the form of leaks rather than official disclosures (Blakeney and Blakeney 2010, pp. 91–2). Geiger referred to the secrecy of negotiations giving rise to considerable concerns and emphasizing 'the feeling of exclusion sometimes perceived by public opinion when it comes to passing new legislation in intellectual property matters' (2010, p. 629). Leith referred in 2011 to the 'veil of secrecy' behind which the negotiations for the Agreement took place, raising questions over democratic accountability (2011, p. 82). These concerns were reiterated at the WTO under the auspices of the TRIPS council meeting by Indian and Chinese delegations in June 2010 (Farrand and Carrapico 2012, p. 394), with India's representative stating that ACTA's negotiations were not only secretive, but exclusionary, preventing countries such as India, Russia, Brazil and China from being actively involved in negotiations (Indian representative at the WTO TRIPS Council 2010). Through bypassing the usual forum for international trade agreements, namely the WTO, 'ACTA negotiating partners have instead opted for a plurilateral approach that circumvents possible opposition from developing countries . . . there will be a concerted effort to transform a plurilateral agreement into a multilateral one' (Geist 2009c). In other words, ACTA would oblige other WTO party states to adhere to an international agreement that they had no ability to negotiate, circumventing accepted processes (see also Ruse-Khan and Jaeger 2009, p. 503; Yu 2011, pp. 1–2). Similarly, Goldsmith and Lessig argued that the US government's intention to sign ACTA as a 'sole executive agreement' that only required presidential approval rather than Congressional scrutiny raised significant constitutional questions (2010).

Concerns were also raised by the expansive scope of ACTA. Geiger in particular expressed reservations concerning the criminal sanctions outlined in the deliberative versions of the Agreement, referring to the definition of infringement on a 'commercial scale' being 'very broad . . . [and that] extreme prudence seems necessary' (2010, p. 631). These concerns were also expressed by Ramalho, who argued that it was debatable whether the European Commission, the chief EU negotiating institution, had the exclusive competence to conclude an international agreement concerning criminal sanctions (2011, pp. 97–8). It has also been argued that the broad wording of the deliberative texts created a substantial risk that individuals downloading infringing material on the internet could also be subject to criminal sanctions (Farrand and Carrapico 2012, p. 394). While, as Geiger has stated, the finalized version of the Agreement removed many of the more controversial aspects concerning liability on the internet, such as those concerning intermediary liability and graduated response measures (2012, p. 172), ACTA was alleged to have retained the overly broad definition of commercial scale (Geiger 2012, pp. 174–5). Leith argues that the finalized version of the Agreement posed significant privacy and data protection concerns and stated that a footnote made a statement that 'suggests that a regime could be adopted to limit liability of or remedies against ISPs, whilst preserving the interests of rights-holders' (2011, p. 83; see also Baraliuc et al. 2013, p. 101).

Nevertheless, ACTA was strongly supported by the European Commission and industry representatives. In the Commission report 'A Single Market for IPRs', it was stated that ACTA constituted 'an important step in improving the international fight against IPR infringements . . . the Commission will table its proposal for an EU decision to sign the agreement' (European Commission 2011, pp. 20–1). A representative from BUSINESSEUROPE stated that ACTA would help 'ensure that counterfeiting and piracy and their damaging effects on investment, creation, innovation and jobs are addressed . . . addressing IP theft online' (Buck 2011, p. 142). IFPI welcomed the signing of the Agreement in early 2012, stating that ACTA 'highlights the EU's ongoing support for intellectual property. We urge the European Parliament to complete the adoption process by giving its assent to the treaty' (Moore 2012b). However, despite strong support for the Agreement on the part of the entertainment industry, heavily involved in both drafting and lobbying for the ratification of the Agreement (see MacKinnon 2012, pp. 106–7), unforeseen and unprecedented political mobilization in the EU against the ratification of the Agreement resulted in traditionally influential network actors being unable to effectively exercise power over decision makers in the EU. In comparison to previous initiatives, European citizens were much more active than usual in urging the European Parliament to reject ACTA. Why, then, was the legislative process for ACTA distinct from previous legislative initiatives at the European level for increased copyright protection? Why, and how, was resistance successful in a field of policy normally characterized by low political salience and extensive industry influence?

Resistance to ACTA: the use of the internet in protest and forming issue networks

It appeared in January 2012 after the signing of ACTA at a ceremony in Japan by the EU and twenty-two Member State representatives (excluding Cyprus, Germany, Estonia, the Netherlands and Slovakia) that the EU implementation of the Agreement was a foregone conclusion (Solon 2012). However, the narrative concerning ACTA is somewhat more complex, and by April 2012, ACTA was described as being 'on its knees' (Fry 2012). In comparison to previous legislative initiatives concerning copyright in the EU, resistance to the passing of ACTA was concerted and far-reaching, as this section shall demonstrate. In particular, the use of the internet as a mobilization tool by activists and the coordination of online and offline action was of particular note. The importance of the internet as a tool of mass communication has been argued by Castells, who has argued that whereas traditional media such as newspapers or television are one-directional forms of communication, 'with the diffusion of the Internet, a new form of interactive communication has emerged, characterized by the capacity of sending messages many to many, in real time' (2011, p. 55). Gil de Zúñiga *et al.* argue that the internet allows for communications in the form of many-to-many, many-to-one and one-to-many forms, 'which combined may take the behavior of expressive participation to a place not easily achieved by more traditional means' (2010, p. 38). In other words, the use of the internet as a means of communication both lowers the costs of political organizing, as well as the ease of organizing politically. Bimber *et al.* state that the reduction of transaction costs makes information-intensive tasks and communicative processes and products readily accessible, meaning that actors seeking to become involved in collective action 'have available to them many alternative forms and strategies. These alternatives are less dependent than in the past on constraints associated with material resources, expertise, location and target of the organizing' (2009, p. 73). For example, to write to friends and family in order to send to them a news story of particular interest, in the pre-internet communication model, may have involved phoning each individual to urge them to buy a copy of that newspaper, or alternatively, cutting out that news story, photocopying it and then distributing it to them in person or by letter. In comparison, through internet communications technologies, that same news story may be in an online version of that newspaper, the link to which can then be emailed immediately to all those family members or friends that have access to the internet. This dramatically reduces the time, effort and money invested in sending that news story. Benkler refers to this change brought about by digital communications technologies as the creation of a 'networked public sphere', in which the individual's position within politics is qualitatively changed, allowing them to be not merely a listener and voter, but a potential speaker (2006, p. 213). This in turn allows for 'direct organization of opinion and action' (Benkler 2006, p. 213), with individual actors and collective organizations using these communications technologies to advance their projects, whether political, social or otherwise (see Downing 2003 generally; Castells 2011, p. 57). Returning to the principles of networks of power and the network society (as described by Castells), this means that on the internet, each individual has the potential to be an active node within the network of power relations active in a particular area of policy. It has been argued that the use of the internet as a form of mass communication for political action has the potential to reinvigorate participative democracy (Krueger 2002; Graber *et al.* 2004; cf. Sunstein 2009).

Prior to the signing of ACTA on 26 January 2012, the Polish government announced their intention to sign and ratify the Agreement, referring to it as a 'success of the Polish EU Presidency' (Odrozek 2012b). In response to this announcement, Facebook pages such as 'Nie dla ACTA' were set up, which according to a post made on the page on 21 January 2012, had over 10,000 views within the first 24 hours of being active. By 22 January 2012, this number had reached 100,000 views. Odrozek reported that central to the concerns of Polish citizens was the anti-democratic nature of the ACTA negotiations, with one activist being reported as stating that 'They promised debates – nothing. They promised openness – nothing. Democracy is being destroyed, the deputies don't know what they are signing, and all this will lead to a situation when bloggers, scientists and entrepreneurs will be qualified as criminals' (Antyweb, as quoted in Odrozek 2012b). According to the BBC, on 26 January 2012, thousands of protestors marched throughout cities in Poland carrying banners with statements including 'No to ACTA' and 'a free internet' (BBC News 2012j). A report by The Associated Press stated that this included 15,000 demonstrators in Krakow and 5,000 in Wroclaw (The Associated Press 2012), and the *International Business Times* newspaper referred to 'over a thousand' protestors congregating in the center of Warsaw (Mezzofiore 2012). These protests were predominantly organized through the creation of a 'Facebook event' by Nie dla ACTA, with social media being used to coordinate the protests (Odrozek 2012a; Masnick 2012b; Gera 2012). Donald Tusk, Prime Minister of Poland, affirmed that Poland would continue with the ratification of ACTA, stating that the protests amounted to little more than 'brutal blackmail' (as quoted in Gera 2012). By 2 February 2012, however, he announced that ACTA would not be ratified, as it 'does not match "the realities of the twenty-first century"' (*The Warsaw Voice* 2012). In February, the Czech Republic, Latvia and Germany also announced that they would delay, if not block the ratification of ACTA (Couts 2012). On 2 February 2012, the Slovenian ambassador to Japan also apologized for signing the Agreement, referring to the 'barrage' of emails and messages on Facebook regarding ACTA. The ambassador stated that ACTA was signed out of 'civic carelessness . . . [there was] too little transparency . . . we, as Slovenian citizens, neglected our civic duty' (Slovenian ambassador to Japan, as quoted in Masnick 2012a). As a result of the protests, EU Commissioner for Trade Karel de Gucht stated that he had referred ACTA to the CJEU, stating that the intention was to 'to assess whether ACTA is incompatible – in any way – with the EU's fundamental rights and freedoms . . . [however] ACTA will not censor websites or shut them down; ACTA will not hinder freedom of the internet or freedom of speech' (de Gucht 2012).

The statements of these public officials coincided with the intensification of protests throughout Europe, with reports of more than 25,000 protestors in Germany and 4,000 in Bulgaria, in addition to thousands protesting throughout France, Romania, the Czech Republic, Poland, Sweden and Croatia on 11 February as a day of protest against ACTA (Arthur 2012b). These protests were organized through online coordination by activist organizations such as FightForTheFuture.org, which ran the website killacta.org, LQDN, and the Facebook group 'Stop ACTA', all of which provided details on the different protests being organized 'in hundreds of locations all over Europe' (La Quadrature du Net 2012d). Protests continued in June, prior to the European Parliament vote on ACTA, with social media being used to coordinate those protests (Neubauer 2012). The activist organization Digitale Gesellschaft was active in this coordination, with its stated main goal being to 'create a broad coalition of organisations and people protesting against ACTA for different arguments, to communicate the criticism against ACTA in a comprehensive way as well as to connect protests taking place online and offline' (Beckedahl 2012). Bennett and Toft argue that while social technologies such as blogs and social networks do not provide 'magic solutions' in the formation of activist networks or completely replace organizations and rallies as a means of building solidarity, they may nevertheless contribute to existing processes (2009, p. 246). In particular, they state, 'forms of activism – particularly those that cross national and cultural boundaries – blur easy distinctions between on- and offline behavior' (2009, p. 246). This is because the organizational activities may occur both on- and offline, or actions may be coordinated online in order to be more effective offline. One example provided by Gil de Zúñiga *et al.* is that of 'Blog for America', an online grassroots blog ran as part of Howard Dean's presidential primary campaign from 2003 to March 2004, allowing members of the public and Dean's campaign team to coordinate events and keep potential voters updated on developments on the campaign trail (2010, p. 39). According to Gil de Zúñiga *et al.*, online activities, such as the running of Facebook events or activist blogging sites such as LQDN, can contribute to the convenient coordination of in-person political activities and the swift mobilization of activists (2010, p. 38). Or, as Castells puts it,

> individual activists who mobilize for specific campaigns, connect with each other over the Internet to debate, to organize, to act, and to share ... Internet networks are essential to bring together the hundreds of local organizations and the thousands of activists that come to the local from the global.
>
> (Castells 2011, p. 342)

In other words, the coordination of protestors and protests against ACTA is achieved through nodal relationships between individuals and collective organizations. What appears to have its origins in the creation of networks of protest in Poland using Facebook as a coordination tool spread to other EU Member States as activist organizations such as FightForTheFuture.org and LQDN used their respective websites to provide information and coordinate offline protests. Through the development of network relations between individuals in different Member States, acting through nodal points such as activist organizations, it was possible to coordinate protests in such a way as to bring public attention to the existence of the Agreement, thereby raising the salience of ACTA. Protest, according to Hintz, constitutes an 'outsider' strategy, questioning the legitimacy of power holders through disruptive action as a means of drawing public attention to a particular 'problem' (2012, p. 136). The reactions of state officials, and the referral of ACTA to the CJEU by the Commissioner for Trade, are indicative of the fact that these protests were successful in raising this awareness.

Resistance to the ratification of ACTA in the EU did not only come in the form of street protests, however, but also came in the form of 'insider' strategies (Hintz 2012, p. 136), in which EU citizens directly lobbied the European Parliament. The protests used to generate public attention to concerns over ACTA were complemented by civil society organizations such as the Open Rights Group and La Quadrature du Net running campaigns urging EU citizens to contact MEPs in order to make their opposition to the Agreement known. LQDN arguably became one of the most important nodes in the resistance to ACTA, providing infrastructure and 'expertise' to activists. This is because, unlike the policy networks comprising media interest representative organizations such as IFPI (as discussed in previous chapters), activist organizations tend to be less stable. According to Mueller, policy networks are typified by corporate actors forming strong and stable network relations, being 'drawn into regularized interaction around a set of laws and regulations in a specific sector' (2010, p. 38). As has been demonstrated in previous chapters, organizations such as IFPI fit well within this definition of a policy network actor, having regularized contact with both the European Commission and Parliament concerning copyright policies, being highly active in influencing the framing of such legislation. In comparison, activists (be they individual or organization-based) form 'looser kinds of relationships, known as *issue networks*' (Mueller 2010, p. 39). These networks are defined as 'a shared-knowledge group having to do with some aspect (or, as defined by the network, some problem) of public policy' (Heclo 1978, p. 103). However, as Mueller indicates, issue networks are less stable, and built around individual causes, rather than developing a strong, regularized role in policy development (Mueller 2010, p. 44). According to Ward and Gibson, these issue networks are loose coalitions that often have no formal membership or recognizable organizational structure, and are generally informal and ephemeral (2009, p. 27). 'Many of the newer direct action networks have simply removed the concept of membership altogether since there are no hierarchies or structures, just activists' (Ward and Gibson 2009, p. 27). Indeed, the function of LQDN in the resistance to ACTA appears to have been that of a central repository for activist action, rather than a civil society organization with established membership – rather than saying there was no structure, however, which particularly from a Foucauldian perspective is impossible, given the nature of social relations, it is more accurate to state that '*the communication process becomes the organizational structure*, making technology inseparable from the social network itself' (Bennett and Toft 2009, p. 254).

In this respect, LQDN constituted a central communication point in a highly decentralized network of activists, providing regular updates on the process of ACTA through the European Parliament and its constitutent sub-committees, raising awareness of perceived repercussions of ACTA, and providing analysis of leaks of the Agreement. For example, on a Wiki created by LQDN, a page titled 'How to act against ACTA' provided information on how to contact elected representatives in the European Parliament, a list of key 'talking points' to use when discussing ACTA, as well as YouTube videos and informational posters which LQDN encouraged internet users to share by email and on social media platforms such as Facebook and Twitter (La Quadrature du Net 2012b). In addition, LQDN provided a Voice Over IP (VOIP) phone service called Piphone that internet users could use to contact MEPs, as well as a tool called 'Political Memory', allowing users to find an MEP by their political grouping, country or committee membership, along with details of their ACTA voting intentions (La Quadrature du Net 2012f). In order to ensure the effectiveness of activists calling the European Parliament, LQDN also provided an instructional video demonstrating how to call an MEP, showing how to use the Piphone to contact an MEP's office and bring up the perceived problems with ACTA in a constructive manner (La Quadrature du Net 2012c). LQDN posted updates on their websites urging EU citizens to contact MEPs prior to the final votes on official positions by European Parliamentary committees analysing ACTA (La Quadrature du Net 2012a) and again prior to the final vote by the European Parliament (La Quadrature du Net 2012e). In this respect, LQDN's involvement in using the internet and digital technologies to coordinate activist activities played an important role in resistance to ACTA. As Bennett and Toft argue, what distributed networks 'lack in terms of traditional organizational resources they often gain in networking capacities through the use of social technologies to facilitate the maintenance and activation of weak ties' (2009, pp. 253–4). While activists in single issue areas often lack the individual resources and expertise possessed by policy network actors such as industry representatives, internet-based coordinators of action such as LQDN are able to assist activists in campaigning more effectively, using digital technologies to provide activists with resources and information they would otherwise lack or find difficult to obtain, such as contact details for and a free and accessible means of calling MEPs to discuss their concerns over ACTA. This then allows those activists to 'more confidently lobby governments and parliamentarians with high-quality information' (Ward and Gibson 2009, p. 30). Through the demonstration of possessed knowledge, activists then present themselves as being informed of those issues, meaning that the phone calls to MEPs are more likely to have impact. As Zimmermann, one of the founders of LQDN, stated prior to the committee votes on ACTA, as soon as citizens stop caring about the 'dull parliamentary process that ACTA is ongoing, they leave a space in which the copyright lobbies engulf. In order to reject ACTA once and for all, we must be watchful of each and every step of its parliamentary procedure' (La Quadrature du Net 2012a). Through providing both information and infrastructure, LQDN was able to keep activists focused throughout the parliamentary process. On 31 May 2012, it was recommended that the European Parliament reject ACTA by the Committees on Civil Liberties, Justice and Home Affairs, Industry, Research and Energy and Legal Affairs (Whittaker 2012), and then by the Committees for Development on 4 June and International Trade on 21 June (La Quadrature du Net 2012e). As the result of what was referred to by the European Parliament as 'unprecedented direct lobbying by thousands of EU citizens who called on it to reject ACTA, in street demonstrations, e-mails to MEPs and calls to their offices', in addition to the submission of an Avaaz petition signed by 2.5 million activists, ACTA was finally rejected by the European Parliament by 478 votes to 39, with 165 abstentions on 4 July 2012 (European Parliament Press Service 2012). In December 2012, the European Commission withdrew its referral of ACTA to the CJEU, signaling the end of the attempt to have the Agreement ratified in the EU (Meyer 2012b).

Networks of power and resistance, unquiet politics and the political salience of copyright policy

As was demonstrated in Chapters 4 to 6 of this book, controversial copyright-related legislation has been passed at the EU level despite strong criticisms and protest from actors including academics and the telecoms industry. However, in this case, an international agreement already signed by twenty-two Member States and the EU's representative was successfully blocked at the ratification stage. What distinguishes ACTA from legislative acts such as the Information Society, Enforcement and Term Extension Directives? It is submitted that the key distinctions are those of the dominant discourse in the ACTA narrative, and political salience. As has been demonstrated in the previous chapters of this book, copyright policy is ultimately an issue of low political salience and high complexity. As it is not the type of issue that normally generates much public attention or impact upon voting intentions, policymakers and parliamentary bodies tend to defer to the wishes of experts in this area. This was seen in the passing of the Information Society Directive, in which civil society organizations found that they were unable to match the lobbying expertise of entertainment industry organizations, and in the passing of the Enforcement Directive, in which IFPI was largely able to steer legislation and manage the framing of discourse concerning copyright enforcement. In the areas covered in Chapters 4 to 6, media coverage of legislative developments was scant to non-existent, and where stories were reported, they were mainly favourably predisposed to those legislative initiatives. With strong network relations between the entertainment industry and policymakers such as the European Commission, an environment of quiet politics allowed for the passing of legislation considered contentious or disproportionate by academics.

While an 'outsider' activity, protest is nevertheless an act that is intended to raise awareness of a particular issue or perceived problem (see, for example, Bennett and Toft 2009, p. 247; Castells 2011, p. 108). Another way of putting this is that protest constitutes an attempt to raise the political salience of a particular issue. Protests are an effective way of drawing media attention, although this attention is not always positive (Castells 2011, p. 108). It would appear that the ACTA protests generated significant media attention throughout Europe. Based on the five UK-based news sources used as a measure of political saliency, there is evidence to suggest that the ACTA protests rendered the Agreement more politically salient. For the purposes of this analysis, a story is considered negative if the framing is negative, focusing on negative aspects of ACTA such as 'censorship', 'secrecy' or 'anti-democratic'. A 'neutral' frame is one in which both positive and negative claims are represented, such as referring to the need to protect intellectual property, in addition to the above made claims. A 'positive' frame is one in which solely positive claims about ACTA are referred to in the story (for more on framing in the context of the Enforcement Directive, see Haunss and Kohlmorgen 2009). In the period between the start of negotiations in 2008 up until the end of 2011, there were seven stories about ACTA on BBC

News, all of which were editorials making negative claims, expressing the concerns of commentators Geist and Thompson (Geist 2008; Thompson 2008; Geist 2009a; Geist 2009b; Thompson 2009; Thompson 2010a; Thompson 2010b). In the *Guardian*, there were ten stories in the same timespan, three of which were presented neutrally, referring to both positive and negative claims (Arthur 2008a; Arthur 2008b; Johnson 2009), and seven of which were negative commentaries (Doctorow 2008; Johnson 2008; Doctorow 2010b; Doctorow 2010a; Doctorow 2010c; Quinn *et al.* 2010; Doctorow 2011). The *Telegraph* had eight news stories, four of which were neutral (Simpson 2008; Warman 2010a; Warman 2010e; Warman 2010d), and four of which were negative (Richmond 2010; Warman 2010b; Warman 2010c; Richmond 2011). In comparison, in the time period between the beginning of protests in January 2012 and the rejection of the Agreement by the European Parliament in July 2012, there were eighteen stories on BBC News, of which seven were neutral (BBC News 2012b; BBC News 2012d; BBC News 2012j; Lee 2012b; Lee 2012c; Lee 2012d; Lee 2012f), and eleven negative (BBC News 2012a; BBC News 2012c; BBC News 2012e; BBC News 2012f; BBC News 2012g; BBC News 2012h; BBC News 2012i; Cellan-Jones 2012; Lee 2012a; Lee 2012e; Moore 2012a). The *Guardian* had sixteen stories in that time period, six being neutral (Arthur 2012a; Arthur 2012b; Arthur 2012c; Arthur 2012e; Arthur 2012g; Plunkett 2012), two being positive commentaries (Lindvall 2012a; Lindvall 2012b), and eight being negative (Arthur 2012d; Arthur 2012f; Arthur 2012h; Halliday 2012a; Halliday 2012b; Halliday 2012c; Lingard and Perrott 2012; Meyer 2012a). The *Telegraph*, in comparison, had only five stories during this six-month period, although all were negative (Warman 2012a; Warman 2012b; Warman 2012c; Warman 2012d; Warman 2012e). The tabloid newspaper used, the *Daily Mail*, had no stories either before or after the protests began.

As Iyengar (1991) has stated, and has been discussed throughout this book, the media framing of events is important in determining potential political responses to a particular issue. This is because the way in which an issue is framed affects what the perceived 'problem' in that issue is. For example, reporting on the Enforcement Directive took an industry favourable view, in which the lack of effective enforcement mechanisms was problematized. The solution, therefore, was stronger protections. This was despite the arguments of the telecoms industry and academics that those posed solutions were disproportionate. However, the way in which the ACTA negotiations and potential ratification were framed was significantly different. It becomes apparent in the ACTA narrative, particularly after the beginning of protests in January, that the frame for the discussion of the Agreement became one of democracy, rather than of intellectual property. Initial news stories, both neutral and negative, discussed the secrecy of negotiations (see, for example, Arthur 2008b; Doctorow 2010b; Warman 2010d). While the fact that the intention of the Agreement was to counter intellectual property infringement was mentioned, the lack of transparency in the negotiation procedure was the main story. With the beginning of protests in January and continuing throughout February, the focus of news stories was on the concerns of protestors, with references to the 'contentious' nature of the Agreement being made (Arthur 2012e), in addition to claims that the ACTA posed a threat to the internet and associated accusations of resultant censorship (Lee 2012d). The dominant discourse from January onwards became one of democratic accountability and perceptions of risks to the free flow of information on the internet. Statements from high profile political actors further reinforced this discourse, such as when the original rapporteur for ACTA, MEP Kader Arif, resigned in protest over the handling of the Agreement, stating that he denounced 'in the strongest manner the process that led to the signing of this agreement: no association of civil society [and] lack of transparency from the beginning' (Arif as quoted in Arthur 2012d). This argument was also referred to in reporting on the protests (Lee 2012a; Plunkett 2012). This discourse in turn began to influence the European Parliament, transforming the discourse of intellectual property protection into a discourse of accountability and responsibility. MEP David Martin, who replaced Arif as the rapporteur for ACTA, stated in April 2012 that the 'intended benefits of this international agreement are far outweighed by the potential threats to civil liberties . . . the European Parliament cannot guarantee adequate protection for citizens' rights in the future under Acta' (BBC News 2012c).

This statement represented a substantial shift in the European Parliament approach to ACTA. In 2010, when negotiations were still ongoing, several groupings within the European Parliament presented a critical resolution against ACTA, deriding the lack of disclosure during negotiations and urging greater transparency in proceedings (Verts/ALE et al. 2010, sec. 5–7). However, this resolution was rejected in a vote by the European Parliament (La Quadrature du Net 2010) in favour of a resolution that reiterated the need to ensure effective protection of intellectual property rights (PPE and ECR 2010, sec. A–D). At the time this resolution was passed, ACTA was still being negotiated in an environment of low political salience, in which news coverage was limited (if still negative), and without much in the way of public attention being paid to the legislative process on what was considered an intellectual property matter. By April, however, the salience of ACTA had increased, particularly in light of protests throughout the EU. According to Gormley, issues become more salient when a threat is perceived (1986, pp. 600–1). When the discourse becomes one of democratic accountability, and perceived threats of censorship, then an issue is more likely to become salient. This has been suggested as being one reason why the anti-ACTA protests were particularly strong in former Soviet states, in which official state censorship had occurred in recent memory (see, for example, Arthur 2012b). The result is that European Parliament deliberations had moved from being conducted in an environment of quiet politics, in which legislatures are likely to defer to the interests of policy network actors such as industry representatives, to an environment of 'noisy' politics, in which the ability of industry representatives to influence legislation is reduced unless 'they can ride out the storm of public attention and shift to a technical battle over bureaucratic regulations that is uninteresting to newspaper readers' (Culpepper 2011, p. 190). However, continued protest action and the coordination of lobbying efforts in the European Parliament by organizations such as LQDN (as discussed earlier) meant that industry representatives were not able to exert significant influence over the course of deliberations. Indeed, in media reporting, supporters of ACTA were discursively on the back foot, seeking to defend the Agreement. For example, the Intellectual Property Office of the UK was quoted in one report as stating that ACTA did not threaten internet 'freedom' as 'it aims to improve the enforcement of existing IPR laws, not create new ones' (BBC News 2012c). In another report, Commissioner de Gucht stated that 'debate must be based upon facts, and not upon the misinformation and rumour that has dominated social media sites and blogs in recent weeks', arguing that ACTA would 'raise global standards for intellectual property rights' (Lee 2012c). Discursively, de Gucht felt obliged to respond to criticisms of the Agreement, qualifying his statement on the protection of intellectual property in light of the pervading discourse, albeit to challenge it. However, as was demonstrated in the previous chapter, micro-resistances taking place within a dominant frame of discourse have the potential to reinforce and validate that discourse. In arguing within the frame of the dominant discourse, namely that of democratic accountability and threats of repressive laws, supporters of ACTA assisted in reinforcing that discourse. In releasing a press statement in which IFPI claimed that protests were stifling democratic discourse, with 'coordinated attacks on democratic institutions such as the European Parliament and national governments over ACTA' (as reproduced in Horten 2012), IFPI was unable to reframe the discourse concerning ACTA at the European level, instead working within the accepted discourse.

It is likely that the effectiveness of the protests and lobbying of the European Parliament by activists was the result of a clear and unified message reiterating the need to reject ACTA on the grounds of democratic deficit and concerns over civil liberties. In this respect, the protests and lobbying effectively constructed a narrative in which ACTA posed a threat to civil liberties, and it was the role of the European Parliament as the representative body for EU citizens to give effect to the wishes of European voters. Bennett and Toft underline the importance of narrative construction as a way of unifying collective actors with differing interests and backgrounds, allowing for multiple narratives (such as ACTA as lacking in transparency, and ACTA as threatening civil liberties) to be incorporated into a single frame (such as 'No to ACTA') (see generally Bennett and Toft 2009). This allowed for a weak-tie network functioning across Member States to present a clear, unified message, in away that was not achieved in attempts to challenge the passing of the Enforcement Directive (as discussed in Chapter 5). By focusing on the issue of democracy, rather than the disproportionate nature of ACTA as a means of protecting intellectual property, civil society organizations such as LQDN were able to 'define problems, set agendas, prescribe solutions, and hold institutions accountable to previously stated policies and principles' (Hintz 2012,

p. 135). In other words, civil society organizations, rather than policy network actors such as IFPI, set the frame of acceptable discourse with regard to ACTA. This discourse ultimately defined the European Parliament committee reports on the Agreement. For example, the Committee on Industry, Research and Energy stated in its reasons for rejecting ACTA that it did 'not ensure a fair balance between the right to intellectual property and the freedom to conduct business, the right to protection of personal data and the freedom to receive or impart information' (Committee on Industry, Research and Energy 2012, para. 5). The Committee on Civil Liberties, Justice and Home Affairs worked specifically within a frame of concern for democracy, stating that 'ACTA comes at a very premature stage and a possible adoption of the Treaty would essentially freeze the possibility of having a public deliberation that is worthy of our democratic heritage' (Committee on Civil Liberties, Justice and Home Affairs 2012, p. 6). The Committee on International Trade, the final committee to report on ACTA, urged rejection stating that 'intended benefits of this international agreement are far outweighed by the potential threats to civil liberties' (Committee on International Trade 2012, p. 6). The final statement on ACTA by European Parliament President Martin Schulz made clear that the discourse within which ACTA was rejected was one of democracy, not intellectual property:

> The decision to reject ACTA was not taken lightly. It followed an intensive, inclusive and transparent debate with civil society, business organisations, national parliaments and many other stakeholders . . . The debate on ACTA demonstrated the existence of European public opinion that transcends national borders. All over Europe, people were engaged in protests and debates. The mobilisation of public opinion was unprecedented. As the President of the European Parliament, I am committed to dialogue with citizens and to make Europe more democratic and understandable.
>
> (Schulz 2012)

The rejection of ACTA constituted an effective act of macro-resistance, transforming networks of power and dominant discourses in such a way that individual citizens rather than industry actors were able to influence the direction of intellectual property policy. This is in noticeable contrast to the passing of the Information Society, Enforcement and Term Extension Directives, and the proposals for a Directive on Collective Rights Management, in which policy network actors such as IFPI largely achieved the preferred framing of legislative responses to perceived problems. Using the language of democracy and accountability as a means to reshape those networks meant that ACTA specifically was resisted/rejected, through the transformation of the issue from being a low salience issue of copyright regulation to a high salience issue of democratic accountability and civil liberties. It is important to note, however, that this does not result in a substantial change to the general networks of power and dominant discourses of intellectual property itself in the EU, and it is arguable whether copyright regulation in itself will become a more politically salient issue. The discourse on copyright protection as a necessity does not appear to have been substantially changed at the European level, including at the European Parliament, the body responsible for the EU rejection of ACTA. The discourse of rapporteur David Martin is particularly interesting in this respect. Speaking after the International Trade Committee vote, Martin stated that 'this was not an anti-intellectual property vote. This group believes Europe does have to protect its intellectual property but Acta was too vague a document' (as quoted in BBC News 2012d). Subsequent to the final vote by the European Parliament, Schulz reiterated in his statement that the vote against ACTA was 'not one against the protection of intellectual property. On the contrary – the European Parliament staunchly supports the fight against piracy and counterfeiting, which harm European companies and pose a threat to consumer health and European jobs' (Schulz 2012). In other words the dominant discourse of intellectual property protection itself has not been substantially altered by the rejection of ACTA. The transformation in this particular instance concerned the framing of ACTA specifically, rather than intellectual property more generally. The presentation by activists of a clear and unified 'No to ACTA' message meant that their attempt to ensure the rejection of ACTA was successful. However, it also meant that the discourse and subsequent debate was limited to the effects of ACTA, rather than resulting in a broader discussion concerning copyright. Indeed, as an institution, the European Parliament appears to remain favourably predisposed to copyright. In May 2013, the European Parliament adopted a resolution on the Transatlantic Free-Trade Agreement (TAFTA), an ongoing negotiation between the US and EU for the creation of a Transatlantic Free Trade Area. In addition to removing trade barriers and tariffs, TAFTA negotiations are also understood to include provisions on intellectual property protection. A wide range of civil society organizations have openly condemned TAFTA as being ACTA '2.0' (Wessels 2013), and being subject to the same concerns over secrecy, in addition to a lack of transparency and democratic accountability (Sutton 2013). The European Parliament, however, rejected amendments by some MEPs criticizing this lack of transparency in negotiations, and the finalized resolution states that 'intellectual property is one of the driving forces of innovation and creation and a pillar of the knowledge-based economy, and that the agreement should include strong protection of precisely and clearly defined areas of intellectual property rights' (European Parliament 2013). It would appear, therefore, that while effective transformation of networks of power was achieved with regard to the framing of ACTA, the networks of power in copyright law and policy remain unchanged.

Conclusion

In the introduction to this book, it was stated that asking 'why are lobbyists unduly influential over the development of copyright law?' was potentially the wrong question to ask, given that all attempts, whether by industry representatives lobbying for stronger protections or academics advising on the optimal duration of copyright, are attempts to influence the legislative process. The more interesting question, on that basis, is 'why are some lobbyists more successful than others in influencing the legislative process?', a question that helps to reconceptualize the way in which copyright policy is formulated. The concept of networks proves to be particularly useful in evaluating influence in the legislative process, with Foucault's networks of power approach providing an effective frame for analysis. If power is conceived as being something that operates, or rather, something that is exercised by one actor over another in order to influence that actor's decisions, rather than something characterized as being a possession of 'the powerful', then a more holistic consideration of the way in which 'power' can influence the legislative process can be achieved. One way of analysing that power in practice is through the concept of political salience more generally and Culpepper's theory on quiet politics specifically. The political salience of an issue will help to determine whether individual citizens (or voters) are likely to take interest and vote for a political representative (or threaten not to vote for that same representative) as a response to action taken on that issue, becoming an active node in the policymaking network, or whether a lack of voter interest will result in corporate actors being able to guide the legislative process. The media, another type of node in the networks of power, plays an important role in assessing political salience by providing an idea of how salient an issue is by the amount of coverage and framing of that issue. Where an issue is of low salience, then if a story is reported at all, it is likely that the framing of that story will be one favourable to business interests. This in part is due to the deference to perceived expertise on the part of those corporate actors. Policymakers are by no means immune to the relative salience of an issue. Where an issue is highly salient, policymakers are more likely to pay heed to the perceived preferences of 'ordinary voters'. Where an issue is not particularly salient, policymakers are also likely to defer to managerial or corporate expertise, based on perceptions that those actors best understand the business sector in which they operate.

It is for this reason that conceptualizing policymaking in terms of networks, both through the Foucauldian notion of governmentality and the theories of networked governance, becomes useful in assessing the way in which copyright law develops. By moving away from a conceptualization of lawmaking as involving a hierarchical relationship, in which 'powerful' European institutions such as the European Commission draft legislation that is then passed by the European Parliament and 'forced' upon Member States, it is possible to see that power relations between actors are multilateral. Legislation is not developed in a vacuum, or to put it another way, the Commission does not create copyright policy in splendid isolation. Drivers for law-making may come from the international level, or from the national level. Policies may be developed or lobbied for by private business interests, by national governments or by academics. There may be significant transference, through the exercise of power by international industry representatives upon national governments, who then exert influence upon

European policymakers, who then draft laws that are then implemented by Member States' parliamentary bodies. By considering copyright in this way, it is possible to begin to assess why certain actors are more influential than others in framing or influencing policies, by focusing on the power relations acting within the networks, rather than assuming a default position of an industry as 'policymaker' and a European institution as 'policy taker'. Instead, policies are formed through the interaction between actors, in which 'problems' are identified, to which legislation is perceived as a 'solution'. The solution, however, is determined by the way that the problem is framed. If, for example, the 'problem' is framed as a lack of effective copyright enforcement mechanisms, then the solution for this problem is legislation that creates or bolsters enforcement mechanisms. The ability to effectively frame a policy, or determine what conduct is a problem, is dependent on perceptions of expertise. In the Foucauldian conceptualization, expertise is key in networks of power. Experts produce knowledge and this knowledge helps to reinforce the networks of power. Through the regular production of expert knowledge and interaction with European institutional actors, industry representatives help to establish a discourse in which they are perceived as being experts, effectively understanding their area of business, knowing the problems that sector faces and what solutions to that problem are advisable. Particularly in areas of high technical complexity and low political salience, the perceived expertise of industry representatives plays a key role in legislative development, as institutional actors will rely upon and defer to that expertise, rather than invest time and labour in seeking to understand complex information that may not be perceived as being of particular importance to citizens. Because of this deference, certain discourses become dominant, such as the discourse that states that increasing protection for intellectual property will result in economic benefit. When this discourse is accepted as constituting a 'truth', then the ability to challenge or resist those discourses is limited, as attempts to do so may fall outside of the accepted bounds of discourse. In practice, this may mean that where a dominant discourse of protection is established, and a lack of effective protection established as being a problem, then attempts to counter this discourse by arguing that the perceived problem does not exist are less likely to be successful than discourses proposing 'solutions' to that existing problem.

The application of this to the development of digital copyright law at the EU level helps to provide insight on how relationships within the networks of power allow for certain discourses to become dominant, resulting in certain legislative responses. Copyright law scholarship can be characterized by opposition to the EU's legislative agenda, with each new development being subject to critique by a range of academics. This critique can be over the effectiveness (or not) of proposed changes, the proportionality of those changes, or the legitimacy of those changes (which is often considered in relation to the role of lobbying on law-making processes). For example, the implementation of the Information Society Directive was criticized on the grounds that it unduly (in the eyes of its critics) expanded the scope of copyright, and restricted the exceptions and limitations to copyright. However, the dominant discourse during the development of the Directive was one of the significant changes (and resultant threats) brought about by the internet. Increases in the scope of copyright were necessary in order to ensure that the possibility to effortlessly and cheaply reproduce copyrighted works would not eliminate the incentives and/or rewards for creation. When a dominant discourse of the late 1990s was that 'the internet will change everything', then opponents to change arguing that reforms were not necessary, or were disproportionate, had less impact than those arguing about the best way to ensure those protections continued to exist. IFPI in particular was a very influential node in the policy network surrounding the Information Society Directive, providing expert knowledge at the pre-legislative stage, and using familiarity with European law-making processes and active connections with European Commission and Parliament actors to ensure the passing of the Directive. IFPI again was particularly influential in the passing of the Enforcement Directive and the subsequent framing of internet intermediaries as having a responsibility to monitor and end infringements of copyright online, providing both data on the losses attributable to piracy and framing a lack of enforcement mechanisms as posing a significant threat to the economic health of the EU. IFPI, as was demonstrated in Chapter 5, is a particularly important policy node in copyright law development at the EU level, taking an active role in producing knowledge that influences policy framing (whether in the form of direct evidence production as in the case of the Enforcement Directive, or through commissioning the production of that evidence as in the case of the Term Extension Directive), and then using inter-institutional connections to ensure legislation is passed. Even where a particular policy is not particularly favoured by IFPI, as in the case of the proposed Directive on Collective Rights Management, they are nevertheless influential in the framing of particular issues. One such example is the way that cross-border licensing has been framed as a problem concerning collecting societies' national roles, best addressed through competition law and the breaking of national monopolies. In each of the legislative initiatives assessed, actors such as IFPI have exerted considerable influence over European institutional actors, largely due to the perception of the expertise that IFPI holds.

Another characteristic of the assessed initiatives is their high complexity and low political salience. Media coverage of the Information Society, Enforcement and Term Extension Directives during their legislative development was negligible based on the news sources analysed, and next to non-existent in popular tabloid newspapers. Where there has been media coverage, particularly in the case of the Enforcement Directive, the coverage has been somewhat favourable to positive claims concerning that legislation, demonstrating the ability of policy network actors to influence the framing of that legislation. By operating in environments of quiet politics, in which media and individual interest in the legislation being adopted is low, policy network actors such as IFPI are subsequently able to exert greater influence over European institutions than opponents to those legislative initiatives. In particular, successful resistance by academics is limited due to the fact that this resistance often comes in the forms of critique in academic publications that arguably have limited reach; while the arguments made may influence and change the perceptions of other academics, the ability to increase the salience of an issue through academic to academic conversations is comparatively weak, due to the low density of network connections. Where academics advise policymaking institutions directly, such as commissioned studies on the impact of extending the term of protection for sound recordings, they are 'combatants' in a 'battlefield of ideas', in which they present a discourse that actively competes with established policy network actors. In this battle of expertise, those arguments that more effectively fit within the dominant discourse are more likely to be accepted as 'true'. If, as is the case with the Term Extension Directive, the limited duration of protection has already been established as the 'problem', then arguments raised on how best to extend that term are more likely to be accepted than those that suggest that the duration of protection is not a problem.

Resistance in the field of copyright law, it is submitted, is dependent on political salience. While salience is not a prerequisite for resistance within the court system, any resistance to extensions of copyright law are limited by the role of the CJEU as an interpreter of the law, working within the framework of the Directives referred to it. While the court may be a useful site of micro-resistance, the ability to affect significant change in the networks of power at a macro level is debatable. The CJEU acts as a potential node for reform, rather than 'revolution'. For macro-level revolution, or transformation of dominant discourses governing copyright law and policy, it is necessary for the copyright to become a politically salient issue. As the European Parliament rejection of ACTA has demonstrated, lobbying in the field of copyright law and policy is not a simple matter of corporations getting the legislation corporations desire. Through the construction of a counter discourse bringing into question the way in which ACTA was negotiated, and the formation of a cohesive issue network operating both online and offline to raise awareness of concerns over ACTA, the Agreement became more politically salient than issues of copyright law have been historically. The media attention, and subsequently the public attention paid to ACTA, is unprecedented in the field of copyright law, resulting in the creation of an environment of 'unquiet' politics, in which a dominant discourse of the responsibility of the European Parliament to fulfill the wishes of voters was established. This has not resulted in the transformation of networks of power in digital copyright law in the EU; instead, it has shown where, and how, resistance is possible. While resistance was successful against ACTA specifically, to change the networks of power in copyright law will require the facilitation and maintenance of a level of political interest in copyright that has not yet been expressed. As Foucault stated, for revolutionary resistance to be successful, relations of power must be attacked through the notions and institutions that serve as their armaments and armour. Should civil society organizations and academics desire to change the networks of power that guide copyright policy, they must raise the salience of copyright, bringing it to the attention of the 'ordinary voter'. By establishing discourses in which the direction of copyright law can be 'problematized', and by encouraging voters to become involved in parliamentary processes, an environment of unquiet politics may be established. If resistance is to be effective, then the revolution must be televised.

Bibliography

Arthur, C., 2008a. 'The right to peer inside your iPod'. *The Guardian*. Available at: www.theguardian.com/technology/2008/jul/10/intellectualproperty.law [Accessed 21 August 2013].

Arthur, C., 2008b. 'What does the Anti-Counterfeiting Trade Agreement (Acta) really mean for you and I?' *The Guardian*. Available at: www.theguardian.com/technology/blog/2008/jul/10/whatdoestheanticounterfeiti [Accessed 21 August 2013].

Arthur, C., 2012a. 'Acta approval stalled by European commission'. *The Guardian*. Available at: www.theguardian.com/technology/2012/feb/22/acta-stalled-european-commission [Accessed 21 August 2013].

Arthur, C., 2012b. 'Acta criticised after thousands protest in Europe'. *The Guardian*. Available at: www.theguardian.com/technology/2012/feb/13/acta-protests-europe [Accessed 19 August 2013].

Arthur, C., 2012c. 'Acta down, but not out, as Europe votes against controversial treaty'. *The Guardian*. Available at: www.theguardian.com/technology/2012/jul/04/acta-european-parliament-votes-against [Accessed 21 August 2013].

Arthur, C., 2012d. 'Acta goes too far, says MEP'. *The Guardian*. Available at: www.theguardian.com/technology/2012/feb/01/acta-goes-too-far-kader-arif [Accessed 21 August 2013].

Arthur, C., 2012e. 'Acta protests break out as EU states sign up to treaty'. *The Guardian*. Available at: www.theguardian.com/technology/2012/jan/27/acta-protests-eu-states-sign-treaty [Accessed 21 August 2013].

Arthur, C., 2012f. 'Acta set to fail after Europe's trade committee votes against it'. *The Guardian*. Available at: www.theguardian.com/technology/2012/jun/21/acta-europe-vote-against [Accessed 21 August 2013].

Arthur, C., 2012g. 'Acta unlikely to be ratified in Europe, says Kroes'. *The Guardian*. Available at: www.theguardian.com/technology/2012/may/08/acta-europe-kroes [Accessed 21 August 2013].

Arthur, C., 2012h. 'YouTube loses music clip copyright battle in court'. *The Guardian*. Available at: www.theguardian.com/technology/2012/apr/20/youtube-music-clip-copyright-court [Accessed 21 August 2013].

Baraliuc, I., Depreeuw, S. and Gutwirth, S., 2013. 'Copyright enforcement in the digital age: A post-ACTA view on the balancing of fundamental rights'. *International Journal of Law and Information Technology*, 21(1), pp. 92–104.

BBC News, 2012a. 'EU court blocks net-filtering bid'. *BBC*. Available at: www.bbc.co.uk/news/technology-17060112 [Accessed 21 August 2013].

BBC News, 2012b. 'EU rejects anti-piracy agreement'. *BBC*. Available at: www.bbc.co.uk/news/technology-18704192 [Accessed 21 August 2013].

BBC News, 2012c. 'Euro MP David Martin dismisses anti-counterfeiting treaty'. *BBC*. Available at: www.bbc.co.uk/news/technology-17728045 [Accessed 21 August 2013].

BBC News, 2012d. 'European trade committee votes to reject piracy treaty'. *BBC*. Available at: www.bbc.co.uk/news/technology-18533268 [Accessed 21 August 2013].

BBC News, 2012e. 'European watchdog warns on Acta'. *BBC*. Available at: www.bbc.co.uk/news/technology-17827566 [Accessed 21 August 2013].

BBC News, 2012f. 'Germany delays Acta signing'. *BBC*. Available at: www.bbc.co.uk/news/technology-16980451 [Accessed 21 August 2013].

BBC News, 2012g. 'Poland protests for online freedom'. *BBC*. Available at: www.bbc.co.uk/news/technology-16757611 [Accessed 21 August 2013].

BBC News, 2012h. 'Polish sites hit in Acta attack'. *BBC*. Available at: www.bbc.co.uk/news/technology-16686265 [Accessed 21 August 2013].

BBC News, 2012i. 'UK ISPs lose file-sharing appeal'. *BBC*. Available at: www.bbc.co.uk/news/technology-17270817 [Accessed 21 August 2013].

BBC News, 2012j. 'Web treaty protests across Poland'. *BBC*. Available at: www.bbc.co.uk/news/world-europe-16735219 [Accessed 19 August 2013].

Beckedahl, M., 2012. 'How to build an anti-ACTA campaign'. *Digitale Gesellschaft*. Available at: https://digitalegesellschaft.de/2012/06/how-to-build-an-anti-acta-campaign/ [Accessed 19 August 2013].

Benkler, Y., 2006. *The wealth of networks: How social production transforms markets and freedom*. New Haven, CT: Yale University Press.

Bennett, W.L. and Toft, A., 2009. 'Identity, technology, and narratives: Transnational activism and social networks'. In A. Chadwick and P.N. Howard, eds, *Routledge handbook of internet politics*. London: Routledge.

Bimber, B., Stohl, C. and Flanagin, A.J., 2009. 'Technological change and the shifting nature of political organization'. In A. Chadwick and P.N. Howard, eds, *Routledge handbook of internet politics*. London: Routledge.

Blakeney, M. and Blakeney, L., 2010. 'Stealth legislation? Negotiating the Anti-Counterfeiting Trade Agreement (ACTA)'. *International Trade Law and Regulation*, 16(4), pp. 87–95.

Buck, P. de, 2011. 'Expectations of European companies as regards intellectual property in Europe and globally'. In F. Gevers and E. Cornu, eds, *The future prospects for intellectual property in the EU: 2012–2022*. Brussels: Bruylant.

Castells, M., 2011. *Communication power*. Oxford: Oxford University Press.

Cellan-Jones, R., 2012. 'The internet is angry: Is it winning?' *BBC*. Available at: www.bbc.co.uk/news/technology-17010553 [Accessed 21 August 2013].

Committee on Civil Liberties, Justice and Home Affairs, 2012. *Draft Opinion of the Committee on Civil Liberties, Justice and Home Affairs for the Committee on International Trade on the compatibility of the Anti-Counterfeiting Trade Agreement with the rights enshrined in the Charter of Fundamental Rights of the European Union*. Brussels: European Parliament.

Committee on Industry, Research and Energy, 2012. *Draft Opinion of the Committee on Industry, Research and Energy for the Committee on International Trade on the compatibility of the Anti-Counterfeiting Trade Agreement with the rights enshrined in the Charter of Fundamental Rights of the European Union*. Brussels: European Parliament.

Committee on International Trade, 2012. *Draft Recommendation on the draft Council decision on the conclusion of the Anti-Counterfeiting Trade Agreement*. Brussels: European Parliament.

Couts, A., 2012. 'ACTA bombshell: Germany refuses to sign anti-piracy treaty amid protests'. *Digital Trends*. Available at: www.digitaltrends.com/international/acta-bombshell-germany-refuses-to-sign-anti-piracy-treaty-amid-protests/ [Accessed 19 August 2013].

Culpepper, P.D., 2011. *Quiet politics and business power: Corporate control in Europe and Japan*. Cambridge: Cambridge University Press.

Doctorow, C., 2008. 'Copyright enforcers should learn lessons from the war on spam'. *The Guardian*. Available at: www.theguardian.com/technology/2008/jul/15/copyright.filesharing [Accessed 21 August 2013].

Doctorow, C., 2010a. 'Digital economy act: This means war'. *The Guardian*. Available at: www.theguardian.com/technology/2010/apr/16/digital-economy-act-cory-doctorow [Accessed 21 August 2013].

Doctorow, C., 2010b. 'The real cost of free'. *The Guardian*. Available at: www.theguardian.com/technology/blog/2010/oct/05/free-online-content-cory-doctorow [Accessed 21 August 2013].

Doctorow, C., 2010c. 'Viacom v YouTube is a microcosm of the entertainment industry'. *The Guardian*. Available at: www.theguardian.com/technology/blog/2010/may/04/viacom-youtube [Accessed 21 August 2013].

Doctorow, C., 2011. 'Beware the spyware model of technology: Its flaws are built in'. *The Guardian*. Available at: www.theguardian.com/technology/2011/mar/15/computers-incorporate-spyware-dangers [Accessed 21 August 2013].

Downing, J.D.H., 2003. 'The independent media center movement'. In N. Couldry and J. Curran, eds, *Contesting media power: Alternative media in a networked world*. Lanham, MD: Rowman & Littlefield.

European Commission, 2010. *Consolidated text prepared for public release: Anti-Counterfeiting Trade Agreement*. Brussels: European Commission.

European Commission, 2011. *A single market for intellectual property rights: Boosting creativity and innovation to provide economic growth, high quality jobs and first class products and services in Europe*. Brussels: European Commission.

European Parliament, 2013. *European Parliament resolution of 23 May 2013 on EU trade and investment negotiations with the United States of America*. Brussels: European Parliament.

European Parliament Press Service, 2012. 'European Parliament rejects ACTA'. *Europarl*. Available at: www.europarl.europa.eu/news/en/pressroom/content/20120703IPR48247/html/European-Parliament-rejects-ACTA [Accessed 20 August 2013].

Farrand, B. and Carrapico, H., 2012. 'Copyright law as a matter of (inter)national security? – The attempt to securitise commercial infringement and its spillover onto individual liability'. *Crime, Law and Social Change*, 57(4), pp. 373–401.

Foucault, M., 1977. *Language, counter-memory, practice: Selected essays and interviews*. D.F. Bouchard, ed. Ithaca, NY: Cornell University Press.

Fry, R., 2012. 'ACTA on its knees'. *Intellectual Property Magazine*, April, pp. 12–13.

Geiger, C., 2010. 'Of ACTA, "pirates" and organized criminality: How "criminal" should the enforcement of intellectual property be?' *International Review of Intellectual Property and Competition Law*, 41(6), pp. 629–31.

Geiger, C., 2012. 'Weakening multilateralism in intellectual property lawmaking: A European perspective on ACTA'. *The WIPO Journal*, 3(2), pp. 166–77.

Geist, M., 2008. 'Trade agreement could hit privacy'. *BBC News*. Available at: http://news.bbc.co.uk/1/hi/technology/7446280.stm [Accessed 21 August 2013].

Geist, M., 2009a. 'Battle over global anti-counterfeit treaty'. *BBC*. Available at: http://news.bbc.co.uk/1/hi/technology/8011895.stm [Accessed 21 August 2013].

Geist, M., 2009b. 'Could piracy blacklist backfire?' *BBC*. Available at: http://news.bbc.co.uk/1/hi/technology/8033382.stm [Accessed 21 August 2013].

Geist, M., 2009c. 'Inside views: The ACTA threat to the future of WIPO'. *Intellectual Property Watch*. Available at: www.ip-watch.org/2009/04/14/the-acta-threat-to-the-future-of-wipo/ [Accessed 17 August 2013].

Gera, V., 2012. 'ACTA protests in Poland: Groups fear copyright treaty will lead to censorship'. *Huffington Post*. Available at: www.huffingtonpost.com/2012/01/24/acta-protests-poland_n_1229110.html [Accessed 19 August 2013].

Gil de Zúñiga, H., Veenstra, A., Vraga, E., Shah and D., 2010. 'Digital democracy: Reimagining pathways to political participation'. *Journal of Information Technology & Politics*, 7(1), pp. 36–51.

Goldsmith, J. and Lessig, L., 2010. 'Anti-counterfeiting agreement raises constitutional concerns'. *The Washington Post*. Available at: www.washingtonpost.com/wp-dyn/content/article/2010/03/25/AR2010032502403.html [Accessed 17 August 2013].

Gormley, W.T., 1986. 'Regulatory issue networks in a federal system'. *Polity*, 18(4), pp. 595–620.

Graber, D.A., Bimber, B., Bennett, W.L., Davis, R. and Norris, P., 2004. 'The internet and politics: Emerging perspectives'. In H.F. Nissenbaum and M.E. Price, eds, *Academy and the Internet*. New York: Peter Lang.

Gucht, K. de, 2012. 'Statement by Commissioner Karel De Gucht on ACTA'. *European Commission*. Available at: http://trade.ec.europa.eu/doclib/press/index.cfm?id=778 [Accessed 20 August 2013].

Halliday, J., 2012a. 'Facebook and Twitter do not need anti-piracy software, says court'. *The Guardian*. Available at: www.theguardian.com/media/2012/feb/16/facebook-twitter-piracy-software-court-ruling [Accessed 21 August 2013].

Halliday, J., 2012b. 'Publishers make bid to close filesharing sites'. *The Guardian*. Available at: www.theguardian.com/technology/2012/feb/16/publishers-bid-close-filesharing-sites [Accessed 21 August 2013].

Halliday, J., 2012c. 'The Pirate Bay to defy international crackdown on filesharing websites'. *The Guardian*. Available at: www.theguardian.com/technology/2012/feb/21/pirate-bay-defy-crackdown-filesharing [Accessed 21 August 2013].

Haunss, S. and Kohlmorgen, L., 2009. 'Lobbying or politics? Political claims making in IP conflicts'. In S. Haunss and K.C. Shadlen, eds, *Politics of intellectual property: Contestation over the ownership, use, and control of knowledge and information*. Cheltenham: Edward Elgar.

Heclo, H., 1978. 'Issue networks and executive establishment'. In A. King, ed., *The new American political system*. Washington, DC: American Enterprise Institute for Public Policy Research.

Hintz, A., 2012. 'Challenging the digital gatekeepers: International policy initiatives for free expression'. *Journal of Information Policy*, 2, pp. 128–50.

Horten, M., 2012. 'IFPI accuses: "protests silence democratic process"'. *IPTEGRITY. COM*. Available at: www.iptegrity.com/index.php/acta/744-ifpi-accuses-protests-silence-democratic-process [Accessed 21 August 2013].

Indian representative at the WTO TRIPS Council, 2010. 'India's intervention to the WTO TRIPS Council'. *Knowledge Ecology International*. Available at: http://keionline.org/node/864 [Accessed 17 August 2013].

Iyengar, S., 1991. *Is anyone responsible?: How television frames political issues*. Chicago, IL: University of Chicago Press.

Johnson, B., 2008. 'Breakfast briefing: MySpace tightens up on scammers'. *The Guardian*. Available at: www.theguardian.com/technology/blog/2009/nov/04/breakfast-briefing [Accessed 21 August 2013].

Johnson, B., 2009. 'What is Acta and what should I know about it?' *The Guardian*. Available at: www.theguardian.com/technology/2009/nov/11/acta-trade-agreement [Accessed 21 August 2013].

Krueger, B.S., 2002. 'Assessing the potential of internet political participation in the United States: A research approach'. *American Politics Research*, *30*, pp. 476–98.

La Quadrature du Net, 2010. 'European Parliament on its way to accept ACTA?' *La Quadrature du Net*. Available at: www.laquadrature.net/en/european-parliament-on-its-way-to-accept-acta [Accessed 21 August 2013].

La Quadrature du Net, 2012a. 'ACTA in parliamentary committees: Urgent citizen participation required'. *La Quadrature du Net*. Available at: www.laquadrature.net/en/acta-in-parliamentary-committees-urgent-citizen-participation-required [Accessed 20 August 2013].

La Quadrature du Net, 2012b. 'How to act against ACTA'. *La Quadrature du Net Wiki*. Available at: https://www.laquadrature.net/wiki/How_to_act_against_ACTA#Contact_your_Elected_Representatives [Accessed 20 August 2013].

La Quadrature du Net, 2012c. [instructional videos – vol.1] 'How to call a MEP (against ACTA)'. *La Quadrature du Net*. Available at: www.laquadrature.net/en/instructional-videos-vol1-how-to-call-a-mep-against-acta [Accessed 20 August 2013].

La Quadrature du Net, 2012d. 'Join the giant distributed ACTA protest all over Europe!' *La Quadrature du Net*. Available at: www.laquadrature.net/en/join-the-giant-distributed-acta-protest-all-over-europe [Accessed 19 August 2013].

La Quadrature du Net, 2012e. '[Major victory] Now let's win ACTA's final round!' *La Quadrature du Net*. Available at: www.laquadrature.net/en/major-victory-now-lets-win-actas-final-round [Accessed 20 August 2013].

La Quadrature du Net, 2012f. 'Tools'. *La Quadrature du Net*. Available at: www.laquadrature.net/en/tools [Accessed 20 August 2013].

Lee, D., 2012a. 'Acta protests spread over Europe'. *BBC*. Available at: www.bbc.co.uk/news/technology-16906086 [Accessed August 21, 2013].

Lee, D., 2012b. Acta: European Parliament's Schulz criticises treaty. *BBC*. Available at: www.bbc.co.uk/news/technology-17012832 [Accessed 21 August 2013].

Lee, D., 2012c. 'EU court to rule on Acta legality'. *BBC*. Available at: www.bbc.co.uk/news/technology-17125469 [Accessed 21 August 2013].

Lee, D., 2012d. 'Europe takes to streets over Acta'. *BBC*. Available at: www.bbc.co.uk/news/technology-16999497 [Accessed 21 August 2013].

Lee, D., 2012e. 'Piracy treaty dealt critical blow'. *BBC*. Available at: www.bbc.co.uk/news/technology-18264856 [Accessed 21 August 2013].

Lee, D., 2012f. 'Top Euro MP quits in piracy row'. *BBC*. Available at: www.bbc.co.uk/news/technology-16757142 [Accessed 21 August 2013].

Leith, E., 2011. 'ACTA: The anti-counterfeiting crack-down'. *Entertainment Law Review*, 22(3), pp. 81–4.

Lindvall, H., 2012a. 'Supporting copyright is not the same as opposing freedom of speech'. *The Guardian*. Available at: www.theguardian.com/music/musicblog/2012/apr/19/copyright-freedom-speech [Accessed 21 August 2013].

Lindvall, H., 2012b. 'Those who want freedom from copyright will really deliver feudalism'. *The Guardian.* Available at: www.theguardian.com/music/musicblog/2012/may/10/freedom-copyright-feudalism [Accessed 21 August 2013].

Lingard, T. and Perrott, O., 2012. 'Keeping the pirates at bay'. *The Guardian.* Available at: www.theguardian.com/media-network/media-network-blog/2012/may/21/pirate-bay-court-order [Accessed 21 August 2013].

MacKinnon, R., 2012. *Consent of the networked: The worldwide struggle for internet freedom.* New York: Basic Books.

Masnick, M., 2012a. 'Full text of Slovenian ambassador's apology for signing ACTA'. *Techdirt.* Available at: www.techdirt.com/articles/20120202/02305917633/full-text-slovenian-ambassadors-apology-signing-acta.shtml [Accessed 20 August 2013].

Masnick, M., 2012b. 'People in Poland come out to protest ACTA in large numbers; Polish gov't calls it "blackmail"'. *Techdirt.* Available at: www.techdirt.com/articles/20120126/03543117549/people-poland-come-out-to-protest-acta-large-numbers-polish-govt-calls-it-blackmail.shtml [Accessed 19 August 2013].

Meyer, D., 2012a. 'Act on Acta now if you care about democracy and free speech'. *The Guardian.* Available at: www.theguardian.com/commentisfree/2012/feb/03/act-acta-democracy-free-speech [Accessed 21 August 2013].

Meyer, D., 2012b. 'ACTA gets final stake through heart as EC drops court referral'. *ZDNet.* Available at: www.zdnet.com/acta-gets-final-stake-through-heart-as-ec-drops-court-referral-7000009070/ [Accessed 20 August 2013].

Mezzofiore, G., 2012. 'Act against Acta: Demonstrators protest against Poland signing'. *International Business Times.* Available at: www.ibtimes.co.uk/articles/287236/20120125/act-against-acta-demonstrators-protest-poland-signing.htm [Accessed 19 August 2013].

Moore, A., 2012a. 'Alan Moore on anonymous rise'. *BBC.* Available at: www.bbc.co.uk/news/technology-16968689 [Accessed 21 August 2013].

Moore, F., 2012b. 'IFPI welcomes ACTA signature'. *IFPI.* Available at: www.ifpi.org/content/section_news/20120126.html [Accessed 23 August 2013].

Mueller, M., 2010. *Networks and states: The global politics of internet governance.* Cambridge, MA: MIT Press.

Neubauer, M., 2012. 'How activists coordinated European opposition to ACTA'. *TechPresident.* Available at: http://techpresident.com/news/22311/germany-activists-help-coordinate-europe-wide-anti-acta-protests [Accessed 19 August 2013].

Odrozek, K., 2012a. 'Poland: Government will sign ACTA despite massive protest'. *Global Voices Online.* Available at: http://advocacy.globalvoicesonline.org/2012/01/25/poland-government-will-sign-acta-despite-massive-protest/ [Accessed 19 August 2013].

Odrozek, K., 2012b. 'Poland: Netizens protest government's plan to sign ACTA next week'. *Global Voices Online.* Available at: http://globalvoicesonline.org/2012/01/22/poland-netizens-protest-governments-plan-to-sign-acta-next-week/ [Accessed 19 August 2013].

Plunkett, J., 2012. 'Acta opposition grows as Pirate Party UK joins day of action'. *The Guardian.* Available at: www.theguardian.com/technology/2012/feb/06/acta-pirate-party-uk [Accessed 21 August 2013].

PPE and ECR, 2010. *Motion for a Resolution to wind up the debate on the statement by the Commission pursuant to Rule 110(2) of the Rules of Procedure on ACTA.* Brussels: European Parliament.

Quinn, B., Kingsley, P. and Jeffery, S., 2010. 'WikiLeaks cables: You ask, we search'. *The Guardian*. Available at: www.theguardian.com/world/blog/2010/dec/22/you-ask-we-search-december-22 [Accessed 21 August 2013].

Ramalho, A., 2011. 'The European Union and ACTA – or making omelettes without eggs (again)'. *International Review of Intellectual Property and Competition Law*, 42(1), pp. 97–101.

Richmond, S., 2010. 'EU concerned about Acta privacy implications'. *Technology – Telegraph Blogs*. Available at: http://blogs.telegraph.co.uk/technology/shanerichmond/100005358/eu-concerned-about-acta-privacy-implications/ [Accessed 21 August 2013].

Richmond, S., 2011. 'EU's new copyright leader doesn't believe private copying should exist'. *Technology – Telegraph Blogs*. Available at: http://blogs.telegraph.co.uk/technology/shanerichmond/100006531/eus-new-copyright-leader-doesnt-believe-private-copying-should-exist/ [Accessed 21 August 2013].

Ruse-Khan, H.G. and Jaeger, T., 2009. 'Policing patents worldwide? EC border measures against transiting generic drugs under EC and WTO intellectual property regimes'. *International Review of Intellectual Property and Competition Law*, 40(5), pp. 502–38.

Schulz, M., 2012. 'European Parliament President Martin Schulz – ACTA wrong solution to protect intellectual property'. *Europarl*. Available at: www.europarl.europa.eu/the-president/en/press/press_release_speeches/press_release/2012/2012-july/html/acta-wrong-solution-to-protect-intellectual-property [Accessed 21 August 2013].

Simpson, A., 2008. 'Airport scans for illegal downloads on iPods, mobile phones and laptops'. *Telegraph.co.uk*. Available at: www.telegraph.co.uk/technology/3357838/Airport-scans-for-illegal-downloads-on-iPods-mobile-phones-and-laptops.html [Accessed 21 August 2013].

Solon, O., 2012. 'The EU signs up to Acta, but French MEP quits in protest'. *Wired UK*. Available at: www.wired.co.uk/news/archive/2012–01/26/eu-signs-up-to-acta [Accessed 19 August 2013].

Sunstein, C.R., 2009. *Republic.com 2.0*. Princeton, NJ: Princeton University Press.

Sutton, M., 2013. 'Transatlantic civil society declaration: Leave copyright and patent provisions out of TAFTA'. *Electronic Frontier Foundation*. Available at: www.eff.org/deeplinks/2013/03/transatlantic-declaration-leave-copyright-patent-issues-out-tafta [Accessed 23 August 2013].

Swiss Federation of Intellectual Property, 2009. *The Anti-Counterfeiting Trade Agreement – Summary of key elements under discussion*. Available at: www.ige.ch/fileadmin/user_upload/Juristische_Infos/e/transparency_paper.pdf [Accessed 15 July 2013].

The Associated Press, 2012. 'Protesters rally across Poland to express anger at international copyright treaty'. *The Hamilton Spectator*. Available at: www.thespec.com/news-story/2231069-protesters-rally-across-poland-to-express-anger-at-international-copyr/ [Accessed 19 August 2013].

The Warsaw Voice, 2012. 'Poland withdraws from ACTA ratification'. *The Warsaw Voice*. Available at: www.warsawvoice.pl/WVpage/pages/article.php/19893/news [Accessed 19 August 2013].

Thompson, B., 2008. 'Making punishment fit the crime'. *BBC*. Available at: http://news.bbc.co.uk/1/hi/technology/7493365.stm [Accessed 21 August 2013].

Thompson, B., 2009. 'Games without frontiers?' *BBC*. Available at: http://news.bbc.co.uk/1/hi/technology/8020890.stm [Accessed 21 August 2013].

Thompson, B., 2010a. 'Is it time to defend our rights?' *BBC*. Available at: http://news.bbc.co.uk/1/hi/technology/8544935.stm [Accessed 21 August 2013].

Thompson, B., 2010b. 'Seeing the big picture on content'. *BBC*. Available at: www.bbc.co.uk/news/technology-11380490 [Accessed 21 August 2013].

Verts/ALE, ALDE, S&D, GUE/NGL, 2010. *Joint motion for a resolution pursuant to Rule 110(4) of the Rules on Procedure on ACTA*. Brussels: European Parliament.

Ward, S. and Gibson, R., 2009. 'European political organizations and the internet: Mobilization, participation, and change'. In A. Chadwick and P.N. Howard, eds, *Routledge handbook of internet politics*. London: Routledge.

Warman, M., 2010a. 'Acta: "close to agreement"'. *Telegraph.co.uk*. Available at: www.telegraph.co.uk/technology/news/7987299/Acta-close-to-agreement.html [Accessed 21 August 2013].

Warman, M., 2010b. 'Europe threatens web openness'. *Telegraph.co.uk*. Available at: www.telegraph.co.uk/technology/news/7400075/Europe-threatens-web-openness.html [Accessed 21 August 2013].

Warman, M., 2010c. 'European Parliament finally debates Acta piracy treaty'. *Telegraph.co.uk*. Available at: www.telegraph.co.uk/technology/news/8077616/European-Parliament-finally-debates-Acta-piracy-treaty.html [Accessed 21 August 2013].

Warman, M., 2010d. 'Secret copyright talks document leaks'. *Telegraph.co.uk*. Available at: www.telegraph.co.uk/technology/news/7535606/Secret-copyright-talks-document-leaks.html [Accessed 21 August 2013].

Warman, M., 2010e. 'Text of secret ACTA talks released'. *Telegraph.co.uk*. Available at: www.telegraph.co.uk/technology/news/7623605/Text-of-secret-ACTA-talks-released.html [Accessed 21 August 2013].

Warman, M., 2012a. 'ACTA referred to European Court of Justice'. *Telegraph.co.uk*. Available at: www.telegraph.co.uk/technology/news/9098744/ACTA-referred-to-European-Court-of-Justice.html [Accessed 21 August 2013].

Warman, M., 2012b. 'ACTA treaty "dead in the water"'. *Telegraph.co.uk*. Available at: www.telegraph.co.uk/technology/news/9203093/ACTA-treaty-dead-in-the-water.html [Accessed 21 August 2013].

Warman, M., 2012c. 'Acta treaty "unacceptable", says European Data Protection Service'. *Telegraph.co.uk*. Available at: www.telegraph.co.uk/technology/internet/9225370/Acta-treaty-unacceptable-says-European-Data-Protection-Service.html [Accessed 21 August 2013].

Warman, M., 2012d. 'European Parliament rejects ACTA piracy treaty'. *Telegraph.co.uk*. Available at: www.telegraph.co.uk/technology/news/9375822/European-Parliament-rejects-ACTA-piracy-treaty.html [Accessed 21 August 2013].

Warman, M., 2012e. 'MEPs reject ACTA piracy treaty'. *Telegraph.co.uk*. Available at: www.telegraph.co.uk/technology/news/9346957/MEPs-reject-ACTA-piracy-treaty.html [Accessed 21 August 2013].

Wessels, A., 2013. 'Do not turn TAFTA into ACTA v2.0'. Available at: http://acta.ffii.org/?p=1743 [Accessed 23 August 2013].

Whittaker, Z., 2012. 'EU sends strongest signal yet to reject ACTA'. *ZDNet*. Available at: www.zdnet.com/blog/london/eu-sends-strongest-signal-yet-to-reject-acta/5039 [Accessed 20 August 2013].

Yu, P.K., 2011. 'ACTA and its complex politics'. *The WIPO Journal*, 3(1), pp. 1–16.

Index

For Product Safety Concerns and Information please contact our EU
representative GPSR@taylorandfrancis.com
Taylor & Francis Verlag GmbH, Kaufingerstraße 24, 80331 München, Germany

www.ingramcontent.com/pod-product-compliance
Lightning Source LLC
Chambersburg PA
CBHW061210220326

41599CB00025B/4595

9 781138 944848